P9-DHD-300

Pirates, Privateers,
& Rebel Raiders
of the Carolina Coast

Pirates, Privateers,

& Rebel Raiders
of the Carolina Coast

LINDLEY S. BUTLER

The
University
of North
Carolina
Press

Chapel Hill
& London

910.4
B 977
2722718

© 2000 The University of North Carolina Press
All rights reserved

Designed by April Leidig-Higgins
Set in Monotype Bulmer by Keystone Typesetting, Inc.
Manufactured in the United States of America

The paper in this book meets the guidelines for permanence
and durability of the Committee on Production Guidelines for
Book Longevity of the Council on Library Resources.

Library of Congress Cataloging-in-Publication Data
Butler, Lindley S.
Pirates, privateers, and rebel raiders of the Carolina coast / by
Lindley S. Butler.
p. cm. Includes bibliographical references and index.
ISBN 0-8078-2553-0 (cloth: alk. paper)
ISBN 0-8078-4863-8 (pbk.: alk. paper)
1. Pirates—North Carolina—Atlantic Coast—History—Anec-
dotes. 2. Pirates—North Carolina—Atlantic Coast—Biogra-
phy—Anecdotes. 3. Privateering—North Carolina—Atlantic
Coast—History—Anecdotes. 4. Sailors—North Carolina—
Atlantic Coast—History—Anecdotes. 5. Sailors—North
Carolina—Atlantic Coast—Biography—Anecdotes. 6. North
Carolina—History—Civil War, 1861–1865—Naval operations —
Anecdotes. 7. United States—History—Civil War, 1861–1865
—Naval operations—Anecdotes. 8. Atlantic Coast (N.C.)—
History, Naval—Anecdotes. I. Title.
F262.A84 B88 2000   359'.009756—dc21   99-086288

04 03 02 01 00   5 4 3 2 1

For T

Contents

Illustrations & Maps

MAPS

Preface

In our contemporary society characterized by a surfeit of violence, why read about pirates and commerce destroyers? What is heroic about bloodthirsty criminals and naval officers who destroyed the livelihood of fisherfolk and sea captains? Simply put, these tales are thrilling adventure stories about that most ancient of plots—the hunter and his prey. Since our primordial days, human beings have found compelling myths of larger-than-life heroes whose stories give us role models for coping with the vicissitudes of life. These real-life sea tales abound with action, suspense, and tragedy about flesh-and-blood historic characters, at least one of whom, Blackbeard, has been mythologized into a romantic figure of popular culture. These men crossed the stage of history at unstable junctures—the early colonial period and the early nineteenth century, eras when our national character was being shaped, and the Civil War, the great American epic tragedy. The phenomenal and lasting popularity of the science fiction odyssey *Star Trek* and the *Star Wars* films suggest a society desperately seeking heroes and a relevant mythology. But history always surpasses fiction as a source for heroism and romance. While the tales in this volume do touch on the dark side, they are mostly about heroic naval officers, dedicated men of principle who gave their best to defend their countries. They all suffered for their service, and one paid the ultimate price. Their countries were flawed, but countries, like all human institutions, reflect the nature of mankind, a mixture of high and low aspirations, of noble and ignoble purpose, and of good and evil behavior.

The eight individuals sketched in this book have a common tie of place: each of them either was a native of North Carolina or else rose to lasting fame or notoriety on her waters. They illustrate the fascinating but barely tapped maritime history of the Old North State, heretofore focused in the popular mind on the unique, splendid land- and seascape of the Outer Banks, its broad strands and its spectacular lighthouses. Not so well known beyond the world of scuba diving is the wealth of historic undersea wrecks that lie in the state's Graveyard of the Atlantic, most vividly illustrated by two discoveries that have generated global excitement—the 1973 find of the USS *Monitor* and the 1996 discovery at Beaufort Inlet of a wreck that is probably the 1718 flagship of Blackbeard, the *Queen Anne's Revenge*.

In earlier ages, navigation on the vast oceans comprised a highly technical science—possibly, until modern times, the most complex field of science. Harnessing the subtle interplay of the forces of wind and current by a sail called for expert knowledge and a decisive character. The wise sea captain was the mariner who left port knowing that no matter how much he had experienced or how calm the sea appeared, life-threatening danger constantly lurked close at hand to overwhelm him when he least expected it. By the eighteenth century, the quest for a means of calculating longitude and the corresponding development of an accurate chronometer consumed the best scientific minds for generations. As students of navigation and the changeable sea, naval officers and sea captains were the cutting-edge specialists of their day, and sea warfare was the most technology-driven form of conflict. The most exciting artifacts being recovered from the ongoing excavation of the eighteenth-century Beaufort Inlet wreck are the numerous well-preserved navigation, surveying, scientific, and medical instruments. To many, these are surprising discoveries to find on a pirate ship, but they illustrate the scientific nature of seafaring in that day as in this.

This book spans an era of 150 years, from the early eighteenth century to the mid-nineteenth century. In 1715 ship and sail design and naval armament had not changed significantly since the introduction of cannon in the late Middle Ages. At the time, Europe was engaged in struggles for continental domination that would not end until 1815. A century of almost continuous warfare spawned new ship types and larger and deadlier naval guns. Tactics were dominated by the battle line of multidecked ships-of-the-line, supplemented with raids by small-boat cutting-out expeditions. Over the next fifty years steam power went to sea, generating great practical innovations. Rifled cannon extended the range of sea combat, and exploding shells multiplied damage and death. The counterpoint to the rifled shell was armor plate, which, coupled with the revolving gun turret, changed naval architecture permanently. Blackbeard would have been perfectly capable of commanding the *Snap Dragon* during the War of 1812, and, conversely, Otway Burns would have been at home on the *Queen Anne's Revenge*, although he would have preferred the size and speed of Stede Bonnet's *Royal James*. Each of the Civil War officers, trained on sailing ships, could easily have captained the *Queen Anne's Revenge*. As skilled as they were, however, all of the pre-1815 mariners would have been lost on the CSS *Albemarle* or the USS *Monitor*, though they would have been fascinated and intrigued by the power and military potential intrinsic in these modern vessels.

As practitioners of warfare at sea—from pirate and privateer to naval commerce raider—the men whose stories are told here shared the same methods over time. Only their motives varied. The pirate and privateer had personal gain at stake and chose the passive approach of preserving the prize, as well as life and limb, if possible. The naval commerce raider, in contrast, was free to attack his declared foe's ability to make war by the destruction of his prey, although prize money was still offered by his government as an incentive.

The common theme running through these stories is the nature of sea warfare. In his brilliant television series, *The Ascent of Man*, first aired in 1973, Jacob Bronowski said of war, "But war, organised war, is not a human instinct. It is a highly planned and cooperative form of theft."[1] Ocean warfare as practiced by pirates, privateers, and naval raiders was without question "a highly planned and cooperative form of theft" adapted to their particularly challenging environment. The eight mariners presented in the pages that follow were all masters of organized theft at sea. They are connected by place, by the practice of their warrior profession, and by what their lives reveal to us about the origins and nature of sea warfare as a human experience.

1. Jacob Bronowski, *The Ascent of Man* (Boston: Little, Brown and Company, 1973), 88.

Acknowledgments

All research is a collective effort, and a number of individuals have greatly helped me in writing this book. Rodney Barfield, former director of the North Carolina Maritime Museum, drew me from inland brown-water navigation into blue-water coastal history through the North Carolina Maritime History Council. As a volunteer diver with the North Carolina Underwater Archaeology Unit of the Division of Archives and History, I was ready when the Beaufort Inlet wreck was discovered. Working with Richard Lawrence and Mark Wilde-Ramsing and their staff, with Phil Masters of Intersal, and with Mike Daniel of the Maritime Research Institute has been one of the most stimulating experiences in my lifetime of studying North Carolina history. Exciting as archival research can be, it simply doesn't compare with an early morning run to the dive site on the *Seahawk* or the *Snap Dragon* to begin a long day of undersea work. A former student of mine, nautical archaeologist David Moore of the North Carolina Maritime Museum, reentered my life at a timely point. His in-depth knowledge of Blackbeard and his liberal sharing of ideas and research has saved me countless hours.

The staffs of numerous archives, libraries, museums, and photographic repositories have been courteous and helpful, particularly those at the North Carolina Division of Archives and History, the Southern Historical Collection and the North Carolina Collection of the University of North Carolina, the Outer Banks History Center, the North Carolina Maritime Museum, the Cape Fear Museum, the North Carolina Museum of Art, the North Carolina Museum of History, the Mariners' Museum, the Maritime Museum of the Atlantic, the U.S.

Naval History Center, the National Archives, the Library of Congress, the Portsmouth Public Library, the Portsmouth Naval Yard Museum, the Chester W. Nimitz Library at the U.S. Naval Academy, and the Gerald B. James Library at Rockingham Community College.

A number of colleagues and friends have contributed more than they know to the successful conclusion of this study. With Gerald Shinn, a longtime friend, I have shared for over thirty years a common interest in Otway Burns and naval adventure fiction, especially that of C. S. Forester. Historian Jerry Cashion of the research branch of the Division of Archives and History has always been there for lengthy discussions of knotty research problems. Fellow historians David Stick and William Powell have continually offered encouragement and inspiration. From the inception of the project, David Perry, editor-in-chief of the University of North Carolina Press, recognized the merit of the proposal. At an early stage in the writing, Burke Davis enthusiastically supported the concept and offered valuable guidance. Portions of the manuscript have also been read by Robert Butler, Claire Helgeson, Gerald Shinn, and George Ferguson, who confirmed the broad appeal of the subjects. I am indebted to the sharp eye and sure hand of my manuscript editor, Ron Maner, who made a solid contribution to the readability and accuracy of the book.

Singularly important to the quality of this book has been my wife, T, who typed and edited the manuscript while teaching her classes and giving up her vacations. The most pleasant times in this challenging process came when we could together pursue and find an apt turn of phrase or jointly compose a line or construct a paragraph. Every writer needs a fine editor, and I have the good fortune to have married one.

Wentworth, N.C.
15 October 1999

Pirates, Privateers,
& Rebel Raiders
of the Carolina Coast

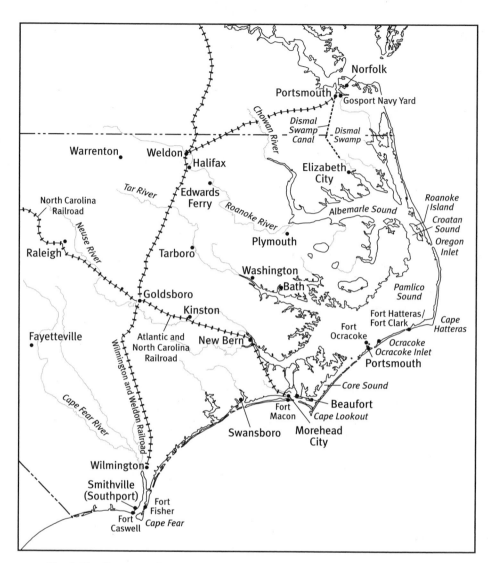

North Carolina coastal waters

*[North Carolina] tis
a place which receives
Pirates, Runaways,
and Illegal Traders.
—Edmund Randolph,
1700*

Introduction

The World of Pirates, Privateers, and Naval Raiders

North Carolina possesses in its rivers, estuaries, tidal marshes, great sounds, barrier islands, and offshore Outer Banks one of the longest shorelines on the Atlantic coast of the United States. The dynamic and ever-changing Outer Banks formation, with its prominent capes—Hatteras, Lookout, and Fear—and their adjacent extensive shoals, encloses the largest sounds on the eastern seaboard. These great capes, the narrow sandy islands, the shallow sounds, and the fickle weather punctuated by fierce northeasters and deadly hurricanes have combined to form the most treacherous stretch of coast in the country and indeed one of the most dangerous in the world. In the aptly named Graveyard of the Atlantic lie buried several thousand ships downed by the twin furies of storms and war. Hundreds of these wrecks, a significant resource of the state's maritime heritage, have been chronicled by coastal historian David Stick and are the reason North Carolina is one of the most popular scuba diving locations in the United States.[1]

For most people the Outer Banks' low dunes, dramatic capes, and

The Union fleet that was part of General Ambrose Burnside's expedition to oc-cupy the North Carolina sound country during the Civil War encountered a stormy Hatteras Inlet in January 1862. (Outer Banks History Center, Manteo, N.C.)

picturesque lighthouses epitomize the Carolina coast. Seen from above, the seemingly fragile, blade-thin islands enclose Albemarle, Pamlico, and Core Sounds, which separate the barrier islands from the mainland by as much as forty miles. Historically, the inhabitants of these sandy strips, described by the royal governor Gabriel Johnston in 1750 as "very Wild and ungovernable,"[2] waged a daily struggle for survival with the ever-encroaching sea. Yet the ocean provided in fish, other sea life, and wrecks to be plundered the means for the "Bankers" to eke out a precarious existence clinging to the sands that were, over time, literally washing away beneath them. Isolation bred self-reliance, a spirit of independence, and strong character, while the watery world nurtured their skills in handling small boats. Each storm left the flotsam of newly sunken ships, including a diverse population of survivors from most of the nations of western Europe and western Africa, many of whom remained to settle on the coast and leave descendants.

The workaday world of the broad sounds' small ports, coastal trade, and fishing that generated distinct boat types is just beginning to be appreciated, although it has long been showcased at the North Car-olina Maritime Museum at Beaufort and known to specialists. It was this unique combination of a dangerous outer coast, shoaly sounds, winding creeks, and vast tidal marshes that provided refuges for pirates and smugglers in an early, more reckless age, honed the skills of small-boat sailors and pilots without peer, and became a setting for privateering and blockade running. With some of the most complex navigable water on the globe and with port development stunted by a coast anchored by landmarks whose very names, Lookout and Fear, evoked wariness and tragedy, it is little wonder that North Carolina would foster piracy, smuggling, blockade running, and naval conflict and would send out on the high seas some of the most successful privateers and naval raiders in the nation's history.

So intertwined as to be virtually inseparable, privateering and piracy are as ancient as the origins of sailing. Piracy, the theft of goods and vessels on the high seas, from early times was considered a capital crime, although the death penalty appears to have had little effect as a deterrent. Privateers were privately owned armed ships licensed by the government in time of war to seize enemy ships or prizes—in effect, legalized, limited piracy. Embedded in the history of every maritime nation are tales of smuggling, wreck plundering, and piratical activity, none more compelling than those of the ancient Greeks. At the very foundation of Western civilization, the epics of Homer—*The Iliad* and *The Odyssey*—delineate vivid portraits of a seafaring culture based on maritime conflict and brigandage. When Odysseus and his crew were caught in the cave of the Cyclops, the one-eyed giant cried:

> Where did you sail from, over the running sea-lanes?
> Out on a trading spree or roving the water like pirates,
> sea-wolves raiding at will, who risk their lives
> to plunder other men?[3]

From the sixteenth to the nineteenth century, sea wolves were an important part of international maritime activity and naval warfare. An intermittent activity in the Middle Ages, privateering came into its own in Western history during the English Tudor period, especially in the heroic age of the Elizabethan "sea dogs"—Sir John Hawkins, Sir Francis Drake, Sir Walter Raleigh, and Sir Richard Grenville. The early sixteenth-century Spanish conquest of Mexico and Peru poured a nearly unimaginable stream of gold, silver, and New World products into the coffers of the Spanish crown. English, French, and Dutch mariners swarmed into the sea-lanes, often with tacit but silent governmental backing, to attack Spanish convoys burdened with the glittering wealth of the Americas. War with Spain came often enough that the prizes could be legally seized by privateers, who were, according to a contemporary observer, "a Nursery for Pyrates."[4] When the wars ended, many of these men found that they could not return to the humdrum world of commerce with its constant scrabbling for sparse profits and instead converted to buccaneering, preying on the shipping not only of their former enemies but indeed of all countries, including their own. Once a person was outfitted with an armed vessel, the lure of easy wealth was too strong to ignore, and the risk of capture was slight unless the level of piracy became so annoying that it triggered a naval reaction from the state. In the Western Hemisphere, English pirates were tolerated primarily because they could be counted on to help defend the British West Indian colonies, and usually they hurt England's Spanish, French, and Dutch rivals far more than they hurt their own countrymen.

In the seventeenth century, pirates established hamlets on remote islands throughout the Caribbean. Some of the earliest outlaw settlers were Frenchmen on the western tip of Hispaniola in modern Haiti. These brigands subsisted chiefly on herds of wild hogs and cattle, whose meat they cured over a wooden frame known as a *boucan*, from which the term "buccaneer" originated. Other strongholds of marauders were established on Tortuga, which they ruled for a time; at Nassau on New Providence Island in the Bahamas; and on Jamaica, where the city of Port Royal became for a while the pirate capital. Despite the fact that by the turn of the eighteenth century the Caribbean was virtually a pirate sea, British officials, still finding the miscreants useful in the frequent wars of the period, were reluctant to root them out. Eventually their blatant arrogance and flaunting of authority, and, most important, the losses they inflicted on English merchants, forced the British government to adopt a double-edged policy of force and reconciliation. Coupled with increased naval strength was an offer of clemency for past offenses. Pirates hounded from the Caribbean by rigorous naval pursuit migrated to the mainland coasts of North and South America, leading eventually to the relocation of several on the Carolina coast where they found temporary refuge in the labyrinth of tidal streams and obscure inlets.

Carolina's isolated backwaters provided a perfect haven for the vagabond pirates, and equally appealing were the weak authority of proprietary officials, the sparse settlement, and the relative poverty of the colony. A low volume of trade and a subsistence economy meant

Founded in 1713, the port of Beaufort, North Carolina, was visited by Black-beard and Stede Bonnet when the *Queen Anne's Revenge* wrecked in 1718. It later was the home of privateer Otway Burns and Captain James W. Cooke of the css *Albemarle*. (North Carolina Collection, Wilson Library, University of North Carolina, Chapel Hill)

fewer customs collectors and a government willing to accommodate merchants or traders who could, by dealing with smugglers and pirates, offer an abundance of low-priced goods. Throughout the North American colonies there was widespread contempt for the Navigation Acts that had been passed in the seventeenth century to assure England's dominance of the colonial trade and the exclusion of foreign competitors, particularly their leading rivals, the Dutch. Beginning in 1651, the series of parliamentary acts required colonial trade to be in English ships with English crews. Later acts enumerated cornerstone products of the imperial trade such as sugar, tobacco, and naval stores that were designated to be shipped to English ports. To ensure that the cargo did not end up in foreign ports, traders were bonded and duties were to be paid at the port of embarkation. In an isolated colony such as Carolina, where transportation costs were already higher than in the Chesapeake, the duties were not affordable. There were so few naval officers and vessels available in the colonies that enforcement was difficult at best and in northern Carolina nonexistent. As a consequence extralegal trading practices became rampant, creating an atmosphere in which bending or breaking the law was the norm. It was no great leap for a merchant routinely buying from smugglers and evading customs officials by stealth and bribery to trade with and protect pirates. An early scholar of Carolina pirates concluded, "There was nothing that contributed so much to the fostering of piracy in the western world as the operation of the English Navigation laws."[5]

During the late seventeenth century and early eighteenth century, England waged three naval wars with the Dutch, growing out of their intense commercial rivalry, and a series of European wars fueled by the great French monarch, Louis XIV, whose overweening ambition had driven him to attempt to dominate the Continent. These conflicts spilled over into the colonial possessions of England, France, Spain, and Holland. Beginning with the 1688–97 War of the League of Augsburg (called King William's War in the English colonies), and continuing through the 1701–13 War of the Spanish Succession (Queen Anne's War), fighting was interrupted by only a brief respite of four years of peace at the turn of the century. In this age of almost unbroken warfare both privateering and piracy flourished, producing Stede Bonnet as well as Blackbeard. As a contemporary described the situation, there were "great Numbers of Seamen turn'd adrift at the Conclusion of a War,"[6] and the vast majority, having little hope of legal employment, found the appeals of freebooting too alluring to resist. Furthermore, there were simply too few royal naval vessels. In 1715, for example, there were only ten on station in North America and the Caribbean to patrol the thousands of square miles of sea-lanes. And because many naval officers supplemented their meager salaries by means of the lucrative but extralegal business of hiring out their vessels to protect merchants and convoys, there was an understandable reluctance on their part to oust the buccaneers in their region.[7]

The reality of the pirate world was markedly different from the romantic image created by fiction and film. Nearly all of the some 2,500 pirates operating in the Caribbean and on the coast of North America were from England, the West Indies, the mainland colonies, or Scotland, with a scattering of Dutch, Spanish, and Portuguese subjects as well. There was a substantial number of Africans, for the most part serving as slaves and performing menial tasks and hard labor such as manning the pumps. Pirates were drawn from the "lowest social classes," or, as one official put it, they were "desperate Rogues." Virtually all were single men with no family ties. Most of them volunteered from captured merchant vessels, but others had served on privateers or in the navy, where, for their daily endurance of near intolerable conditions and harsh discipline, they received low wages, which were paid erratically. Pirates had it no worse, other than the overcrowding of large crews on small vessels, and in many ways the pirate's world was attractive, especially the chance to share in the loot of a valuable prize. The life of a seaman in the early eighteenth century was fraught with constant danger, and as a pirate he was at no greater risk apart from the fact that if he was caught he faced certain death on the gallows.[8]

A pirate community was a "little Commonwealth,"[9] organized on democratic principles, with a majority vote ruling on most decisions, including such important choices as the direction of the cruise or whether to take a prize. As scholar Marcus Rediker has aptly described their community, the pirates created "a rough, improvised, but effective egalitarianism that placed authority in the collective hands of the crew."[10] Captains were elected for leadership ability and seamanship and could be deposed by a vote of no confidence. Other elected leaders were the quartermaster, who served as the ship's first officer, crew spokesman, and prize master; the boatswain or bos'n, who supervised the sails and rigging of the ship; the gunner, who maintained the cannon and powder; first and second mates; a carpenter; and often a surgeon. Most pirate ships carried musicians whose duty was secondarily to provide entertainment but chiefly to play during battle or while the crew performed such onerous tasks as weighing the anchor.

All pirate groups drew up, and all members signed upon joining, a set of rules known universally as "the articles," a term probably based on the Articles of War that governed naval vessels. It may seem absurd to compare pirate governing concepts with the American constitutional process; nevertheless, pirates elected their captain, whose authority was based on consent of the governed. It is unlikely that any of the rogues had heard of John Locke and natural rights philosophy, but these outlaws were rebels to the core, who thrived on defiance of established institutions. At the very least, they were sociopaths in rebellion against authority, especially the strict hierarchical social order based on absolute power and buttressed by stern discipline that ruled the sea. No captain of a naval or merchant vessel would have believed that a seagoing community could be organized on democratic principles, but pirates were living proof that such an alternative was possible. Just by existing, these piratical democracies were a threat to the prevailing social order, and the ruffians never lost an opportunity to show their contempt for those in authority.

Given the image of pirates as crude and uncivilized, their governing documents contained some surprising provisions. Even pirates saw the need for rules within their communities, usually curbing such antisocial behavior as desertion, theft, assault, and sometimes sodomy and rape. Other matters commonly addressed were health and safety regulations and compensation for injury. The articles devised for the *Revenge*, commanded by Captain John Phillips, in 1723 were the following:

1. Every Man shall obey civil Command; the Captain shall have one full Share and a half in all Prizes; the Master, Carpenter, Boatswain and Gunner shall have one Share and [a] quarter.

2. If any Man shall offer to run away, or keep any Secret from the Company, he shall be maroon'd, with one Bottle of Powder, one Bottle of Water, one small Arm and Shot.

3. If any Man shall steal any thing in the Company, or game to the Value of a Piece of Eight, he shall be maroon'd or shot.

4. If at any time we should meet another Marooner (that is *Pyrate*) that Man that shall sign his Articles without the Consent of our Company, shall suffer such Punishment as the Captain and Company shall think fit.

5. That Man that shall strike another whilst these Articles are in force, shall receive *Moses*'s Law (that is, 40 Stripes lacking one) on the bare Back.

6. That Man that shall snap his Arms, or smoak Tobacco in the Hold, without a Cap to his Pipe, or carry a Candle lighted without a Lanthorn, shall suffer the same Punishment as in the former Article.

7. That Man that shall not keep his Arms clean, fit for an Engagement, or neglect his Business, shall be cut off from his Share, and suffer such other Punishment as the Captain and the Company shall think fit.

8. If any Man shall lose a Joint in Time of an Engagement, he shall have 400 Pieces of Eight, if a Limb, 800.

9. If at any Time we meet with a prudent Woman, that Man that offers to meddle with her, without her Consent, shall suffer present Death.[11]

Additional rules included in the articles signed on the vessel of Bartholomew Roberts prohibited gambling and the concealment of boys or women for sexual partners. Fighting among the crew was forbidden, with quarrels among shipmates settled by duels on shore.[12]

In the early eighteenth century pirates targeted small ships, sloops, and a new type of vessel, the schooner, which dominated coastal commerce in the colonies. These craft, usually lightly armed and sailed by crews of fewer than ten men, were easy prey for the fast sloops that the sea rovers favored. Although most pirate ships carried no more than ten or twelve guns, they usually expected to take their prizes by board-ing from small boats; therefore, their own vessels were packed with crews of eighty or more. Derived largely from Hollywood extrava-ganzas, the popular belief is that the brigands overwhelmed a ship with numerous broadsides, which would considerably damage their poten-tial prize, and then swarmed on board armed to the teeth, taking the vessel in a bloody battle. On the contrary, in this period most pirate encounters involved little more violence than showing the black or red flag and giving the targeted ship a "shot across the bow." The truth is that most merchant ships lacked enough crew to man the few guns they had to defend the vessel. Knowing that when no resistance was offered the merchant seamen had little to fear undermined their will to fight for their ship. Usually pirates readily acquired new volunteer recruits from their prizes.

Their well-deserved terrible reputation for torture, murder, and rape had been earned by pirates in the seventeenth century, when England, France, and Spain were almost continually at war. This reputation for cruelty followed pirates into the eighteenth century as an underlying threat in any dealings with them, and those who chose to do battle with pirates and lost were often brutalized. If routine ques-tioning of captives identified an abusive or unjust captain, the desper-ados did not hesitate to punish him by flogging or worse. If pirates sus-pected that valuable plunder was hidden on a prize, then torture was readily employed to extract knowledge of its whereabouts. Edward Low, an exceptionally cruel buccaneer, was known to have burned a captive alive and to have hanged monks from his ship's rigging until they were nearly dead.[13] There were, of course, psychopathic pirates; but the brutality must be set in the context of an age when ship's discipline was maintained by the sadistic cat-o'-nine-tails, and slaves and criminals were routinely punished by whipping, branding, and the disfigurement of ear cropping.

Caribbean piracy in the seventeenth century had been centered in Port Royal, Jamaica. However, vigorous suppression by Sir Henry Morgan, himself a former privateer and buccaneer, during his tenure as lieutenant governor of the island (1676–87), coupled with a devas-tating earthquake in 1692, scattered the surviving marauders through-out the islands. Eventually they reconcentrated at Nassau on the island of New Providence in the Bahamas, forming a new base until another former privateer, Woodes Rogers, arrived as the island's governor in July 1718. Rogers came armed with a naval contingent and a royal pardon that had been passed on 5 September 1717, known as the Act of Grace, which granted pirates a year in which they could request a pardon for past offenses. Relentless pursuit, especially by the famous reformed pirate Benjamin Hornigold, swift trials, mass executions, and the Act of Grace soon brought an abrupt end to the so-called Golden Age of Piracy.

Certainly by the seventeenth century the interdependence of piracy and privateering was well established. Piracy was a legacy to Europe from the ancient world, but the earliest privateers in England originated in the thirteenth century with the practice of allowing the owner of a lost ship to seek reprisal and compensation by in turn taking a vessel from the offending country. The commission authorizing this action was called a letter of marque and reprisal. The concept evolved from permitting individuals to redress personal grievances into an official policy of issuing letters of marque and reprisal during a war to anyone willing to venture the expense of outfitting an armed vessel and risking it in attacks on the enemy. The state thereby expanded its naval forces without any public expense, and the privateers were allowed to keep a substantial portion of profits from the sale of their prizes.

When an English privateer hijacked a ship, it was brought into port, condemned in admiralty court, and sold for the prize money, which was distributed to the owners and crew of the ship that had captured it. Initially the court was located in London, but after 1662 vice-admiralty courts were established throughout the colonies. The first colonial court was opened in Jamaica, which rapidly became the center of both privateering and buccaneering in the Caribbean.

If a vessel of the Royal Navy took a prize, the government received the owner's share, with the remainder of the spoils distributed among the officers and crew of the ship, including the fleet admiral, the squadron commander, and the crews of any other naval vessel in sight of the capture. Needless to say, the promise of prize money was a key incentive for recruitment into the navy, even though seizing prizes was only incidental to the navy's primary goal of protecting the nation and its commerce. On the other hand, since the sole purpose of the privateer was to take prizes, most sailors preferred service on a privateer, where not only was the possibility of prize money much greater, but the discipline and living conditions were more tolerable than on a man-of-war. Privateering became even more lucrative after a 1708 English law ended the requirement of sharing the proceeds with the government.

Like the pirates of an earlier era, privateers based their tactics on having a fast ship with which to catch plodding merchant vessels and to run from stronger adversaries. Normally no privateer sought extended combat, especially with a naval vessel; but over time merchant vessels became more heavily armed, some carrying more than twenty guns. Once the prey was in range, the privateer quickly closed the gap to board and take the vessel by hand-to-hand combat on the deck. All privateers avoided traditional naval combat, a cannon duel at short range, since cannon fire would only damage a prize and might disable the privateer, bringing the cruise to a premature end.

The privateering and piracy tactics of the early eighteenth century continued throughout the century's two remaining colonial conflicts, King George's War (1740–48) and the French and Indian War (1754–63), both of which were extensions of renewed European struggles for power. With the onset of the American Revolution in 1775, the new American confederation strained its meager resources to send little more than a token fleet of several dozen warships to sea but then quickly fell back on the ingrained colonial practice of issuing letters of marque to hundreds of eager mariners. They and their merchant investors drew on the time-honored traditions of piracy, smuggling, and wreck plundering to capture some six hundred ships, or prizes—three times the number taken by the Continental Navy. According to naval historian Edgar S. Maclay, in both the American Revolution and the War of 1812 privateers were "the most important if not the predominating feature of our early sea power."[14] In the nation's infancy, privateering introduced many of our most capable naval officers to combat at sea. The effectiveness of the privateers contrasted sharply with the weakness of the few naval vessels the government could afford. Since the fledgling republic's defense budget was severely limited, the Revolutionary experience reinforced the need to base naval defense strategy on a small fleet supplemented by privateers.

Privateering has been well delineated as "simply a volunteer navy, dependent upon its own enterprises and courage for pay,"[15] and in the early nineteenth century it was still relatively easy and not too expensive to outfit a ship. The law regulating privateering, passed by Congress in June 1812, required that when an individual or group of investors had secured an armed vessel, they could apply through the local customs official to the secretary of state for a letter of marque and reprisal for each cruise. Privateers were admonished to treat their victims "with all the justice and humanity which characterizes the nation of which you are members." When a prize was seized, it was brought into port and condemned in the United States district admiralty court. The prize and its contents could then be sold at auction. After federal import duties were paid on the sale, the remaining prize money, excluding a small percentage for disabled crewmen and widows and orphans of deceased crewmen, was distributed, with the ship owners receiving half and the officers and crew dividing the remainder. Also included in the prize money was a government bounty of $20 paid for each prisoner.[16] Whereas sea battles and defense of the country continued to be the primary mission of the navy, privateers made a significant complement as an informal extension of the navy, preying on the enemy's merchant fleet and exacting at times a heavy toll by aiding in interdiction of their supply lines, hampering their trade, and enhancing naval blockades.

The War of 1812 was fought largely over maritime issues and national self-respect. Since gaining its independence from Great Britain in 1783, the weak American republic had been unable to defend either its commerce or its seamen. Europe had been at war since the onset of the French Revolution, with hostilities intensified by Napoleon's rise to power, and over the course of more than twenty years of worldwide conflict both the British and French had seized American shipping. In the decade prior to the War of 1812 the British had taken over 917 American prizes and the French had captured 558. Only the British navy, however, which had increasing difficulty keeping its vast array of ships manned, had resorted to impressing, or drafting by force, American sailors—over 6,200 of whom the British coerced into service.[17] Diplomatic protests, hollow threats, and an embargo had all failed to secure the right of Americans to sail on the high seas unmolested. To this day a fundamental foundation of American foreign policy is "freedom of the seas." For many Americans the issue was one of continued British arrogance and domination, and they concluded that a second war of independence was necessary to secure international respect. When war was declared in 1812 in response to the British government's failure to rescind its Orders in Council (the decree authorizing seizure of American ships), the United States was suddenly faced with the challenge of having to defend its coast with sixteen vessels, the largest of which were heavy frigates, against the world's foremost navy, comprised of over six hundred ships (some sources say nearly a thousand ships), of which about one hundred were in the western Atlantic.[18] This formidable fighting force was manned by officers and crews battle tested by more than 20 years of continual warfare at sea.

Faced with such long odds, the young republic had no choice but once again to augment its tiny fleet with hundreds of privateers set to prey on the merchant vessels of Great Britain. Captain Johnston Blakeley of the regular navy and privateer captain Otway Burns represent both aspects of commerce raiding. By the end of the war the navy had put to sea twenty-three vessels that captured 254 naval ships and merchantmen, destroying most of them. The 517 privateers took 1,345 prizes, nearly all merchant craft; but about 300 of the raiders were captured early in their cruises or failed to take prizes. Furthermore, over half of the prizes were recaptured by the British, who had established in February 1813 an effective blockade of the American coast that bottled up the larger ships of the United States Navy and hampered the marauding privateers. Despite using men-of-war to convoy flotillas of merchantmen, British vessels remained at high risk, and the fear of loss drove insurance rates to new heights, greatly increasing the cost of shipping. On the other hand, the British blockade and privateers exacted a much heavier toll, effectively sweeping American commerce from the high seas. The annual exports of the United States plummeted from $108 million in 1807 to $7 million in 1814.[19]

Privateering has been such an integral component of the United States' naval establishment that this country remains the sole major maritime power to reserve by constitutional provision the right to commission privateers, although we have not used privateers since the War of 1812 (excluding the few commissioned by the Confederate government in the Civil War). In truth, in an age of air domination and satellite surveillance, privateering is impractical; but commerce raiding by surface ships and submarines nearly won the Battle of the Atlantic for Germany and was decisive in defeating Japan in the Pacific in World War II, the last epic naval conflict in history.

North Carolina chief justice Walter Clark, in public addresses delivered at the dedication of a monument at the tomb of Otway Burns in 1901 and a statue to the famous privateer in Burnsville in 1909, elucidated a populist interpretation of the demise of modern privateering. He concluded that the destruction wrought on British merchant shipping in the Revolution and the War of 1812 and the devastation of the U.S. merchant fleet by Confederate raiders in the Civil War forced the wealthy businessmen, merchants, bankers, and traders of the great maritime nations to lobby their governments for an end to privateering. In Clark's words, "The eminent buccaneers of Wall Street wish war to be confined to wounding and killing of sailors and soldiers (who have small interest in war), but that their own property should be held sacred on the high seas." From Clark's viewpoint, however, privateering might serve as a powerful deterrent to war. As he stated it, the "surest way to create a desire for peace among the influential element of the enemy is for privateers to lay rude hands upon their floating wealth."[20]

It was precisely the laying of rude hands on the enemies' floating wealth by British, French, and American privateers, who took thousands of prizes in the Napoleonic Wars, that convinced the European naval powers to end the practice. In the Declaration of Paris in 1856, following the Crimean War, the Europeans agreed to abolish privateering; but the United States, which had had to rely on privateering so heavily for self-preservation, refused to sign the treaty. Ironically, just five years later, at the onset of the Civil War, the Confederacy began to issue letters of marque, causing the outraged United States to condemn captured rebel privateers and threaten to execute them as pirates. The determination of the Confederate government to retaliate in kind quickly forced the United States to reverse its position and extend to captured Confederate privateers and naval high seas raiders the status of prisoners of war.

In 1861 the U.S. Navy was manned by experienced officers who boasted years of sea duty but were untested in combat. The only war since 1815, the brief Mexican War (1846–48), had afforded few opportunities for naval combat beyond coastal raids and a single major amphibious landing at Veracruz. Of the active duty officers, about one-third, 671, were native Southerners, of whom fewer than half, 321, would resign and join the Confederate States Navy.[21] Naval officers, most of whom spent years away from their home country, were to some extent citizens of the world. Nevertheless, a sailor living in the restricted universe of a ship at sea, or spending years in foreign lands, often possessed an even greater depth of commitment to the nation than did his fellow citizens who remained at home. Furthermore, in an age when personal honor was held in high regard, the oath to defend the Constitution was not taken lightly by anyone. The dilemma with which all Southern-born army or naval officers struggled weighed their devotion to home against the grave seriousness of breaking that sacred oath. They knew, as well, that the country they left might accuse them of desertion and treason, although in practice most of the resignations were accepted without rancor.

Between the War of 1812 and the Civil War significant changes had taken place in naval technology, shipbuilding, and armament. When a sailor entered the navy in the 1830s, the sailing ships on which he served and the guns he handled had been designed in the eighteenth century. By 1861 the advent of steam power had so revolutionized sea transportation that most naval vessels were propelled by a combination of sail and steam, and the sailing vessels still in commission were considered obsolete. Smooth-bore cannon were being replaced by ever-larger rifled cannon that could hurl an exploding shell with greater accuracy, range, and penetrating force, although vessels continued to be armed with a mixture of both smooth-bore and rifled cannon. Armored warships, or ironclads, introduced to the modern world by the French and British, were designed to be impervious to the massive rifled cannon. Based on experience with armored floating batteries in the Crimean War, both the British and French navies developed armored steam-sailing vessels just prior to the American Civil War, but none had yet seen battle.

Sectional issues and the contest over slavery that had threatened the unity of the nation, simmering for decades, finally erupted in the election of 1860 when the splintering of the Democratic Party paved the way for the election of Republican Abraham Lincoln. Although Lincoln advocated a moderate policy of gradual emancipation with compensation for slaveholders, he was unacceptable to the South, and his election triggered the promised secession of South Carolina on 20 December. North Carolina was deeply divided over the question of secession, having citizens with strong Union sentiment, especially in the eastern port towns and the western Piedmont and mountain counties. The nation teetered toward disintegration when six more Southern states withdrew from the Union early in 1861 and then, along with South Carolina, met in February in Montgomery, Alabama, to form a new nation, the Confederate States of America.

Montgomery was flooded in the spring of 1861 with Southern naval officers who had resigned from the U.S. Navy, where they had been accustomed to service in a fleet of well-armed, blue-water sloops and frigates powered by sail and steam. One can imagine their disappointment when they were faced with the flimsy tugboats, small river steamers, and harbor ferries armed with one or two cannon that the individual states and the Confederate government had managed to scrape together. The only bright spot that augured well for the future of the navy and shore defense was the Union's hasty abandonment and only partial destruction of the vast Gosport Navy Yard near Norfolk, which was seized by Virginia naval forces on 20 April.[22] The ships and most of the buildings were in ruins, but much heavy equipment survived, as well as the great prize of some 1,200 large naval guns. Although most of the cannon were obsolete smooth-bores, many of them would be rifled and would serve the South well throughout the war. Certainly the Confederacy, which lacked a heavy industrial infrastructure, could not otherwise have produced high-quantity cannon in any reasonable length of time.

The energetic and forward-thinking Confederate secretary of the navy, Stephen R. Mallory of Florida, had to create a navy almost overnight in a country that had little maritime heritage, scant commercial shipping, and only a nascent industrial infrastructure. Considering these obstacles, the Confederacy would amaze the world by building a sizable ironclad defense force, purchasing and outfitting a fleet of high seas cruisers, repeatedly penetrating the inexorable Union blockade, and pioneering successfully the development of novel and experimental submarines, mines, and torpedo boats. Ironclads were a particularly high priority for Secretary Mallory, who realized that the Confederate government, starting from nothing, had no other way to challenge the sea supremacy of the United States Navy.

The Confederacy, with no navy of its own and few ships of any kind available, was in a position similar to that of the United States in its infancy, when it had resorted to privateering to mount a significant naval presence. The fall of Fort Sumter and President Lincoln's call for troops to suppress the rebellion brought an immediate response from Confederate president Jefferson Davis, whose proclamation of 17 April 1861 on national defense encouraged citizens to apply for letters of marque and reprisal for "private-armed vessels." Davis's follow-up message to the Confederate Congress requesting swift consideration of legislation that would authorize privateering stated, "In the absence of a fleet of public vessels it will be eminently expedient to supply their place by private-armed vessels, so happily styled by the publicists of the United States 'the militia of the sea.' "[23] Congress responded quickly to the president by passing the law on 6 May. Although North Carolina was not yet officially out of the Union, Governor John W. Ellis's response to the Confederate president was: "We have on these waters some bold and Skilful Seamen who are ready to go out as privateers at once. . . . The enemy's commerce between N. York and all the West Indies and South American ports could be cut off by privateers on the coast of No. Ca."[24]

In the first months of the war, as letters of marque were issued, twenty-five privateers put to sea from several ports, most successfully from New Orleans and Charleston. New Orleans, the South's largest and wealthiest port, had both investment capital and numerous vessels available for privateering. In addition to the usual assortment of sailing craft and river steamers, Crescent City privateers launched the nation's first ironclad ram, the *Manassas*, and built a prototype submarine. Confederate privateering reached its apogee in the early months of the war and resulted in some forty prizes, but as the war progressed the ever-tightening noose of the Union naval blockade made it increasingly risky to sally out to sea and practically impossible to slip prizes back for condemnation proceedings in the diminishing number of open Southern ports. As a result, any idled craft that were suitable were converted to blockade running, which, fueled by inflationary prices, became the most lucrative business in the Confederacy.

While the blockade restricted egress from the larger Southern ports, on the North Carolina coast the little-known Hatteras and Ocracoke Inlets were fortified and became harbors for commerce raiding by the fledgling North Carolina state navy and privateers. Following the outbreak of war in mid-April, Governor Ellis, foreseeing the inevitable secession of his state, refused military support to the United States and confiscated Federal property. Defense preparations, including repairs to existing fortifications at Beaufort Inlet and Cape Fear and new forts at Hatteras, Ocracoke, and Oregon Inlets, were accelerated by the state's secession on 20 May 1861. After Ellis's untimely death in late May, the feverish pace of placing the state on a war footing continued unabated under the new governor, Henry T. Clark.

North Carolina's minuscule navy was charged with defending the state's long coastline, protecting its vast inland waters, and harassing enemy shipping at sea. Derisively known as the "mosquito fleet," the motley collection of five shallow-draft local steamers and tugboats, each armed with one heavy cannon, saw action in May at Hatteras and Ocracoke Inlets. The first vessel to be commissioned, the *Winslow*, proved most successful at chasing and boarding Union merchant shipping, but she was capably aided by her consorts—the *Raleigh*, the *Beaufort*, the *Ellis*, and later the *Edwards*. Captured vessels were sailed to New Bern, where they were condemned in a state district court, which granted prize money for the fleet. When, later in the summer of 1861, the state transferred its navy to the Confederacy, the little fleet came under the command of Commodore Samuel Barron. With prizes accumulating, the "mosquito fleet" was joined by other Confederate naval vessels and privateers. Up to this point, the limited Union naval forces off the Outer Banks had done little more than observe the Confederate raiders, and their mounting frustration was expressed in a letter to Secretary of the Navy Gideon Welles from an officer on the USS *Cumberland*, who wrote that "the coast of Carolina is infested with a nest of privateers that have thus far escaped capture, and, in the ingenious method of their cruising, are probably likely to avoid the clutches of our cruisers."[25]

Public outcry in the North over the outrageous "nest of pirates"[26] at Hatteras and lobbying by Northern commercial interests and marine insurance companies precipitated the Federal government's organizing a combined army and navy expedition, the first Union naval offensive of the war. In late August a fleet of seven heavily armed men-of-war appeared off Hatteras accompanied by transports bearing a small invasion force. Over a two-day period the lightly armed and poorly constructed defenses were overrun, and the North celebrated its first victory of the war. Admiral David Dixon Porter later wrote, "This was our first naval victory, indeed our first victory of any kind, and should not be forgotten. The Union cause was then in a depressed condition, owing to the reverses it had experienced. The moral of this affair was very great, as it gave us a foothold on Southern soil and possession of the Sounds of North Carolina if we chose to occupy them. It was a death-blow to blockade running in that vicinity, and ultimately proved one of the most important events of the war."[27]

Union occupation of the inlet fortifications ended Confederate privateering on the Outer Banks, but a sizable expedition would be needed to conquer the North Carolina sound country. A second incursion into the Carolinas came just a month later when Port Royal Sound in South Carolina was taken by a large combined force, which shelled the Confederate forts into surrender and brushed aside another lightweight "mosquito fleet" of river gunboats and tugs. The harbor at Port Royal Sound became a vital base for sustaining the Union blockade along the southeastern coast. The initial success at Hatteras in North Carolina was exploited in February 1862 by a flotilla of over a hundred ships and the largest Union amphibious force yet gathered. This massive expedition crushed the outmanned Confederate defenses on Roa-

From behind a line of obstructions across Croatan Sound, the Confederate "mosquito fleet" engaged Union ships bombarding Roanoke Island on 7 February 1862. (Outer Banks History Center, Manteo, N.C.)

noke Island and destroyed the remaining Confederate gunboats in a naval action at Elizabeth City. Further Union victories at New Bern and Fort Macon resulted in permanent occupation of northeastern North Carolina and opened a backdoor threat to the South's great naval base at Norfolk.

These obscure but strategically important operations provided an arena for James W. Cooke to demonstrate his ability as a commander in North Carolina's "mosquito fleet" gunboats. The North Carolina coast was also the setting for Cooke's exploits in 1864 as captain of one of the South's most successful ironclads, the css *Albemarle*. In that same year, New Bern saw a dramatic cutting-out expedition commanded by John Taylor Wood, a pioneer of naval commando tactics.

After the failure of the misguided cotton embargo, it dawned on the Confederate leadership that the agricultural South could not develop in time the heavy industrial infrastructure to support modern warfare. The alternative was to use cotton to purchase arms and equipment abroad and import them through the Union blockade of Southern ports. Shipbuilders in Great Britain responded to the Confederacy's plight by constructing small, fast steamers made to order to run the blockade by short voyages from the transshipping points of Bermuda and Nassau.

An 1853 view of Wilmington, on the Cape Fear River, then North Carolina's largest port. Through blockade running it became the most important port in the Confederacy. (Outer Banks History Center, Manteo, N.C.)

As the war dragged on, the increasingly decrepit Confederate economy stumbled toward failure and would have collapsed sooner had not blockade running staved off defeat by slipping into the country crucial goods purchased abroad. Although most of the runners were privately owned, many by foreigners, both the Confederate government and state governments wholly or partially owned blockade runners and purchased cargo space for badly needed weapons, ammunition, medicine, food, and textiles. At first any available vessel was used, but soon craft designed for speed were built—low, nimble, narrow, and equipped with powerful engines. In an early use of camouflage, they were painted gray to blend invisibly into the sky and sea. The state government of North Carolina went into blockade running early in the war and ultimately owned several vessels. One of the most successful of the blockade runner captains was John N. Maffitt, who was raised in the Cape Fear valley and was almost unique in making the transition from cruisers to blockade runners. As more Southern seaports were occupied or closed, Wilmington became the most important point of entry into the Confederacy. Thanks to the protection of the redoubtable Fort Fisher, Wilmington was the last major port remaining open, the center of blockade running, and the only Confederate port to harbor high seas raiders.

The early demise of privateering left the Confederate navy as the sole offensive striking force capable of high seas commerce raiding. Secretary Mallory envisioned a fleet of long-range cruisers vigorously waging "guerrilla warfare of the sea,"[28] with the goals of ravaging the enemy's merchant fleet, disrupting the Northern economy, lowering Northern morale, and luring enough Union warships away to weaken the blockade. To a surprising degree these objectives were achieved, although, of course, a dozen raiders were not able to affect the outcome of the war. Realizing that the South had too few ships suitable for overseas cruising and too little time to build new ones, Secretary Mallory sent James D. Bulloch to England in the summer of 1861 to acquire and equip armed cruisers capable of remaining at sea for long periods. Dogged at every step and often thwarted by Union embassy officials, Bulloch nevertheless secretly managed to put to sea the finest of the Confederate cruisers—the css *Florida*, the css *Alabama*, and the css *Shenandoah*. A master at staying one step ahead of Union authorities, Bulloch used dummy trading companies and foreign purchasers to launch apparent merchant vessels that were then commissioned and armed at a rendezvous near some remote island.

When, in 1872, Great Britain agreed, after protracted arbitration in the *Alabama* claims settlement, to pay the United States $15.5 million in damages attributed to Confederate cruisers that had originated in Britain, it was determined that Bulloch's three cruisers and their four tenders had accounted for over 80 percent of the claims. The *Florida*, commanded first by John N. Maffitt, went to sea in August 1862 on a seven-month cruise, accumulating numerous prizes. Sailing a few days later, the *Alabama*, under Raphael Semmes, the South's foremost commerce raider, embarked on a nearly two-year voyage in which she garnered over sixty prizes, sank the uss *Hatteras* in the Gulf of Mexico, and met with a spectacular demise in a battle with the uss *Kearsarge* off Cherbourg, France. James I. Waddell's *Shenandoah*, the last of the great cruisers to be commissioned, finally ended her thirteen-month-long, globe-encircling odyssey six months after the war was over. Meanwhile, in 1864 John Taylor Wood created a near panic on the northeastern coast when he sailed the css *Tallahassee*, a converted blockade runner, from Wilmington on a sensational cruise to Halifax, Nova Scotia, taking numerous prizes as he went.

The depredations inflicted in three years of war by eleven cruisers led to the destruction of nearly two hundred prizes, sweeping the U.S. merchant fleet from the high seas. While the cruisers sank just 110,000 tons of shipping, vessels totaling 800,000 tons were sold to foreign owners, and about as many ships sought the protection of foreign registry, in which they remained after the war. Financially, the doubling or even tripling of marine insurance rates had a greater impact than the actual loss of prizes. The United States in 1861 had a merchant fleet second in the world only to that of Great Britain, and in just four years that fleet was reduced to a third of its prewar vessels.[29] Not until the twentieth century did the American merchant fleet recover from the effects of the Civil War. The damage wrought by the Confederate cruisers to the economy of the United States was "more effective than any other single effort by the Confederacy during the war."[30]

Not being a seafaring nation, the Confederacy could barely comprehend how solid were the achievements of its tiny naval service of just over five thousand men—less than one-tenth the size of the Union navy. In the final analysis, however, the stunning successes of the ironclads, the undersea warfare of mines and submarines, the commando raids, and the cruisers must be balanced against the failure to break the strangling grip of the blockade, the loss of the Mississippi valley, and the inability to protect the coast from invasion. With the realization that their defeats were due more to the nation's limited industrial capacity than to any failings of naval officers and sailors, the services's esprit de corps remained high. But the few triumphs remind us of the truth of John N. Maffitt's observation, "The grand mistake of the South was neglecting her navy."[31]

From pirate to privateer to naval high seas raider, these North Carolina heroes and rogues shared similar personalities and experiences. They were all skilled seamen and decisive, imaginative leaders who possessed a deep thirst for adventure, at times pursuing danger with a reckless abandon. Although they all courted death repeatedly in the arena of naval combat, only three lost their lives as a result—Stede Bonnet, Blackbeard, and Johnston Blakeley. Blackbeard alone was killed in action. While these men who sailed so frequently in harm's way may have been extraordinarily fortunate, it is likely that their skill at sea and their sharply honed instincts had more to do with their survival than did mere luck. Clearly these mariners could have succeeded, and most did, in the routine but important existence that is the lot of most of the world—day-to-day work and family responsibilities. But once they had tasted the excitement of high seas theft, raids, smuggling, or naval combat, they never again felt so alive as when they were on a quarterdeck sailing or steaming at full speed in a chase as hunter or prey, approaching a strange sail with battle impending, or confronting the awful power of the natural elements as they rode out an intense offshore storm.

*A most cruel
hardened Villain,
bold and daring
to the last degree.*
—*Captain Charles
Johnson, 1724*

Blackbeard

The *Queen Anne's Revenge* Scourges the Carolinas

The morning wind freshened to near gale force as scuba divers gathered on the municipal dock in Beaufort. The inlet was choppy and the weather marginal, but aborting the expedition was out of the question. Just hours before, a decade-long quest by Intersal, Inc., had on the last scheduled day of the search finally located a wreck that could be the long-sought and elusive *Queen Anne's Revenge*, the powerful forty-gun flagship of one of the most notorious pirates in history—Blackbeard. It was 1996, 22 November, 278 years to the day since Blackbeard had been killed in a savage fight at Ocracoke Inlet. If indeed this wreck was the *Queen Anne's Revenge*, it would be one of the most important marine archaeological discoveries ever in North Carolina's Graveyard of the Atlantic, which holds the remains of thousands of wrecked ships spanning the last four hundred years of naval warfare and marine disasters.

The trail that led to the discovery of the Beaufort Inlet wreck began in 1982 with a research project of David Moore, a North Carolina native and a graduate student in the maritime history program at East Carolina University. Over the course of his professional career as a marine archaeologist, Moore compiled a comprehensive study of Blackbeard and his ships, dreaming that one day he would be able to find and excavate the *Queen Anne's Revenge*. In 1986, Phil Masters, a Florida treasure hunter who was seeking the Spanish treasure ship *El Salvador*, which was lost near Beaufort Inlet in the mid-eighteenth century, applied for a search permit from the North Carolina Underwater Archaeology Unit. Delving into the unit's files at their Fort Fisher office, Masters came across Moore's report from which he gleaned leads to research the pirate wrecks himself. In 1988 Masters formed Intersal, Inc., in Boca Raton, Florida to finance excavation of treasure and historic ships. He then received a North Carolina permit to survey the coast in and around Beaufort Inlet, searching primarily for the *El Salvador* but secondarily for the *Queen Anne's Revenge* and its consort the *Adventure*, which had been wrecked at the same time. In 1988–89 Masters sent Jim Whitaker to Beaufort with remote sensing equipment to survey the inlet, and Whitaker located a number of underwater anomalies potentially worthy of further investigation.

Since the Beaufort Inlet project was one of several treasure hunts engaging Intersal's limited resources, work on it was intermittent. Years went by with no success. With time running out on an annual permit in 1996, in a last-ditch effort Intersal brought in an experienced wreck diver, Mike Daniel, who located five promising wreck sites in the inlet. Early in the morning on 21 November, the last day of the scheduled survey, divers Ray Giroux and Eugene Brunelle descended on the west side of the inlet and came upon a large mound of debris heavily concreted with marine growth. Clearly visible were large anchors and three cannon. With mounting excitement Daniel joined his divers, and during the day the elated team identified more cannon and recovered several artifacts from the pile—a large bronze bell, a gun barrel, lead items, barrel hoops, and cannon balls. Observing that the number and size of the cannon and the large anchors were appropriate for a vessel the size of the *Queen Anne's Revenge*, they dared hope that the bell would bear a date or an identifying inscription.

A call to Fort Fisher brought the unit head, Richard Lawrence, and his chief conservator, Leslie Bright, to Beaufort for the confirmation dive with Phil Masters and Ray Giroux on the following day. Despite rough water and rising wind, the dive was completed, and the state archaeologists came to the conclusion that this wreck could indeed be the *Queen Anne's Revenge*. As Bright carefully began to remove the marine encrustation from the bell, excitement grew as "1709" was painstakingly revealed, a date nine years prior to the loss of the *Queen Anne's Revenge*. The inscription, IHS MARIA, identified the bell as Spanish in origin, possibly a ship's bell or plunder from a church or mission. The gun barrel was from an English brass blunderbuss. The lead pieces were identified as a cannon touch hole apron, which protected the powder charge from dampness, and a twenty-one-pound deep-sea sounding weight. One of the two iron cannon balls was, appropriately, a four-pounder, but the other, a twenty-four-pound ball, may have been fired from nearby Fort Macon, which mounted cannon of that size during the Civil War. As a result of the worldwide interest generated by this find, Intersal, Inc., formed a nonprofit corporation, Maritime Research Institute, to study historic wrecks.

The cleaning and conservation of the eclectic mix of artifacts consumed the next few months. With the artifacts brilliantly prepared for exhibit, the North Carolina Division of Archives and History held a joint press conference with Intersal in Raleigh on 3 March 1997. The conference opened with Governor James B. Hunt's official announcement that the waters of Beaufort Inlet might hold the remains of one of the largest and most famous pirate ships that ever sailed. The governor was followed by the division director, Jeffrey J. Crow, who declared in his opening remark that this was "the most important underwater archaeology discovery since the USS *Monitor* was found off Cape Hatteras in 1973."

With a working hypothesis that the wreck might be the *Queen Anne's Revenge*, archaeologists from the Maritime Research Institute, the Underwater Archaeology Unit, and the North Carolina Maritime Museum conducted technical dives on 15 April and 2 July 1997. The wreck was pinpointed again and its condition examined, but work was limited by poor visibility. Less than two miles offshore in shallow water, twenty-two to twenty-six feet deep, the site is on a clear, sandy bottom in an area with moderate current. With the realization that the ship could be excavated, a major investigation involving nine different agencies, universities, and museums was scheduled for the month of October.

On 3 October a flotilla of research vessels, including Intersal's *Pelican III*, the Underwater Archaeology Unit's *Snap Dragon*, and the University of North Carolina at Wilmington's *Seahawk* anchored over the wreck to begin a month of surveying, mapping, and excavation.

Principal divers, supervised by field director Mark Wilde-Ramsing, came from Maritime Research Institute, the Underwater Archaeology Unit, the Maritime Museum, and East Carolina University. Through the month of October the expedition uncovered an astonishing array of artifacts, including fifteen cannon, three large anchors, a grapnel, numerous barrel hoops and ballast stones, large quantities of eighteenth-century glass and ceramics shards, musket balls, and a sheet-lead pump screen. Most telling were bagged lead shot, lead shot in a bottle fragment that may be the remains of a crude hand grenade, and two marked English pewter plates. On a day of high drama, Cape Fear Community College's large research vessel, the *Dan Moore*, was brought in on 23 October to raise two of the cannon, each weighing about a ton. Six days later the excavation culminated in a crowded press conference at the Maritime Museum in Beaufort at which Crow announced that the archaeologists were "95 percent certain" that the wreck is the flagship of the infamous Blackbeard.

In September and October 1998, the research team reconvened at the Gallant's Channel docks of the Maritime Museum to continue their archaeological examination of the Beaufort Inlet wreck. Despite some days lost to sharp southwest winds and choppy seas, over a six-week season the divers uncovered a section of the hull and an astonishing array of artifacts. A sizable cache of musket balls and swan shot and three more cannon were located. More pewter plates and chargers were recovered, as well as two intact early eighteenth-century wine bottles. The new artifacts that generated the most excitement were parts of brass surveying and navigational instruments and a minuscule amount of gold dust. Several hundred feet south of the wreck divers found a well-preserved kedge anchor, which indicated that an attempt had been made to free the doomed ship from the sandbar.

At this early stage of archaeological research, all the evidence points toward this wreck's being the *Queen Anne's Revenge*, a two-hundred-ton vessel, over ninety feet long, that may have carried forty guns. The more than two thousand artifacts already recovered, as well as the anchors and ship's fittings, suggest a ship of that size, and no other known wreck at this location had armament of such a number and size. Furthermore, the multinational origins of the assemblage of recovered objects would be expected on a pirate ship that pillaged vessels sailing from many different countries. Nevertheless, it must be said that years of excavation in which thousands of appropriate artifacts are recovered will come to naught if the investigation yields in an undisturbed context artifacts made after 1718. Even if the ship turns out not to be the *Queen Anne's Revenge*, however, it is the earliest wreck ever found in North Carolina waters and has the potential to illuminate a little-known historical era in which the future course of the state was set. A comprehensive examination of any shipwreck from the early eighteenth century is a major archaeological event deserving the extraordinary attention that this discovery has already attracted. A projected museum at Gallant's Channel will become the repository of the artifacts and the center of the lengthy preservation process necessary to make possible the exhibition of artifacts immersed in the sea for nearly three hundred years.[1]

After extensive research, excavation, and conservation the Division of Archives and History should eventually be able to prove whether or not the Beaufort Inlet wreck is the *Queen Anne's Revenge*. Some of the thousands of artifacts will be displayed at the Maritime Museum and other appropriate facilities around the state. The artifacts should bring to life "the fiercest pirate of all," illuminating a colorful era that is still, after nearly three hundred years, only partly understood. Through the portal of the Beaufort Inlet wreck may come insight into this giant of a man who was "Superior in Roguery"[2] to his contemporaries and strode so boldly on the stage of history. Was Blackbeard merely a bizarre larger-than-life character whose brief piratical career was "a tale," to borrow Shakespeare's phrase, "full of sound and fury, signifying nothing"? Perhaps it is more likely that through him we will gain a better comprehension of the lives of early eighteenth-century seamen and pirates and their world of maritime commerce in the American colonies.

Documentation on Blackbeard is so sparse that he is to this day a historical figure who barely emerges from the shadows; what we do know of him covers a period of less than two years of his life. Nothing of certainty is known about his parentage, his birthplace, or even his name. Those who have written narratives about him have repeated dubious tales that have little foundation in fact. Even Captain Charles Johnson, in *A General History of the Pyrates*, had little to say about Blackbeard's early life. In his first edition Johnson had Edward Thatch, a native of Jamaica, going to sea as a boy and serving on privateers in Queen Anne's War. In his second edition Johnson's revision had Edward Teach originally from Bristol, England, later sailing out of Jamaica on privateers, and finally becoming a pirate under Benjamin Hornigold.[3] One early reference declares that Blackbeard was born in

Jamaica, where his mother and a brother were still living in 1740. Other contemporary sources connect him to Philadelphia, from which he supposedly sailed as a mate on merchant vessels, and London, where one of his wives was living. Although extensive searches by scholars in Bristol, Jamaica, and London have unearthed nothing about him or his origins, as a merchant seaman he surely passed through the major ports of England and the colonies, and it is to be expected that he spent some time in Jamaica since the island had a long history as a pirate and privateer stronghold.[4]

A major obstacle in researching Blackbeard is simply that we may not know his real name. A high percentage of the primary documents record Blackbeard's name as "Thatch" or some phonetic derivation thereof. The earliest use of "Teach" is in an issue of the *Boston News-Letter* of November 1717, but this same paper uses "Bennet" for Stede Bonnet.[5] In the Carolinas, Blackbeard is almost always referred to in the documents as Edward Thatch, though occasionally his last name is given as Tach or Thache. It also may be that both Thatch and Teach were aliases, but on the Carolina coast Blackbeard was Edward Thatch. As late as 1733, when surveyor Edward Moseley, who had known Blackbeard as an adversary, was preparing his great map of North Carolina, he labeled the traditional site of Blackbeard's final battle near Ocracoke Inlet as Thatches or Thatch's Hole. How then did "Teach" become the preference? It must be attributed first to the only newspaper in the North American colonies, the *Boston News-Letter*, and, more decisively, to the pervasive influence of the later editions of Johnson's *General History of the Pyrates*, which has been the basis for most pirate narratives published from 1724 to the present.

Although with little provocation pirates might resort to senseless "barbarities," prizes often fell to them simply because of the fear inspired by their legendary savagery. Of all the pirates in history, Blackbeard is singled out as the master of creating and perpetuating an image that terrorized his victims and companions alike. Admittedly, Captain Johnson may have done as much for Thatch's larger-than-life image as did the rogue himself, with vivid descriptions of his "remarkably black ugly Beard" that consisted of a "large Quantity of Hair, which like a frightful Meteor, covered his Whole Face."[6] One eyewitness, Henry Bostock, who was captured by Thatch near Puerto Rico on 5 December 1717, reported that "the Captain by the name (as he thinks) of Capt Tach . . . was a tall Spare Man with a very black beard which he wore very long."[7] Captain Johnson fleshed out the classic

Edward Thatch, Blackbeard, gained notoriety from Captain Charles Johnson's *General History of the Pyrates*. This portrait of the infamous buccaneer appeared in the second edition of the work (1724). (North Carolina Division of Archives and History, Raleigh)

portrait, which has entered popular culture, saying, "This Beard was black, which he suffered to grow of an extravagant Length; as to Breadth, it came up to his Eyes; he was accustomed to twist it with Ribbons, in small Tails, after the Manner of our Ramillies Wiggs, and turn them about his Ears: In Time of Action, he wore a Sling over his Shoulders, with three Brace of Pistols, hanging in Holsters like Bandaliers; and stuck lighted Matches under his Hat, which appearing on each Side of his Face, his Eyes naturally looking fierce and wild, made him altogether such a Figure, that Imagination cannot form an Idea of a Fury, from Hell, to look more frightful."[8]

There is little wonder that before such a monstrous apparition, bearing down in his sinister black vessel, flying the red "no quarter" banner and the black-and-white death's head, decks bristling with cannon, rails jammed with equally fierce visages, his victims' resistance would melt, particularly if word had passed among the common sea-men that immediate surrender meant little risk to themselves. Despite the specter of a probable gallows ending, men could be found on most merchant ships eager to join the "brethren of the coast," to break out of their miserable lives if only for a brief while, to experience the freedom offered by a colorful outlaw on the high seas with all of the perceived excitement, the potential wealth, and the exhilaration of danger that surrounded him.

Blackbeard's unpredictable and terrifying behavior, coupled with his frightening appearance, cultivated among his followers the notion that he was the "Devil incarnate." As if to prove them right, he amused himself once by creating a hell aboard ship. "A little flushed with Drink," Blackbeard shut himself and several of his men in the hold with burning pots of brimstone. Declaring himself best able to with-stand the suffocating smoke, he finally gave them air after they repeat-edly begged him to open the hatches. In another drinking bout, Black-beard disabled his sailing master, Israel Hands, by secretly drawing pistols under the table, blowing out the candle, and randomly dis-charging the weapons, wounding Hands in the knee. His explanation was that "if he did not now and then kill one of them, they would forget who he was."[9]

Charismatic, physically domineering, and fearless in battle, Black-beard was a natural leader who understood the subtleties of handling his restless crew, as the following journal entry reveals: "Such a Day, Rum all out:—Our Company somewhat sober:—A damn'd Confusion amongst us!—Rogues a plotting;—great Talk of Separation.—So I look'd sharp for a Prize;—such a Day took one, with a great deal of Liquor on board, so kept the Company hot, damn'd hot, then all Things went well again."[10]

Although the early life of Blackbeard remains shrouded in mystery, in 1717 he burst suddenly onto the pirate scene, creating an unforgetta-ble persona that "frightened *America* more than any Comet that has appeared there [in] a long Time." How did this man who had "often distinguished himself for his uncommon Boldness and personal Cour-age" as a privateer become such a dominant figure of his age and ultimately a global icon of piracy?[11] He first appeared in Jamaica as a seaman during Queen Anne's War under privateer Captain Benjamin Hornigold, from whose tutelage came a number of pirates of this era.[12] After the war Hornigold sailed the brigantine *Ranger* as a pirate, but his choice to take only French and Spanish ships meant that he passed up too many potentially rich English prizes to suit his crew. Soon Hornigold's men deposed him, electing Samuel Bellamy as their cap-, tain and sending Hornigold off in a captured sloop of eight guns with such crew members as remained loyal to him, including Blackbeard.

Hornigold shifted his base to Nassau on New Providence Island in the Bahamas, which had become a haven for several hundred logwood cutters and freebooters evicted by the Spanish from the Bays of Campeche and Honduras. The Nassau rendezvous gradually attracted buccaneers from all over the Caribbean, who organized themselves into a community under the nominal command of Captain Henry Jennings. Faced with this new outlaw stronghold athwart the main shipping lanes between North America and the West Indies, the British government sent out a new governor of the Bahamas, Captain Woodes Rogers, a well-known privateer and navigator. Rogers arrived in the summer of 1718 with two naval vessels and a royal pardon for all pirates who would surrender. Like most of his partners in crime, Hornigold took the pardon at that time. He then joined the governor in his quest to end piracy in the Bahamas.[13]

Before he accepted the pardon, however, Hornigold had become one of the pirate chieftains of Nassau, and sometime in 1717 he raided the North American coast, taking a shallop from Havana with a cargo of flour, a Bermuda-based sloop from which he looted wine, and a valuable cargo from a ship out of Madeira. On the coast of Virginia, Hornigold cleaned his ship by careening it, or rolling the hull on its side to remove marine growth and barnacles. He then returned with Blackbeard to the Bahamas rendezvous, where in the fall of 1717 they met Stede Bonnet, who had suffered a major battle with a Spanish man-of-war that had seriously damaged his ship, the *Revenge*, cost him about half his crew, and left him gravely wounded. With his sloop refitted and ready to sail, Bonnet, who was still recuperating from his injuries, engaged Blackbeard to captain the *Revenge* on another voyage north to the American mainland.[14]

This cruise of the *Revenge* off the busy Delaware capes and Virginia coast under Blackbeard's command reaped a bonanza of eleven prizes. The first capture came on 29 September near Cape Charles, Virginia, when the sloop *Betty* was plundered of Madeira wine and sunk. Moving north, the *Revenge* arrived off the Delaware capes and on 12 October took a ship under a Captain Codd, which had 150 passengers, mostly indentured servants bound for Pennsylvania. Codd reported that the pirate captain was "one Teach, who formerly Sail'd Mate out of this Port [Philadelphia]." Except for personal looting, what cargo was on board was tossed into the sea. Shortly thereafter, the *Revenge* stopped two outward-bound snows, or large, two-masted merchant vessels—the *Spofford*, laden with a thousand barrel staves for Ireland, and the *Sea Nymph*, carrying wheat. Both cargoes were thrown overboard. The *Sea Nymph* was kept and the prisoners put aboard the *Spofford*. On 22 October the sloop *Robert* of Philadelphia and the ship *Good Intent* of Dublin were stopped and robbed of supplies. Two wine-laden sloops from Madeira were welcome prizes, enthusiastically plundered. One was released without her masts to drift ashore, while the other was sunk. Next taken was a sloop with thirty indentured servants from London, followed by a sloop from Curaçao with a cargo of cocoa, which was also thrown overboard. The master, a Captain Goelet, was given the *Sea Nymph*, which was loaded with the indentured servants from London. Goelet made port in New York on 30 October and reported that before he left he saw the pirates take another sloop and a snow. A Captain Farmer of Jamaica was stopped twice by pirates, the last time by Blackbeard, who removed his masts, anchors, cables, and money and set him adrift to be stranded on Sandy Hook.[15]

Leaving Delaware Bay, the brigands returned to New Providence, where they were reunited with Hornigold. In November their combined flotilla sailed toward the Leeward Islands. Unbeknown to the pirates, the previous spring, on 24 March 1717, the two-hundred-ton *Concorde* under Captain Pierre Dosset with a crew of seventy-five men had embarked from Nantes on a slave trading voyage to West Africa and the French West Indies. Arriving on the Guinea coast on 8 July, Captain Dosset purchased 516 slaves. The ship also had on board over twenty pounds of gold dust, cocoa, and some copper. Sailing west from Guinea on 2 October, the vessel was struck with illness. Within two months sixteen crewmen had died and thirty-six were down with scurvy and dysentery, leaving less than half the crew able to serve the ship. Sixty-one slaves also perished. On 17 November some one hundred miles from their destination of Martinique, the *Concorde* was waylaid by two pirate craft described by Lieutenant François Ernaud as one of twelve guns and 120 men and another of eight guns and 30 men. Although the French slaver was armed with at least fourteen cannon, the reduced crew could not work both armaments and ship. They had little choice but to surrender to the pirates who had raked them with "two volleys of cannons and musketry." The pirates sailed their prize south into the Grenadines, where the many islets afforded numerous hideaways. Off Bequia they plundered the "cream" of the cargo and were overjoyed to hear from Louis Arot, a newly recruited fifteen-year-old cabin boy, that there was gold on board. A threat to cut the throats of the ship's officers loosened tongues and quickly revealed the treasure. Four crewmen from the *Concorde* freely joined the pirates, while ten others, including a pilot, three surgeons, two carpenters, a cook, a gunsmith, and a black trumpeter, were forced into piracy. Now Blackbeard could dine in grand style, savoring French cuisine served on silver plate, accompanied by music. Of the 125 slaves taken by the pirates, the French eventually recovered all but 65. The remaining French crewmen were set ashore with the slaves, and the pirates gave their smaller vessel, a forty-ton Bermuda sloop, to the French.[16] Blackbeard assumed command of the prize, which he named *Queen Anne's Revenge*, probably as an insult to the reigning British monarch, George I.[17] Hornigold, now enriched with the plundered gold, sailed with Blackbeard for only a few days, then left and headed for Nassau and retirement. The *Revenge* was returned to Bonnet.

With her armament more than doubled—to nearly forty guns—the *Queen Anne's Revenge* was destined to become one of the most famous pirate ships of the era. Blackbeard, now commanding a ship that was a match for any royal naval vessel in the hemisphere, embarked on a year-long ravishment of trade in the Americas that would make him one of the most famous pirates in history. The day after the *Queen Anne's Revenge* was taken, the pirate flotilla of three ships encountered the *Montserrat Merchant*. The captain was ordered on board and questioned about shipping and the whereabouts of the HMS *Scarborough*, the thirty-gun man-of-war stationed in the Leewards. The pirates bragged about cutting out a French ship at Guadeloupe and burning part of the port town. On 30 November the sloop *New Division* from Antigua was stopped, queried about local shipping, and then allowed to proceed.[18]

The *Queen Anne's Revenge* and the *Revenge* swept across the Caribbean from the Leeward Islands to the Virgins, capturing and destroying a French vessel loaded with sugar off St. Christopher. On 5 December they plundered and burned the sloop *Margaret*. Off St. Vincent the ship *Great Allen* was looted, and, after the crew was set ashore, it too was burned. The collusion of Blackbeard and Bonnet in late 1717 was recorded by Captain Francis Hume, the commander of the *Scarborough*, stationed at Barbados. Hume identified two craft seen sailing through his area as "a Pyrate Ship of 36 Guns and 250 men, and a

Sloop of 10 Guns and a 100 men." Although Captain Johnson thought that Blackbeard had bested the *Scarborough* in a lengthy sea battle, there is no reference to such an encounter in Hume's correspondence or the frigate's log. With Hume in pursuit, the pirates always managed to stay one island ahead and disappeared to the west toward their eventual rendezvous in the Bay of Honduras.[19]

From the Virgin Islands and a winter layover in Nassau, Blackbeard headed alone for the Central American coast, the fabled Spanish Main, a well-known pirate rendezvous from the logwood-cutting days. By March 1718 *Queen Anne's Revenge* had arrived off the Turneffe Islands in the Bay of Honduras to take on fresh water. In early April Bonnet's *Revenge* dropped anchor nearby with a crew near mutiny after their recent defeat by a merchant ship. Bonnet's men secretly appealed to Blackbeard to remove Bonnet, and while entertaining Bonnet on board the *Queen Anne's Revenge*, Blackbeard persuaded him to move to more comfortable quarters aboard the larger ship. The *Revenge*'s crew then voted in Richards, one of Blackbeard's officers, as their captain. Shortly thereafter, an eighty-ton sloop from Jamaica named the *Adventure* arrived, also planning to take on water. The *Adventure*'s master, David Herriot, expected to see other Jamaican vessels but instead found Blackbeard's flotilla. Firing a single gun, Richards hoisted the black flag on the *Revenge*, whereupon Herriot surrendered his ship. He and his crew were forced into piracy, with Israel Hands, another of Blackbeard's close cohorts, given command of their ship.[20] Blackbeard was in effect now commodore of a formidable pirate fleet—the *Queen Anne's Revenge*, the *Revenge*, and the *Adventure*. This squadron, mounting over sixty guns, was more than a match for the dispersed Royal Navy, whose few vessels in the hemisphere were scattered throughout the Caribbean and the North American colonies.

Spreading out across the Bay of Honduras in small boats to search for prizes, the pirates found moored on the coast the *Protestant Caesar*, the very ship that had defeated Bonnet's *Revenge* several days earlier. Bonnet evidently exaggerated the strength of their adversary to the point that Blackbeard believed they needed reinforcement. Furthermore, Blackbeard was determined to take the *Protestant Caesar* quickly to ensure that Captain William Wyer "might not brag when he went to New England that he had beat a Pirate." In preparation for the battle, on 5 April the pirates located and boarded four sloops out of Jamaica. One of the sloops was burned when it was learned that the owner refused to allow pirates on as crewmen, but the other three, including Thomas Newton's *Land of Promise*, were commandeered temporarily by Blackbeard to double the size of his force.

Meanwhile, following the night battle with the *Revenge*, the *Protestant Caesar* had arrived in the Bay of Honduras on 1 April to pick up a cargo of logwood. For a week the New Englanders cut and loaded the wood unmolested, but on the morning of 8 April they were approached by five vessels—a large ship and a sloop flying "Black Flags and Deaths Heads" and three sloops displaying red or "Bloody Flags." Captain Wyer mustered the crew on deck and asked them if they would defend their ship. The men replied that if the strangers were Spaniards, "they would stand by him as long as they had Life," but they would not fight pirates. Wyer sent his second mate in the pinnace to reconnoiter the fast-closing flotilla. Upon learning that the ship had forty guns and 300 men and the sloop was none other than the *Revenge* that they had driven off ten days earlier, the crew, unwilling to face such overwhelming odds, and "believing they would be Murthered," abandoned ship and fled into the forbidding jungle. Three days later Blackbeard coaxed Captain Wyer on board under a promise of protection and told him that he had been wise to desert the *Protestant Caesar* because the *Revenge*'s crew would have exacted a terrible vengeance. He then told Wyer that he must burn the ransacked merchant ship because she was from Boston and "he would burn all Vessels belonging to New England for Executing the six Pirates at Boston." The next morning Captain Wyer watched his livelihood go up in flames. When Blackbeard released Captain Newton's sloop, Wyer and his crew were able to return to Boston with Newton.[21]

Weighing anchor, the pirate fleet followed a circuitous route north, stopping at Grand Cayman to relieve a turtle boat of its fresh meat, and then skirting the west coast of Cuba, passing by Havana. Off Cuba they took a small Spanish sloop, which they retained as a tender for carrying supplies. In the Bahamas the flotilla dropped anchor at the "Spanish wrecks," the well-known site of a lost treasure fleet and a favorite stopover, where the buccaneers spent some time carousing ashore and diving for bullion on the wrecks scattered along the reef.

Resuming their northward journey toward the mainland, the pirates boarded a brigantine and two sloops. By mid-May they had arrived off Charleston harbor in South Carolina and for a week blockaded the port, taking prizes and holding hostages for ransom. The blockade, a famous incident of the period, "struck a great Terror to the whole Province of Carolina."[22] Coming on the heels of a long Indian war and a recent raid by the pirate Charles Vane, this notorious episode reinforced the sense of helplessness the Carolina authorities felt at being beleaguered by a horde of vandals. As a result, it became a turning point, for the colonial governors of Virginia and South Carolina began to rally what little force they had in a determined effort to rid the southern coast of the pernicious pack of sea wolves. The five vessels waylaid off Charleston during that week enriched the pirates by nearly £1,500 in gold and silver and the usual supplies. Blackbeard's ransom demand for the release of the ships and hostages, which included Samuel Wragg, a member of the colonial council, was surprisingly low—a chest of medicine worth about £400. Although this may appear to be a peculiar and insignificant payment to a brigand of Blackbeard's reputation who was in control of the port, medicine was expensive and not easily procured. Governor Robert Johnson at first balked at the idea of giving the villains anything; however, a hostage, Mr. Marks, was escorted ashore by the swaggering Captain Richards, who swore to the governor's council that if the ransom were not paid immediately, the captured vessels would be burned and the heads of the hostages would be presented to the governor. At that, Governor Johnson reluctantly agreed to send the medicine chest.

Locked in the holds of their vessels, the hostages lived in stark terror that their lives might end at any moment. Blackbeard, "putting on a terrible Countenance" and suspecting "foul Treachery," threatened twice to kill his captives when the emissaries he sent to Charleston failed to appear at the appointed hour. Both times he was dissuaded from the bloody deed by Councilman Wragg. The first episode occurred when the boat sent ashore capsized, delaying the return of Marks and Richards. The timely arrival of a message from Marks explaining the incident mollified Blackbeard until the second deadline was not met. This time the negotiations had been successful, but Richards and his companions had scattered into town to drink with acquaintances and could not be found. Pandemonium reigned in the port as Blackbeard arrayed his fleet of eight vessels, including the five prizes, in preparation to attack the town; but at the last moment the boat carrying Marks, Richards, and the medicine chest was seen pulling out from shore. Upon their arrival on board, Blackbeard released the hostages and sailed away.[23]

The pirate fleet worked slowly up the coast to North Carolina, seeking a place to careen their vessels, and in early June came to Topsail Inlet, now Beaufort Inlet. The *Revenge*, the *Adventure*, and the

Spanish sloop safely entered the harbor. When the deep-draft *Queen Anne's Revenge* attempted to cross the bar, she struck hard. Efforts were made to warp the vessel off the bar by setting a kedge anchor south of the wreck, but she was grounded too firmly. Blackbeard sent word to Israel Hands in the *Adventure* to come to his aid, but as the *Adventure* tacked toward the flagship she ran aground and was lost as well. Apparently most if not all of the crew members were rescued by the *Revenge* and the Spanish sloop and initially were taken to the little fishing village of Beaufort at the head of the inlet. Even though Blackbeard was a skilled seaman, North Carolina inlets were notorious for drifting sandbars and shifting channels, and it seems unlikely that any of the pirates was familiar with Topsail Inlet. Suspicion was aired in court depositions that Blackbeard had intentionally grounded his ships to reduce the number of pirates with whom he would have to divide the spoils. Lending credence to the notion of a conspiracy to downsize his group, which was reported to number nearly four hundred men, was Blackbeard's subsequent action of fleeing the scene with forty crewmen, sixty slaves, and most if not all of the loot. Furthermore, when Herriot sought restitution from Blackbeard for the loss of his ship, he and two dozen of his men were marooned on a desolate sandy island nearby, probably Bogue Banks.[24]

An intriguing mystery is what happened to the nearly two hundred pirates who seem to have disappeared after the wrecks. Although there is no record that any of them drowned, it is likely that some did. Several others later surfaced in Virginia, and there is mention of still others in New York and Philadelphia. The remainder must have scattered into thinly settled North Carolina, but there was little to hold them in that poor backwater unless they sought to escape the gallows by blending into the yeoman farmer and fishing communities.

Leaving the scene of this disaster with a select crew in the Spanish sloop, which he armed with eight guns and christened the *Adventure*, Blackbeard headed for Bath, North Carolina's oldest town and the governmental center of the colony, to take the pardon offered under the Act of Grace. Incorporated in 1705, this tiny village of a dozen or so houses on Bath Creek, a tributary of the Pamlico River, included the townhouse of Governor Charles Eden and the residences of the colony's former chief justice, Christopher Gale, and current secretary and collector of customs, Tobias Knight. Blackbeard's arrival in Bath coincided with a critical juncture in North Carolina politics. Over the previous decade the province had endured the political upheaval of a coup d'état by Thomas Cary in 1708 and Cary's Rebellion, a counter-coup orchestrated by Governor Edward Hyde in 1711. Furthermore, the colony had been severely buffeted by crop failures, a yellow fever epidemic, and the devastation of the Tuscarora War of 1711–15. With the end of the war the colony began to experience an economic recovery that coincided with the arrival of Blackbeard. The infamous pirate and his gang, although not desirable citizens, provided welcome cheap trade goods and hard cash to a long-depressed community whose grateful merchants and tavernkeepers kept their questions to themselves.[25]

The fallout from years of political struggle had left the colony's leadership in disarray and bitterly divided. In 1718 an opposition faction headed by Edward Moseley, with his ally Colonel Maurice Moore, faced off against the government, represented by Governor Eden, Secretary Knight, and Councilman Thomas Pollock. Moseley, characterized by his biographer as perhaps "the single most important political figure" of the era, had immigrated to northern Carolina in 1704 and rapidly risen in the General Assembly to the speakership and the Proprietary Council. Described as a "chief contriver" in Thomas Cary's seizure of power in 1708, Moseley was eclipsed when Cary was overthrown in 1711, and his denunciation by Pollock led to a lifelong enmity between them. Colonel Moore, the son of a governor of South Carolina and North Carolina's most renowned Indian fighter, served in the Tuscarora War and then led a contingent from North Carolina to aid the South Carolinians in defeating the Yamassee. His victory over the Cape Fear Indians in 1712 opened that region to settlement. Governor Eden had arrived from England in 1714, settling first in Bath and later purchasing a plantation in Bertie County west of the Chowan River. Eden was ably supported by Pollock, a longtime council member and twice acting governor as president of the council. Pollock's decade-long animosity toward Moseley resurfaced now in the 1718 pirate controversy. Knight was a long-term council member who had been the colony's secretary since 1712 and had been named chief justice in 1717.[26]

Doubtless paving the way with generous gifts, Blackbeard ingratiated himself with Governor Eden and Secretary Knight. Accompanied by twenty of his men, the wily pirate approached the governor and received pardon under the Act of Grace, not for any genuine commitment to reform but rather for "a more favorable Opportunity to play the same Game over again."[27] He and his men were granted permission to go to St. Thomas in the Virgin Islands to seek commissions as privateers. As for the Spanish sloop taken off Cuba, the governor convened a vice-admiralty court that declared the vessel a legitimate prize.

Blackbeard was a flamboyant curiosity landing in the midst of a backwater frontier society of rather drab genteel poverty. Tall in stature, volatile and formidable in personality, his pockets heavy with gold that he gratuitously spread among his new neighbors, Blackbeard overnight became a sensation—the center of a society feasting on the swirl of notoriety and wealth that surrounded him. In short order he wooed and won the hand of the sixteen-year-old daughter of a planter, and the couple were married by the governor, who often performed this service in the absence of clergymen. A contemporary wrote that the 1718 marriage was a convenience for Blackbeard "to put a Gloss to his designs," to disarm his opponents by ostensibly settling into the domestic life of the colony.[28]

Captain Johnson would have us believe that this young lady was Blackbeard's fourteenth wife, although there is mention in other sources of only one other, a wife in London. If Johnson is correct, the wedding day of Mrs. Thatch was a dark day indeed for her, because her husband soon abandoned her to roam at sea, returning periodically for connubial visits at the plantation home "where his Wife lived, with whom, after he had lain all Night, it was his Custom to invite five or six of his brutal Companions to come ashore, and he would force her to prostitute her self to them all, one after another, before his Face."[29] From time to time Blackbeard would appear at other plantations where he bestowed gifts of rum and sugar and then "revell'd Night and Day," and it was rumored that he took "Liberties" with the planters' wives and daughters. It would seem that when the overbearing buccaneer went to sea, the little community must have heaved a collective sigh of relief—none with greater happiness than the new Mrs. Thatch.

After only a few weeks ashore, Blackbeard bade goodbye to his new bride and acquaintances, boarded the *Adventure*, and sailed off through Ocracoke Inlet, setting a course directly east toward Bermuda. En route he relieved several English ships of their supplies and then in August captured two French-owned ships out of Martinique, one carrying a valuable cargo of sugar and the other carrying cocoa. Consolidating the plunder on one craft, Blackbeard ordered all of the French crewmen onto the stripped vessel and sent her on her way. The sugar ship he kept and sailed back to Ocracoke. Once in Bath, Black-beard and four of his men approached the governor and signed an affidavit stating that the ship had been found drifting at sea, aban-doned by her crew. The vice-admiralty court declared the French vessel a derelict, enabling Blackbeard to claim salvage rights. He then began divesting himself of the cargo. Through sale, trade, or gift Governor Eden acquired sixty hogsheads of sugar, and Chief Justice Knight obtained twenty. Concerned that his prize might be recognized and become evidence against him, Blackbeard declared to the gover-nor that the vessel was so unseaworthy she was likely to sink and be-come a hazard to navigation. He was granted permission to burn her.[30]

For the next four months Blackbeard remained in North Carolina, sometimes at Bath, other times at his camp at Ocracoke, and still other times at sea. He traded and pilfered at will and amused himself so-cializing with the planters of the region. No traveler on the colony's inland waters was safe from molestation as Blackbeard and his minions ranged across the sounds, the rivers, and the coastal inlets. One such encounter was vividly recorded in a hearing before the council. Wil-liam Bell of Currituck testified that on the evening of 14 September he and two crewmen were in his periauger anchored at a landing on the Pamlico River. Around midnight he observed another periauger being rowed upriver. When the strangers returned just before dawn, Bell's craft was boarded by an unknown man who demanded a dram of rum, to which Bell replied that it was too dark to draw any. Incensed, the intruder "called for a sword," demanding that Bell put his hands behind him to be tied and swearing that "Damnation Seize him he wou'd kill [him] . . . if he did not tell him truly w[h]ere the money was." When Bell asked who his accoster was, the stranger replied that "he came from Hell w[h]ere he woud carry him presently."[31] The frightened Bell began to struggle, whereupon his assailant called for help and was joined by four black companions who subdued Bell and his two crew members—a boy and an Indian. In the fight the brigand's sword broke as he struck the hapless Bell, whose craft was then ran-sacked. The thieves made off with £66 10s. in cash, a pistol, a box of tobacco pipes, a half barrel of brandy, fifty-eight yards of crepe, and a silver cup. Upon leaving, they prevented pursuit by tossing Bell's oars and sails overboard. The next day Bell went to Chief Justice Knight to report the crime. Although he then told Knight that he suspected other culprits,[32] ten days later Bell implicated Blackbeard in testimony during an investigation of Knight's role in the affair.

With such incidents multiplying all across the region, local merchants and "some of the best of the Planters" realized that the governor, who had neither police nor a military force, was powerless. Consequently, they secretly sent representatives to the governor of Virginia, Alexander Spotswood, who was an inveterate enemy of piracy, having for some time battled a number of buccaneers—most recently Charles Vane and Richard Worley—who had beleaguered the Virginia coast. Spotswood, who had two Royal Navy ships at his disposal, welcomed the intelligence from North Carolina on the whereabouts of an old menace, Blackbeard. The governor was convinced that Blackbeard was fortifying Ocracoke Inlet as a new rendezvous for his cronies, and indeed a rumor was abroad that a pirate gathering, which had drawn in the notorious Vane, had already taken place. Ocracoke Inlet was the entrance through the Outer Banks to North Carolina's interior sounds and its little ports of Bath and New Bern. If Blackbeard succeeded in establishing a permanent base at Ocracoke and attracting other pirates, he would control virtually all trade in North Carolina and could easily strike at the much richer colonies of Virginia and South Carolina. Spotswood jumped at the chance "to extirpate this nest of pyrates" and to rid the Atlantic coast of one of its most wicked predators.

After consulting with captains George Gordon of the *Pearl* and Ellis Brand of the *Lyme*, Spotswood conceived a combined land and sea invasion of North Carolina to trap the pirates. Unwilling to risk his naval vessels in the shallow and treacherous Ocracoke Inlet, Spotswood hired two sloops, the *Jane* and the *Ranger*, and two North Carolina pilots. Captain Brand commanded the combined operation and marched south at the head of the land forces. Lieutenant Robert Maynard, first officer of the *Pearl*, was given command of the sea forces and chose the *Jane* as his flagship. Described by his commander as the oldest officer on station in the American colonies, Maynard was anxious to distinguish himself in action to open the door to promotion. The smaller *Ranger* was commanded by an officer named Hyde from the *Lyme*. The sloops were hastily equipped with small arms and possibly swivel guns, but no carriage guns. With pirate gold beckoning, some fifty-four sailors and marines volunteered readily for the expedition. Further incentive was provided by an act of the House of Burgesses that offered rewards for the conviction or death of pirates in North Carolina or Virginia. Blackbeard was singled out with a reward of £100, and various sums were promised for lesser officers, down to £10 for each pirate.³³ At least in Williamsburg no one questioned whether the Virginia assembly had the right to pass such legislation regarding the colony's southern neighbor, but of course it did not.

Because of rumors about the relationship between Blackbeard and Governor Eden, Spotswood did not inform authorities in North Carolina about his plans or request permission to enter the colony. Now with military and naval contingents poised to invade illegally, it was too late. Captain Brand's forces hacked their way south through the trackless Dismal Swamp and were met at Albemarle Sound by Moseley, Moore, and Captain Jeremiah Vail, who escorted them the rest of the way to Bath, where they arrived on 23 November. Meanwhile, Lieutenant Maynard's sloops weighed anchor and after a four-day voyage sighted Ocracoke Inlet in the fading twilight of 21 November. Although Maynard could see the masts of a vessel that he thought was Blackbeard's, he anchored offshore near the shoals, waiting uneasily until dawn to enter the treacherous waters of the inlet.

Blackbeard's men had sighted the approaching unknown vessels from their lookout point on a hummock near their camp, but they apprehended no cause for alarm. After all, the vessels could have been merchants bound for the North Carolina ports. That evening Blackbeard entertained a passing ship captain, Samuel Odell, and three of his crew. Any lingering ill effects from carousing all night were dispelled at daybreak when the two unidentified vessels were sighted cautiously working their way toward the *Adventure* through the labyrinth of shoals. Blackbeard ordered his ship's anchor cable cut and drifted with the current toward the intruders. To reconnoiter his course, Maynard launched a small boat to sound the depths and find a channel. Approaching too close to the *Adventure*, the boat was driven off by musket fire. Taking the helm, Blackbeard turned his sloop toward shore, hoping to draw the pursuing Maynard onto a hidden sandbar directly in his path. Within minutes the *Jane* and the *Ranger* were aground on the shoal. Using sweeps, or oars, and taking advantage of the remainder of the rising tide, Maynard hoped to break free of the bar before the rapidly closing *Adventure* engaged his ships.³⁴

At hailing distance, Blackbeard bellowed, "Damn you for Villains, who are you? And from whence come you?" Maynard replied, "You may see by our Colors we are no Pyrates!" When Blackbeard responded with an invitation to come on board, Maynard shouted, "I cannot spare my Boat, but I will come aboard of you so soon as I can

The encounter between Lieutenant Robert Maynard and Blackbeard in the battle at Ocracoke on 22 November 1718 as pictured in Captain Charles Johnson's *Lives and Exploits of English Highwaymen* (1842). (Mariners' Museum, Newport News, Va.)

with my Sloop!" Such a saucy retort sparked Blackbeard to raise his glass of liquor and drink a toast to his adversaries, calling them "Cowardly Puppies" and saying, "Damnation seize my Soul if I give you Quarters, or take any from you." In the eighteenth century denying quarter meant taking no prisoners, and Maynard ended the spirited exchange by acknowledging that he expected neither to give nor to receive "Quarters" from the pirate.[35]

With his enemies now at short range and motionless, Blackbeard ordered the *Adventure* to come about and fired a deadly broadside of swan and partridge shot that swept the decks of the *Jane* and the *Ranger*, mowing down nearly half their crews. Hyde and his officers were killed or wounded, and the *Ranger* remained out of the fight until near the end. Although the *Adventure* now drifted onto the shoal, Blackbeard was not troubled. He was sure the battle was all but won. As a ruse, Maynard and his remaining crew hid below the deck. After the *Jane* ground across the shoal, William Butler, the pilot, headed directly for the stranded *Adventure*. To Blackbeard it appeared that nearly everyone had been hit. When the *Jane* plowed into the *Adventure*, the pirates tossed grappling hooks, followed by a barrage of homemade grenades crafted from rum bottles filled with powder and shot. Through the billowing smoke that obscured the deck Blackbeard leaped on board the *Jane*, followed by most of his men. To their surprise and consternation, a swarm of Maynard's sailors and marines poured out of the hold to confront them. The swirling hand-to-hand melee—with pistols, wildly swinging cutlasses, bloody axes, and bludgeons—lasted but a few minutes. Blackbeard headed straight for Maynard, both firing their pistols almost simultaneously. Blackbeard missed. Maynard's ball struck the hairy giant in his chest, but it did not slow him down. Blackbeard bored in relentlessly on Maynard, wielding his cutlass with such force that it broke the lieutenant's sword. Maynard fell back to recover and drew another pistol as Blackbeard raised his blade to finish his foe. As he brought his cutlass down on Maynard, Blackbeard was suddenly staggered by a savage blow from behind that left blood spurting from his neck. His sword glanced off, merely cutting Maynard's hand. Surrounded by his enemies, and weakened by multiple cuts and gunshots, the pirate chieftain collapsed on the deck. His demise took the fight out of his remaining followers. Those who were able attempted to escape by jumping overboard into the bloodstained water. They were shot by the victors as they half stumbled, half swam through the shallows. One body was found days later floating in the marsh, located by the vultures circling overhead.

At this moment the *Ranger* finally came up, and her crew boarded the *Adventure*. In the scuffle one of the British sailors was killed by his own men, but the few pirates on board were quickly subdued. Going below decks, Maynard's men found Odell and his companions, who had cowered in the hold during the battle, restraining Caesar, one of Blackbeard's black pirates, who had been given orders that if they lost the battle he was to light a fuse to the powder and blow the sloop and its occupants to kingdom come. Rummaging through Blackbeard's cabin, the boarders salvaged gold dust, silver plate, and papers allegedly incriminating Secretary Knight and certain New York merchants in Blackbeard's piratical activities.[36]

The casualties had been horrendous—a testimony to the bloodiest six minutes ever fought on Carolina waters. Of the nineteen pirates, six of whom were black, ten were killed and the rest wounded. There are varying reports of Maynard's losses, but Governor Spotswood recorded twelve killed and twenty-two wounded, over half of the force. Maynard completed the grisly task of severing Blackbeard's head and tied it as a trophy to the bowsprit of the prize *Adventure*. Eventually, he sailed back with it to Virginia, where for several years the skull was displayed on a post on shore as a warning to other pirates. The

Lieutenant Maynard's trophy, Blackbeard's head, hung from the bowsprit of his sloop as he sailed back to Virginia from Ocracoke. (North Carolina Division of Archives and History, Raleigh)

harrowing day left the British exhausted. The three sloops dropped anchor in the little bay (today known as "Teach's Hole") where Blackbeard had set up camp, and the crews went ashore, ransacking the camp, in which a large awning sheltered twenty-five hogsheads of sugar, 11 tierces and 145 bags of cocoa, a barrel of indigo, and a bale of cotton. Maynard's force remained on Ocracoke a fortnight, resting, recuperating from wounds, and searching for "Blackbeard's treasure."[37]

In fact, Maynard was out of touch with his commander, Captain Brand, for so long that Brand sent out canoes searching for him, finally establishing contact. Maynard sailed up to Bath with his prize sloop, loot, and trophy head. Brand had collected eighty hogsheads of sugar from Secretary Knight and the governor. Knight's sole mistake had been denying that he had any sugar, but Brand searched his barn and found twenty containers of sugar and two bales of cotton hidden under fodder. Captain Brand later stated that the governor had been completely forthcoming and cooperative. Among the several pirates who were arrested in the vicinity of Bath was Blackbeard's former sailing master Israel Hands, also known as Hesikias Hands. All of the plunder and prisoners were loaded onto the flotilla and returned to Virginia. The *Ranger* dropped anchor at Kiquotan, now Hampton, on 1 January 1719 and was followed two days later by the *Adventure* and the *Jane*. Unloaded from the three sloops were about five tons of cocoa, a large quantity of sugar, two bags of cotton, and over seven hundred pounds of bread. The sale of the *Adventure* and the loot recovered by Maynard and Brand brought about £2,250, which was eventually divided among the crews of the naval vessels.[38]

The government in North Carolina was left in a shambles. The reputations of Governor Eden and Secretary Knight had been tarnished by their dealings with Blackbeard; furthermore, there could be little respect for a government so weak that it could not defend the colony or keep the peace. Moseley and Moore, the governor's chief opponents, did not want to lose the prospect of having the embarrassed governor removed and their own influence thereby enhanced. In a reckless move, they broke into the home of Deputy Secretary John Lovick to ransack the province's records for further evidence connecting the governor to Blackbeard. After denying Lovick entry into his own home for a day, they were arrested by the provost marshal on charges of breaking and entering. In addition, Moseley, who had publicly denounced the governor to rally support for himself, was charged with sedition. Moseley, Moore, and their companions were tried, convicted, and fined by the General Court.[39]

Maynard and Brand returned to a heroes' welcome in Virginia, but the disposition of the prize money led to bickering among the various participants that would take four years to settle. When compared to other accounts, Maynard's self-serving report of the battle at Ocracoke Inlet exaggerated his heroics. He did not help his reputation when, contrary to customary practice, he divided the loot from the *Adventure* only among his own crew, excluding the other participants. Governor Spotswood soon had second thoughts about the legality of his hasty invasion of a neighboring colony and began a lengthy correspondence to justify his actions with officials in London and the Lords Proprietors of Carolina.[40]

The trial of Blackbeard's men in Williamsburg in March 1719 resulted in the execution of all except Israel Hands, who escaped the gallows by receiving a pardon. During the trial, four of the black pirates gave depositions that compromised Secretary Knight. The evidence was sent to North Carolina with a recommendation that Knight be tried as an accessory to piracy. Knight, now suffering a lengthy illness, had resigned as chief justice and left public life behind. He was tried before the council in May 1719 and gave a masterful defense of his actions the previous year. He refuted each charge, establishing that Israel Hands's testimony was hearsay, the depositions of the black pirates were invalid because slaves could not testify in court against a free person, and the sugar found on his premises was being stored there as a courtesy. An eyewitness, Edward Chamberlain, testified that Knight's alleged night meeting with Blackbeard had not occurred. The court found him not guilty, and two weeks later he died.[41]

Charles Eden held the office of proprietary governor from 1714 until his death in 1722. Captain Johnson initially characterized him as a partner-in-crime with Blackbeard but subsequently retracted this description, stating that the governor did not have "any private or criminal Correspondence with this Pyrate" and that he "bore the Character of a good Governor and an honest Man." Eden's problem was that he had neither police nor military support and had to endure in silence "the outragious Insolencies" of Blackbeard, who threatened "to destroy the Town with Fire and Sword, if any Injury was offer'd to him or his Companions." The governor and Blackbeard also followed proper legal procedure: after taking the pardon, the pirates had a clean slate. Blackbeard shrewdly brought the Spanish sloop to the colony's vice-admiralty court to be lawfully condemned as a prize, and the Martinique sugar ship was legally declared a salvageable derelict.[42]

Modern readers may snicker at what appear to be preposterous claims, but the record indicates that Blackbeard committed no piracy after taking the pardon in June 1718. Although bribery could have influenced the courts in which he appeared, Blackbeard's alleged crimes in North Carolina were reviewed in legal hearings after his death, producing no evidence that would have convicted him in any court in the colonies or England. The unauthorized invasion of North Carolina by forces from Virginia, the killing of Blackbeard and his men at Ocracoke, and the pillaging of Blackbeard's possessions, as well as the illegal seizure of the sugar and cocoa from Governor Eden and Secretary Knight, had to be justified by portraying Blackbeard as an evil and monstrous criminal and by blackening the names of Governor Eden and his cronies.

Is the frightening legacy of Blackbeard true or not? We will never really know. We do know that in his day he was a celebrated and infamous pirate. While some of his victims were badly treated, by the loss of their property, there is no evidence that he ever murdered anyone. His word could be believed; he traded as often as he plundered. Captain Johnson expressed some admiration of him when he characterized Blackbeard as "that courageous Brute, who might have pass'd in the world for a Heroe, had he been employ'd in a good

Cause."[43] A master of image making, he manipulated his crew, his pirate peers, and the public to create a lasting portrait of "the fiercest pirate of all," and it is this portrait that subsequent historians have swallowed whole for nearly three hundred years. The mythologizing of Blackbeard began immediately. Within months after his bloody death at Ocracoke, in the streets of Boston a young Benjamin Franklin was hawking the ballad of "a Sailor Song on the Taking of Teach or Blackbeard the Pirate," which ended,

> And when we no longer can strike a blow,
> Then fire the magazine, boys, and up we go!
> It's better to swim in the sea below
> Than to swing in the air and feed the crow,
> Says jolly Ned Teach of Bristol.[44]

Well into a new excavation season on the wreck at Beaufort Inlet, the divers, bleary from the fatigue of long hours underwater, gather on the dock each morning just after dawn. As they collect their scuba gear and trudge out to the boats, someone will lighten the heavy mood by glancing around, squinting at the bright sunlight sparkling on the water, and singing out, "Such a day!" The rejuvenated divers, descending on the wreck once more "to swim in the sea below" with the shades of Blackbeard and his cohorts, recover artifacts from the Golden Age of Piracy—artifacts that after nearly three centuries cut through the myths, the exaggerations, and the contradictions that have obscured the life of the fiercest pirate of them all.

The Major was but ill
qualify'd for the Business,
as not understanding
maritime Affairs.
—*Captain Charles*
Johnson, 1724

Stede Bonnet

The Gentleman Pirate of the *Royal James*

In deepening twilight a trim sloop cast off and stealthily edged out of the Careenage, Bridgetown's narrow harbor, past the grim walls of old Fort James into gently curving Carlisle Bay of Barbados. On her stern the freshly painted name *Revenge* faded into the gloom as the ship picked up speed in a light offshore breeze and began to roll slightly in the low swell. Her dapper captain, who had been pacing the deck with his head down, suddenly looked up and turned toward the island of his birth, absorbing the beauty of royal palms silhouetted on the shore above phosphorescent surf. In his mind's eye were white sandy beaches, brilliant blue sky, verdant canefields rippling in the wind, the stepped-gable Jacobean skyline of the city, and his own townhouse south of the bridge. His gaze finally rested on the now-tiny pinpoint of light on the wharf, a lantern held by the wife he was abandoning. For a brief moment he pictured his three small children asleep at home in the nursery. Although his family and friends had been told that he was

Stede Bonnet of Barbados left his family and the respectable life of a planter to become a notorious pirate. (Library of Congress, Washington, D.C.)

embarking on a short trading voyage, he knew that he would never again see the island, for he had chosen to become a pirate.

What could have been passing through the mind of Stede Bonnet, the most unlikely pirate who ever sailed the high seas? Was he troubled about his decision, or was he elated to escape the confining life of a West Indian sugar planter? Was he sad about leaving his family of two little boys and a toddler daughter, or was his domestic life in turmoil? His friends and acquaintances in Barbados would never understand why this respected and well-to-do gentleman planter left their island world for a career of high seas crime that would lead inexorably to a violent end. The bloody course set that day, which brought him in less than two years to a South Carolina gallows, was so perplexing to his fellow Barbadians that they could only conclude he must be mentally unbalanced.

In his 1724 history of piracy, Captain Charles Johnson wrote that Bonnet "had the least Temptation of any Man to follow such a Course of life," as he was "a Gentleman of good Reputation" who had a considerable fortune and "the Advantage of a liberal Education." Although Bonnet had been "generally esteem'd and honoured" on the island before he left to pursue a life of crime, because of his status his fellow planters "afterwards rather pity'd than condemned" him. To his peers the only explanation that made sense was that "this Humour of going a Pyrating, proceeded from a Disorder in his Mind, which had been but too visible in him, some Time before this wicked Undertaking; and which is said to have been occasioned by some Discomforts he found in a Married State."[1]

From Johnson's sketchy portrayal some later writers have inferred that Bonnet was a foppish and haughty aristocrat with noble connections in England. Other narrators have inflated his rank as major in the island militia into a commission in the regular British army. Although the Bonnet family, and Stede Bonnet in particular, possessed wealth and high position in the island society, not too much should be made of his colonial social status. Like most so-called aristocrats in the English colonies, the Barbados plantocracy consisted of first- or second-generation nouveau riche whose progenitors had arrived in their new home in modest circumstances at best, if not as indentured servants or transported criminals. Taking a somewhat jaundiced view of the island's society, Henry Whistler wrote in his 1655 journal, "This Illand is the Dunghill wharone England doth cast forth its rubidg: Rodgs and hors and such like peopel are those which are gennerally Broght heare. A rodge in England will hardly make a cheater heare: a Baud brought over puts one a demour comportment, a whore if hansume makes a wife for sume rich planter."[2]

In fact, the same could easily have been said about Virginia and other colonies on the mainland or in the West Indies. As one scholar has noted, the colonies were settled by "the offscourings of the mother country."[3] Why, then, were the colonies populated by the social refuse of England? Except for adventurers, younger sons seeking their own fortunes, or those morally compromised and exiled to the colonies, members of the great families of England, who already possessed wealth, power, and status, simply had little reason to risk the early grave that awaited so many immigrants to the Americas.

The island on which Stede Bonnet turned his back in 1717, although already in decline, had been the center of the British Caribbean and the most prosperous English colony in the Americas. Settled in 1627, Barbados became part of a proprietary patent from the Crown to James Hay, Earl of Carlisle. Political turmoil characterized the early years of the colony's government as rival claimants jockeyed at first for ownership and then for control of the island; but by 1639, when a representative assembly was established, Barbados began to evolve toward virtual self-government. From the earliest time of settlement in a jungle-covered landscape, the colonists had rapidly cleared the heavy forest and on the fertile soil established plantations for commercial agriculture. Because of the prevailing winds and ocean currents, Barbados, a solitary dot located out in the Atlantic east of the Windward Islands, was the first landfall of vessels bound from Europe to the West Indies. Passengers on ships approaching the island first saw the windswept, rocky east coast with its high cliffs and, on the northern end, the craggy hills of the Scotland district. Skirting the coral reefs of the south coast, they sailed alongside a lush green plateau adorned with plantation manor houses. Understandably, the island soon came to be called "Little England."

By mid-century the Barbadian colonists had founded an incredibly rich society whose leaders rivaled Londoners' ostentatious display. These early planters were singularly determined in searching for a cash crop that would generate wealth to match what tobacco had produced in Virginia. Finding conditions unsuitable for tobacco, they tried indigo and cotton before finally settling on sugar, from which they reaped huge profits. In a short time the island's rolling central plateau was covered with capital- and labor-intensive sugar plantations, which absorbed the small holdings of yeoman farmers. These operations' voracious appetite for workers consumed white indentured servants, chiefly Scots and Irish, and demanded African slaves, who became the dominant labor force and ultimately the overwhelming majority of the population. The sugar plantations generated a prosperity that in the late seventeenth century was unrivaled in all of British America, so that Barbados was known as the "fair jewell" of the Crown.[4]

Stede Bonnet's grandfather, Thomas Bonnet, arrived on the island in the first generation of settlers and over his lifetime acquired holdings in the parishes of St. Michael and Christ Church. In this era of rapid growth in the island's population, economy, and society, Thomas Bonnet prospered, leaving at his death in 1676 a plantation of over four hundred acres, one of the great Barbadian estates of the period. The Bonnet holdings straddled the parish boundary a few miles southeast of Bridgetown, the island's principal city, where for a time Thomas Bonnet owned a townhouse on High Street. He was a vestryman of St. Michael Parish, although his plantation manorhouse was located in Christ Church. The bulk of his estate Thomas left to his younger son Edward.[5]

To Edward Bonnet and his wife, Sarah, a son, Stede, was born in 1688, and on 29 July the boy was christened in Christ Church parish. Since Stede Bonnet's father died when he was six years old, the youth's property was under a guardianship until he was an adult, and there is reason to believe that his mother also died while he was young, leaving him an orphan. At age twenty-one he married Mary Allamby, on 21 November 1709, in the Cathedral of St. Michael in Bridgetown. The Bonnets had four children—Allamby, who died sometime before 1715, and Edward, Stede, and Mary, all of whom were less than five years old when their father abandoned them. Mary Allamby's father, William, was a wealthy planter who probably provided a substantial dowry at the time of his daughter's marriage and who, upon his death in 1713, left a significant bequest to his yet-unborn grandchild Edward Bonnet.[6] From the island census of 1715, we know that Major Bonnet was then living in the Parish of St. Michael, "over the bridge," which would be just south of the harbor in Bridgetown. His land and tax levy indicate a successful planter of means but not great wealth. His land-holdings and status in Barbadian society led to his receiving the rank of major in the island militia. Because of the large number of inden-tured servants and slaves in the population, the island landowners had organized an extensive militia to provide both internal security from a revolt of laborers and defense from external invasion. After Stede Bonnet left his family, Mary moved to St. Thomas Parish, where she died in 1750, leaving property to her surviving children, Edward, Stede, and Mary.[7]

Unlike other pirate leaders, who customarily hijacked ships that they then made their own, Bonnet had at his own expense armed his ten-gun sloop and manned it with a crew of more than seventy men. With little knowledge of sailing, he relied on his quartermaster and officers, a practice that cost him respect among the crew, for tradition held that a pirate captain was selected by his men for able seamanship and leadership qualities. By paying his crew wages, which was un-heard of among buccaneers, Bonnet hoped to gain their allegiance; but his initial ignorance of pirate custom and his awkwardness at sea contributed to his eventual ouster as captain. Bizarre as it may have seemed to his contemporaries, Bonnet's decision to become a pirate could not have been a secret, for the excessive armament and crew that could be seen going onto the *Revenge* surely betrayed her captain's intent to ply a privateer's, if not a pirate's, trade.

Clearing Carlisle Bay, Bonnet set his course northwest toward the crowded sea lanes of the North American mainland. Arriving off the Virginia capes, at the entrance to Chesapeake Bay, Bonnet sighted and plundered in quick succession the *Anne*, the *Endeavour*, and the *Young* from Scotland and England and the *Turbet* from Barbados. Operating with no base for supplies, pirates lived off their prizes, rifling them for food, wine, rum, water, clothing, sails, cordage, spars, ammunition—in short, for anything needed to keep them at sea. Three of the craft were released, but the *Turbet* was burned, purportedly to keep news of Bonnet's activities from Barbados. The *Revenge* gradually worked her way north along the coast to New York, taking a sloop off Long Island, and at Gardiner's Island, which had a long association with smuggling and was friendly to sea rovers, Bonnet purchased supplies and released captives.

Heading south in August 1717, Bonnet waylaid two prizes on 26 August off the entrance to Charleston, South Carolina—a brigantine from Boston, which was cast adrift after being stripped, and a Barbadian sloop with a rich cargo of slaves, rum, and sugar. Having been at sea now for possibly six months, the *Revenge* badly needed to be overhauled, so the Barbadian sloop accompanied the *Revenge* to a remote North Carolina inlet, probably Cape Fear, where the pirate vessel was careened and repaired. In warm southern waters marine growth was rampant, and the destructive teredo worm, unless checked, could quickly ruin a vessel by boring into its hull. In this period the only way to combat the ubiquitous mollusk was by frequent careening, or rolling the ship on its side, to expose the hull for burning and scraping off barnacles and seaweed and then replacing damaged planks. After the captured sloop's tackle was used to careen the *Revenge*, the prize was dismantled for timber and spare rigging. The remains were then burned.[8]

Bonnet left North Carolina in September and headed south to the well-known pirate rendezvous on New Providence (Nassau) in the Bahamas. On the way he tangled with a heavily armed Spanish man-of-war, a kind of ship pirates always avoided if possible, and the ensuing clash left him temporarily disabled, cost him half his men, and very likely damaged the *Revenge* badly. Bonnet and the *Revenge* were lucky to have escaped the Spanish ship. Arriving in New Providence, while the *Revenge* was being refitted, Bonnet met Blackbeard and his mentor, Benjamin Hornigold, and apparently agreed to let Blackbeard command his vessel while he was recuperating. With the near disastrous encounter with the Spanish warship fresh on his mind, Bonnet needed little extra incentive to add two guns to the repaired *Revenge* and double his crew. It was probably on this cruise that Blackbeard observed Bonnet's weaknesses and may have begun scheming to sever the Major's tenuous hold on his sailors.

With Blackbeard in command, the *Revenge* returned north to Delaware Bay, where in the month of October the pirates terrorized the bay by plundering eleven vessels, mostly sloops, throwing the cargoes overboard and casting the numerous captives adrift in demasted hulks. The pirates told their captives that a "Consort Ship of 30 Guns" was due to reinforce them soon. This companion craft was probably the *Ranger* commanded by the noted pirate leader Benjamin Hornigold, with whom Blackbeard was in league. On 12 October the ship of a Captain Codd was despoiled by the *Revenge*, which he described as carrying twelve guns, having 150 crewmen, and being commanded by "one Teach," who was identified as having sailed at one time from Philadelphia. Codd's narrative further records: "On board the Pirate Sloop is Major Bennet [Bonnet], but has no Command, he walks about in his Morning Gown, and then to his Books, of which he has a good Library on Board, he was not well of his wounds that he received by attacking of a Spanish Man of War, which kill'd and wounded him 30 or 40 Men."[9]

By November, Hornigold's *Ranger* and the *Revenge* were back in the Caribbean, where on the seventeenth they took a fourteen-gun French slaver, the *Concorde*, which Hornigold gave to Blackbeard, who doubled her armament and renamed her the *Queen Anne's Revenge*. Since he had recovered from his wounds, Bonnet resumed command of the *Revenge*. At this time Hornigold left his consorts, who continued a leisurely pace through the Leeward Islands, where they took several vessels in November. On 19 December, the pirates stopped a sloop, and near St. Christopher they sank a French sugar ship. In vain, the HMS *Scarborough* pursued the pirates from island to island but always arrived too late to confront them.[10]

During the winter Blackbeard and Bonnet separated, and Bonnet may have returned to New Providence, since pirates followed the seasons' change, much like modern vacationers. As Captain Johnson explained, "Pyrates generally shift their Rovings, according to the Season of the Year; in the Summer they cruise mostly along the Coast of the Continent of America, but the Winters there, being a little too cold for them, they follow the Sun, and go towards the Islands."[11]

Early in 1718 Bonnet sailed the *Revenge* south to the coast of Cen-

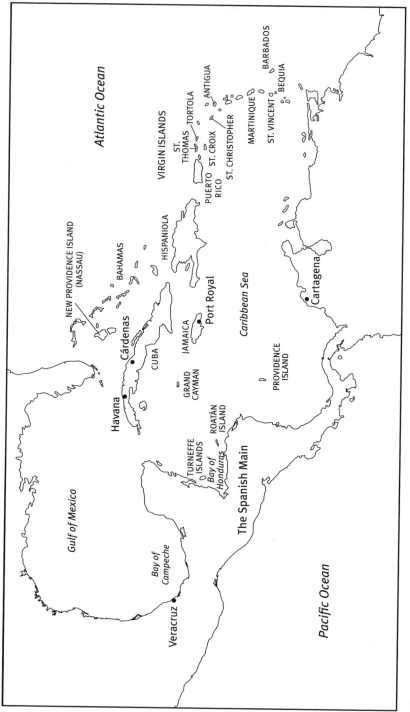

The Caribbean and the Spanish Main

tral America, the legendary Spanish Main, which was crowded with poorly defended shipping. If Captain Johnson is to be believed, by this time Bonnet's personality weaknesses and poor seamanship had so undermined discipline on the *Revenge* that "Confusion seem'd to attend all their Schemes."[12] As the *Revenge* approached the Spanish Main off Honduras on 28 March, Bonnet spotted a large ship, the four-hundred-ton *Protestant Caesar* of Boston, commanded by Captain Wyer, near Roatán Island. Since he carried twenty-six guns and a fifty-man crew, Wyer decided to defend his ship against the stranger if necessary. Gradually closing with the merchant ship, the *Revenge* crossed the stern of the *Protestant Caesar* at nine o'clock that night and opened fire with cannon and a volley of musket fire. Wyer returned fire with his stern chase guns and muskets. Bonnet hailed the merchant ship, calling on its crew to cease fire or no quarter would be given. Undeterred, Wyer mauled the pirates for three hours until they withdrew about midnight. Beaten, the *Revenge* sailed into the darkness, captain and crew alike angered by the failure of their violent encounter with a mere merchantman.[13]

Arriving in the Turneffe Islands, just off the coast of modern Belize, to take on fresh water, Bonnet was surprised to find the *Queen Anne's Revenge* riding at anchor. Still smarting from their recent defeat, Bonnet's crew informed Blackbeard of the nearly intolerable situation on board, whereupon the wily and charismatic schemer quickly won them over and plotted to remove Bonnet from his ship. One evening Blackbeard, who was entertaining Bonnet on the *Queen Anne's Revenge*, persuaded his guest to move into his ship's more spacious quarters. When Bonnet acquiesced to Blackbeard's wishes, possibly relieved to be free of the headaches of command, his clothing, books, and personal property were brought on board. One Richards, a trusted lieutenant of Blackbeard, was named captain of the *Revenge* by Bonnet's former crew. Although Bonnet appeared to be living the life of a gentleman passenger, with no cares or responsibilities, he was described as falling into a melancholy state and becoming nearly overcome with shame. Virtually a prisoner and dominated by the forceful Blackbeard, he confided to the few of his crew who would listen that he was ready to forsake his criminal life if he could find exile in Spain or Portugal and never see another Englishman.[14]

Under Captain Richards the *Revenge* initiated the capture of a Jamaican sloop, the *Adventure*—forcing her captain, David Herriot, and crew to join the pirate band—which now gave Blackbeard a powerful flotilla of three ships. In early April in the Bay of Honduras the pirates looted four Jamaican sloops and the heretofore lucky *Protestant Caesar*, which the crew of the *Revenge* gleefully plundered. The pirates then headed north, taking a Spanish sloop off Cuba and retaining it as a supply vessel. In mid-May they arrived off Charleston, the principal port of South Carolina, where Blackbeard established a blockade, looting at least five prizes of their cargo and specie and ransoming hostages from Charleston for a valuable chest of medicine.[15]

Leaving a relieved Charleston, the pirates sailed up the coast to North Carolina, searching for a place to rest and refit their vessels. Topsail Inlet (now Beaufort Inlet), which they reached in early June, appeared to be the ideal location, for it opened onto an isolated and spacious deep-water harbor with the small fishing village of Beaufort on the north shore. The *Revenge* and her smaller consorts easily entered, but the larger *Queen Anne's Revenge* stuck fast on the bar at the mouth of the inlet, and the *Adventure*, attempting to aid Blackbeard's flagship, was also lost. Although it was believed at the time that Blackbeard had grounded the vessels on purpose to eliminate most of his crew and avoid sharing the plunder with the four hundred men reportedly sailing with him, it is also true that the inlets of the Graveyard of the Atlantic are known for constant change. In fact, whether the wrecks were planned or accidental, Blackbeard marooned a number of men on an offshore island and departed in the Spanish sloop with a few of his crewmen and all of the loot.[16]

After the losses in the inlet, Blackbeard returned the *Revenge* to Bonnet. Realizing that he still had time to be pardoned for his past crimes, Bonnet left his ship in the harbor and traveled to Bath to seek a pardon from North Carolina governor Charles Eden under the terms of the Act of Grace, the royal proclamation of the previous year. Learning there that the Holy Roman Empire (Austria) was still at war with Spain, Bonnet shrewdly asked the governor for a clearance to go to Danish-ruled St. Thomas in the Virgin Islands to seek a letter of marque to attack Spanish shipping. Upon his return from Bath with his clearance papers, Bonnet was dismayed to find that Blackbeard had absconded with most of the booty and the bulk of the supplies in the Spanish sloop, which he had named the *Adventure* and armed with eight guns. He had also removed fourteen of Bonnet's best crewmen, leaving only five men on board the *Revenge*.[17]

When Bonnet returned, he first collected several pirates who had been abandoned in the "poor little village" of Beaufort north of the harbor, and then he rescued Herriot and the twenty-five marooned men from a certain slow death by starvation. The grateful Herriot agreed to join Bonnet as quartermaster in what he thought would be a privateering venture. From a local resident's bumboat selling apples and cider, Bonnet heard that Blackbeard was on Ocracoke with a small crew. Incensed over the shabby treatment he had endured from Blackbeard, Bonnet hoped he could surprise and overpower his betrayer and possibly recover some of the plunder. With a crew of forty men Bonnet sailed at once, but Blackbeard had already left Ocracoke on a cruise.[18]

Low on supplies, Bonnet headed the *Revenge* north to the scene of his early successes—the cruising ground near the busy shipping lanes off the Virginia capes. South of Cape Henry in July Bonnet stopped a small coastal vessel known as a pink, taking ten or twelve barrels of pork and about four hundred pounds of bread and exchanging eight or ten casks of rice and an anchor and cable. He may still have genuinely planned to seek the privateering commission, for this pretense of trading with his captives was selectively continued for a time. To separate himself from his previous depredations, he began using the aliases Captain Edwards and Captain Thomas, and changed the name of the *Revenge* to the *Royal James*.[19]

Off the coast of Virginia Bonnet reaped a rich harvest, taking thirteen prizes in two months. His next capture was a sixty-ton sloop from which he pilfered two hogsheads of rum, a hogshead of molasses, and two slaves. Two ships bound for Scotland and laden with tobacco were relieved of part of their cargo. From a sloop headed to Bermuda he acquired twenty barrels of pork and some bacon, giving in return two barrels of rice and a hogshead of molasses. Another Glasgow-bound vessel yielded only combs, pins, and needles and in turn received a barrel of pork and two barrels of bread. Off Assateague Island Bonnet stopped a North Carolina schooner from which calfskins were taken for gun covers, and breaking his pattern of releasing his prizes, he kept the schooner as a tender for supplies. Bonnet may have seized a pink reported taken on 20 July off the Virginia capes.[20] Contrary to the image of bloodthirsty pirates that had descended from an earlier time, none of these encounters involved violence or injury. Like other pirates of his era, Bonnet usually obtained the surrender of his victims by bravado and bluster.

Sailing north to the entrance of Delaware Bay off Cape May, Bonnet boarded and released two large snows and a ninety-ton sloop. Then at the end of July came the fateful captures of two prizes that would send Bonnet and his crew to the gallows. On 29 July off Cape May the fifty-ton sloop *Fortune*, commanded by Thomas Read, was sighted coming down the bay from Philadelphia. Bonnet sent a boarding party led by Robert Tucker, his quartermaster. In one of the few incidents of sense-less violence in Bonnet's career, Tucker "fell to beating and cutting People with his cutlass" and injured one man on the arm.[21] The *Fortune*, which had been bound for Barbados, was laden primarily with provisions—bread, oil, ham, and flour—which Bonnet did not need at that time; nevertheless, he decided to keep the vessel as a store ship, bringing Read on board the *Royal James*, which then moved with its consorts to an anchorage inside Cape Henlopen. Two days later, on 31 July, the *Francis*, a thirty-five-ton sloop out of Antigua under Captain Peter Mainwaring, sailed into the bay and dropped anchor near the three ships. That evening about nine o'clock a dory with five men on board approached the *Francis*. When hailed from the deck to identify themselves, they replied falsely that they were from Captain Thomas Richards of St. Thomas and Captain Thomas Read of Philadelphia. A rope was let down to bring the visitors on board, allowing the bandits to scramble up to the deck, where they "clapp'd their Hands on their Cutlasses," and Captain Mainwaring realized that his ship was lost. Mainwaring was rowed over to the *Royal James*, where, he later reported, he was treated "very civil"; indeed, after two months as a prisoner in their company, Mainwaring had no complaints about the treatment that he and his men received from their captors. Back on the *Francis*, as James Killing would testify in subsequent legal proceedings, when the pirates "came into the Cabin, the first they begun with was the Pine-Apples, which they cut down with their Cutlasses. . . . They asked me what Liquor I had on board? I told them some Rum and Sugar. So they made Bowls of Punch, and went to Drinking of the Pretenders Health, and hoped to see him King of the *English* Nation: Then sung a Song or two."[22]

The next morning, 1 August, the pirates brought the *Francis* along-side the consort schooner, rigged a hoist, and began to transfer mas-sive hogsheads and barrels. Peering into the cargo spaces and ran-sacking the captain's cabin, Bonnet's crew discovered with mounting excitement the richest booty they had seen in their many months at sea. From the depths of the hold came some 1,800 gallons of rum, 1,575 gallons of molasses, and about 800 pounds of sugar. There were smaller amounts of cotton and indigo and a new anchor cable. The captain's chest was looted of three dozen French, Spanish, and Portuguese gold and silver coins, a pair of silver buckles, and a silver watch. The total value of the plunder was about £500—over half accounted for by the rum. With so much rum on board, about forty gallons for each man, the ship was literally awash in liquor—truly a pirate's heaven. Captain Mainwaring said that the men on the *Royal James* "were all very brisk and merry, and had all things plentiful, and were a-making Punch and drinking." The excessive drinking in celebration of such good fortune inevitably got out of hand, leading to such insubordination that Bonnet took the unusual measure of flogging two of the crew.[23]

While the cargo transfer was under way, Bonnet ordered that two captives, a passenger's wife and Captain Read's son, apparently the only woman and child on board the prizes, be taken ashore. He sent the dory with five armed and sober crewmen to leave them at the Hore-Kills, now Lewes, Delaware. As they left, Bonnet warned young Read that "if any of the Inhabitants offer'd to hurt the Hair of the Head of any Person belonging to his . . . crew, he . . . would put to death and destroy all the Prisoners he had on board, and would also go ashore and burn the whole Town."[24]

That night, with the *Royal James* in the van, the pirate flotilla of four vessels left the cape and headed south. By dawn the *Francis* lagged so far behind that Bonnet, suspicious that the ship's crew might attempt to flee, shouted over his speaking trumpet that if they did not close the gap he would fire on them and sink them. Sufficiently chastised, the *Francis* obeyed. As the pirates and their prizes neared Cape Fear, Bonnet shared with his crew the specie of between £400 and £450, each member receiving £10 to £11—so much for the romantic notion of pirate treasure! On 12 August the four ships entered the mouth of the Cape Fear, sailed a short distance upriver, and anchored near the west bank at the mouth of a stream now known as Bonnet's Creek. This refuge was likely the same place that Bonnet had used to careen and refit a year earlier. The *Royal James* was leaking badly and needed a major rebuilding, but another concern was to lie over until the hurricane season was past. Bonnet and his men would remain there with their captives until 29 September, living on the provisions from the two prize sloops.[25]

Shortly after Bonnet's flotilla had settled into its anchorage, a six-ton shallop under John Dalton and Jonathan Clarke from Charleston sailed into the river and right into the hands of the pirates, thereby becoming the last prize taken by Bonnet's men. The shallop was kept to be broken up for repairs to the *Royal James*. The next day Dalton and Clarke fled into the trackless forest. They became separated, and Clarke wandered aimlessly until, half-starved, he managed to find his way back to the pirate camp. Unfortunately for Bonnet, Dalton succeeded in escaping and made his way overland to Charleston to raise the alarm that there were pirates staying at Cape Fear.

Several incidents occurred at the Cape Fear anchorage that illustrate how the outlaws intimidated their captives to force them into piracy. The *Royal James* was careened and rebuilt largely by slaves, while the crew took their ease. Bonnet punished Jonathan Clarke, the erstwhile escapee, by forcing Clarke to work with the slaves and threatening to "make him the Governor of an island"—that is, maroon him—when they left. Thomas Gerrard, a free mulatto from Antigua, was told that unless he joined the pirates he would be enslaved for life. Rowland Sharp, from Bath, hid in the woods but nearly starved and had to return. Upon his refusal to sign the articles, he was told he would be shot and must choose his executioners, but his fellow crewmen begged successfully for his life. As food supplies dwindled, the pirates found abundant provisions on the *Fortune*, pillaging some 1,500 pounds of bread, 500 pounds of ham, 20 barrels of flour, and a variety of personal items. For refitting the *Royal James*, the *Fortune* yielded seven iron-bound blocks, a fathom of rigging, and a pump.[26]

Back in Charleston, the port had undergone another pirate blockade—this time by the infamous Charles Vane. Aroused by their inability to protect themselves and dismayed by Dalton's news, the South Carolina council and Governor Johnson, fed up with losing trade and periodically being held hostage, determined to rid themselves of the villains, calling for action from the city's military leaders. Colonel William Rhett, highly respected for his previous leadership in defending the colony from Indian attacks and foreign privateers, stepped forward and offered to command a punitive expedition to attack the unknown brigands on the Cape Fear. The governor responded by issuing Rhett a commission as vice admiral. By trade a merchant and sea captain, Rhett (1666–1723) had been for a generation one of the most influential leaders in Charleston. A longtime assemblyman, he had served terms as speaker of the house and had been for some time the colony's receiver general of quitrents. His high stature in South Carolina dated from 1706, when he played a crucial role in saving the colony from a French and Spanish invasion during

Queen Anne's War. As the colony's naval commander, he had crushed a French privateer fleet while the governor, Sir Nathaniel Johnson, defeated the Spanish military forces ashore.[27]

Two eight-gun sloops were outfitted for the expedition—the *Henry*, with a crew of seventy men commanded by John Masters, and the *Sea Nymph*, with a crew of sixty men commanded by Fayrer Hall. As fleet admiral, Rhett chose the *Henry* as flagship. On 14 September, while the ships were completing preparations at Sullivan's Island at the entrance to Charleston harbor, a merchantman from Antigua arrived with the report that his ship had been ravaged by the pirate Charles Vane just outside the harbor. Two other ships had been captured, one of them a slaver from West Africa carrying a cargo of ninety slaves. The slaves had been transferred to a pirate sloop commanded by Yeats, a partner of Vane; but Yeats, who had secretly decided to take the royal pardon, sailed at night into the North Edisto River and surrendered. Vane, angered by Yeats's betrayal and hoping to capture the turncoat, lingered at Charleston and continued to harass the port, taking two more prizes. Learning from released prisoners that Vane had sailed south, on 15 September Rhett ordered the *Henry* and the *Sea Nymph* to sea, setting a course in pursuit of Vane, who was the immediate threat to the city.[28]

After diligently searching the inlets south of Charleston to no avail, Rhett abandoned his quest for Vane and turned back toward Cape Fear, his original objective. At dusk on 26 September, as he was gingerly entering the unfamiliar Cape Fear River, Rhett sighted three sloops at anchor but then ran aground as night fell. Bonnet in turn became aware of the South Carolinians and sent three canoes of armed men downriver to reconnoiter and possibly board the unknown craft. The pirates retreated hastily when they discovered that the visitors were heavily armed. That night both sides feverishly prepared for the impending battle. In the midst of driving his crew to have the *Royal James* ready, Bonnet took the time to write a bombastic missive to the governor of South Carolina, threatening that if he won the day he would descend on Charleston and exact his vengeance by burning all the shipping in the harbor.[29]

Although Bonnet's ten guns and crew of 45 men on the *Royal James* were outnumbered by a combined force of sixteen guns and 130 South Carolinians, the pirates were ignorant of Rhett's exact strength. Bonnet, whose plan was to escape to the open sea, got the *Royal James* under way first on the morning of 27 September and set sail downstream, hoping to surprise the enemy in a running engagement. Rhett's strategy was to sail his sloops upriver toward the *Royal James*, pin her between his ships, and then board her. With guns roaring, Bonnet kept near the shore to prevent being surrounded. Almost simultaneously, all three of the vessels ran aground in the shallows. The *Henry* grounded close off the bow of the *Royal James*, within pistol range, but the *Sea Nymph* was stuck too far away to help her. The changing tide caused the *Henry* to list toward the *Royal James*, exposing her deck to galling fire from the pirates, who were protected since their vessel had heeled away from the enemy. Neither ship could bring cannon to bear, since the *Henry*'s guns pointed toward the water and the pirates' guns were aimed too high.

For five hours the pirates swept the *Henry*'s deck with a murderous fire from muskets, pistols, and possibly swivel guns, inflicting heavy casualties among Rhett's men. The fighting was spirited. The outlaws shouted a stream of oaths and epithets, gesturing with their hats for the South Carolinians to come on over. Despite their heavy losses, Rhett's men countered their tormenters with "chearful Huzzas" and yelled that they would board as soon as they could. Another contemptuous gesture from the pirates was "a Wiff in their bloody Flag,"[30] which means they knotted the flag as a signal to invite the South Carolinians on board. Throughout the battle Bonnet restlessly paced the deck, exhorting his men to sustain their morale and threatening to shoot anyone who quit. One captive, Thomas Nichols, who despite severe threats had never joined the pirates, did refuse to fight, and Bonnet drew his pistol to shoot him. Just at that moment, however, Bonnet was distracted when one of his favorites fell dead at his side, and Nichols scurried to safety in the hold.[31]

When the tide came in, the *Henry* was refloated before the *Royal James*, and after making repairs to the ship's rigging, Rhett bore down on the pirates to board and finish them off. Vowing to fight to the death, Bonnet had George Ross, the ship's gunner, prepared to light a fuse laid to the magazine to destroy them all, but his weary crew, exhausted by the six-hour battle, lost their nerve at the last moment and ran up a white flag. Bonnet had no choice but to surrender when Rhett promised to plead for mercy for his captives, even though the battle had cost him dearly. The *Henry* reported ten killed and fourteen wounded, totaling about one-third of her crew. Fortunately, the *Sea Nymph*, which had been out of range most of the time, suffered only two killed and four wounded, although two of the wounded died later, raising Rhett's final death toll to eighteen. Among the pirates seven men were killed and five were wounded, of whom two soon died. Rhett took thirty-six prisoners to Charleston.

After freeing the captive *Fortune* and *Francis*, Rhett's flotilla left the Cape Fear on 30 September and three days later entered Charleston harbor "to the great Joy of the whole Province." The pirates were brought ashore and housed under close guard in the watch house. Bonnet was ensconced in the provost marshal's house, where in several days he was joined by his master, David Herriot, and bos'n, Ignatius Pell, both of whom had agreed to testify against their companions. Despite the presence of a twenty-four-hour armed guard, on the night of 24 October Bonnet and Herriot escaped, while Pell chose to remain in custody. Traditionally it is believed that Bonnet disguised himself in women's clothing and that sympathetic townsmen may have bribed the sentries. Bonnet's being on the loose brought to the surface all the anxieties of the citizens, who had suffered greatly under the threat of piratical raids. Without foundation, they assailed the colony's officials, accusing the governor and council of colluding with the pirates and accepting bribes to secure Bonnet's release. Governor Johnson's decisive response—offering a £700 reward for Bonnet's return and dispatching deputies to seek him out—brought the accusations to an end.

Bonnet and Herriot fled toward North Carolina in a small boat, but contrary winds and a storm turned them back to Sullivan's Island, only a few miles from Charleston, where they set up a hideout on the north end of the island. When word reached Governor Johnson that Bonnet's party was nearby, he sent in the stalwart Colonel Rhett to arrest them at night. After an exhausting search through the island's tangled scrub, Rhett's posse located the pirates' camp. As they crept through the underbrush to surround it, a scuffle broke out. Fearing that Bonnet would slip away again, Rhett's men shattered the darkness with gunfire, killing Herriot and wounding "one *Negroe* and an *Indian*." Bonnet surrendered and was returned to Charleston on 6 November.[32]

On 28 October, while Bonnet was still at large, a session of the vice-admiralty court was convened for the trial of the surviving crew of the *Royal James*. Nicholas Trott (1663–1740), the vice-admiralty judge and South Carolina's chief justice, as well as William Rhett's brother-in law, was the presiding judge on a panel consisting of himself and ten assistant justices. Like his brother-in-law, Trott had been one of the most powerful men in the colony for a generation. An able jurist, he had begun his public career as the colony's attorney general in 1699. He served in the colonial assembly, was elevated to the council, and became chief justice in 1703. Trott capped his long years in public service by codifying and publishing the laws of the province.[33] The unfortunate pirates hauled before the bar in Trott's court could expect little sympathy. Trott detested pirates, considering them "Enemies of Mankind" who had endangered his city far too long.

On the first day a grand jury was impanelled to hear the evidence against the alleged pirates. Trott's charge to the jury was a lengthy oration that reviewed the law on piracy from ancient times, drew moral homilies from the Bible, defined a pirate as "A Rover and Robber upon the Sea" and characterized the wretches standing before him as "Brutes and Beasts of Prey." He reminded the jury that the whole province of Carolina had long suffered from "The Evil of *Piracy*," stressing that many of the South Carolinians who had gone to Cape Fear to rid the colony of pirates had paid with their lives "by the hands of those inhuman and murdering *Criminals*" and that "the Blood of those murdered Persons will cry for Vengeance and Justice Against these Offenders."[34] In this atmosphere it must have come as no surprise that the jury returned bills of indictment over the next two days for two incidents of piracy—the taking of the *Francis* and the capture of the *Fortune* in Delaware Bay.

Since the captains and crews of the captured vessels were present, there were ample witnesses. Thirty of the prisoners entered not guilty pleas; of the remaining three, two pleaded guilty on both charges and the other prisoner admitted guilt on one indictment. Following customary procedure, the prisoners were not allowed a defense counsel. Their response, which seemed to be the only course open to them, was to claim they had been forced into piracy against their will under threat of harm or marooning. Indeed, with some twenty-five of Bonnet's crew having been marooned by Blackbeard in North Carolina, they had a plausible argument; but Trott and the attorney general, Richard Allein, emphasized several points: how easily they were persuaded to serve Bonnet, whether they had participated in the ship seizures, whether they had signed the articles, how willing they were to fight at Cape Fear, and primarily whether they had accepted any of the plunder. The chief witnesses were their former comrade Ignatius Pell, Captains Peter Mainwaring and Thomas Read, James Killing, mate of the *Francis*, and Francis Griffin, mate of the *Fortune*.[35]

On 30 October Attorney General Allein's charge to the trial jury echoed Trott's diatribe, describing piracy as an "odious and horrid" practice that imperiled trade, to the extent of ruining "not only *Carolina*, but all the *English Plantations* in *America*."[36] The defendants were grouped for trial based on their time on the *Royal James* and their level of participation in the plundering. When all the evidence was heard, Trott, after another interminable sermon condemning piracy and murder, on 5 November pronounced the death sentence on twenty-nine of the thirty-three pirates who had been indicted. Four of the prisoners—Thomas Nichols, Rowland Sharp, Jonathan Clarke, and Thomas Gerrard—were able to prove to the court's satisfaction that they had been forced into piracy and that they had not shared in looting the prizes. Nichols had neither signed the articles nor shared in the plunder; furthermore, in the battle at Cape Fear he had refused to fight and had nearly been shot by Bonnet for that refusal. The remaining three had signed the articles under duress. Clarke had attempted escape and then been "damned" by one of the slaves and threatened with being worked as one of them. Sharp, too, had fled but lost his way and returned nearly starved, only to face a promised execution by firing squad. Gerrard, the West Indian mulatto, joined on pain of lifelong enslavement, but he did not share in the pillaging.[37] On Saturday, 8 November, at White Point, twenty-two of the pirates were executed by hanging. The official record does not reveal whether the sentences of the seven other convicted pirates were commuted.

On 6 November, the day after the trial ended, Bonnet must have created a stir when he was brought into Charleston as a prisoner once again. Four days later the court met to arraign and try him for seizure of the *Francis* and the *Fortune*. When he was called, he pleaded not guilty, and the trial proceeded on the indictment for the *Francis*. The assistant attorney general, Thomas Hepworth, made the opening statement to the jury, stressing Bonnet's many piracies and murders and characterizing him as "the great *Ringleader* of them; who has seduced many poor ignorant Men to follow his Course of Living and ruined many poor wretches." Witnesses who appeared at the trial of the crew—Ignatius Pell, Peter Mainwaring, Thomas Read, and James Killing—testified that Bonnet was in fact the captain or commander of the pirates who had ordered the plundering of the *Francis*. Bonnet did interject on his behalf that he had not forced anyone to sail with him. A witness testified that he had had a clearance to go to St. Thomas. In summation of his defense, Bonnet reasserted the claim that he had not given his consent for robbing the vessels and that he had been overruled by his crew. When asked if he took the *Francis*, he presented perhaps his weakest defense, replying that it "was Contrary to any Inclinations" and that he actually had been asleep when the prize was seized.[38] It is easy to imagine Justice Trott's court having to suppress grins if not outright laughter at that answer. The jury found him guilty as charged.

When the court convened the next day, 11 November, to hear the *Fortune* case, Bonnet changed his plea to guilty. Trott adjourned the session and reconvened the court the next morning. In another tedious religious discourse, the overbearing Trott charged Bonnet with thirteen piracies and the murder of eighteen men in the battle at Cape Fear. Referring to the men killed, Trott thundered, "Their *Blood* now cries out for *Vengeance* and *Justice*," and he ruled that Bonnet must pay with his life and suffer "in the Lake which burneth with Fire and Brimstone." The judge was convinced that Bonnet had fallen away from his religious teachings and urged him to seek repentance to save his soul. He then pronounced the age-old ritual sentence, telling Bonnet "That you . . . shall go from hence . . . to the Place of Execution, where you shall be hanged by the Neck till you are Dead. And the God of infinite Mercy be merciful to your Soul."[39]

In the course of the month that Bonnet spent awaiting his end, he lost his nerve and solicited the pity of the community. Townspeople, especially the young women, began to plead for his life. The governor turned a deaf ear to these supplications, chiefly because Bonnet had earlier embarrassed him by escaping and was held responsible for Herriot's death. Governor Johnson also rejected a proposal to send Bonnet to England for a review of the case, even though Rhett agreed to accompany him to speak on his behalf. Bonnet's last letter to the governor was an abject plea for mercy, claiming that he had truly had a change of heart and would live an exemplary life if pardoned. He implored the governor "to look upon me with tender Bowels of Pity and Compassion; and believe me to be the most miserable Man this Day breathing." Bonnet's appeal to the governor's Christian charity went unanswered. Johnson was unmoved by Bonnet's deathwatch religious conversion and let the sentence stand.[40]

As Bonnet waited, November proved a busy month for Carolinians set on eradicating piracy from their shores. In late October the pirate Christopher Moody had taken vessels off Charleston, forcing the governor to outfit an expedition of four armed ships to seek him out. As the trial of Bonnet's crew was ending, Johnson himself set sail to

On 10 December 1718 Bonnet was hanged on a gallows at White Point in Charleston, South Carolina. (North Carolina Division of Archives and History, Raleigh)

capture Moody. In a bloody action off Charleston, Johnson's fleet attacked and boarded a pirate ship that they thought was Moody's but that turned out to be commanded by Richard Worley, who was killed in the melee.[41] About a week later at Ocracoke Inlet Blackbeard was killed in a sharp fight with Lieutenant Robert Maynard's Virginia expedition. Blackbeard's death on 22 November ended pirate supremacy on the Carolina coast, although there continued to be occasional incidents over the next several years.

On 10 December, the citizens of Charleston gathered for the spectacle of Major Stede Bonnet's final passage to the White Point gallows that had claimed the lives of most of his men. Accompanied by a militia escort, the drumbeat sounding his death knell, the cart bore the stooped Bonnet, who held a wilted bouquet in his manacled hands. To witness the once-proud gentleman reduced to such a low state evoked conflicting emotions in the crowd. Those who saw him as a monster jeered; some sensed the tragedy and wept; still others felt the degradation of the moment and stood silent. The pirate chieftain lost his last shred of dignity, nearly fainting as he approached the scaffold. In a stupor, he was held upright by the marshal's deputies as the noose was tightened around his neck. With the crack of a whip the cart jolted away, leaving his body swaying in the cold wind.

Bonnet was buried near his men in the muddy marsh below the tide line so that no trace of him would be left. For the first time in two generations Carolinians could breathe freely as they laid in an obscure and watery grave the last of the pirate nemeses who had plagued their region, threatening to strangle overseas commerce, the lifeblood of their colonies.

Otway Burns [was] a
terror to all the British
in American waters.
—*John Hill Wheeler,*
1884

Otway Burns

The *Snap Dragon* Sweeps the Western Atlantic

A scant five years after the death of Otway Burns, North Carolina's famous privateer hero of the War of 1812, his first biographer wrote, "From my earliest childhood the adventures of the Snap Dragon, when commanded by Otway Burns, have been rehearsed in my hearing by old tars, many of whom are now dead and in a few years perhaps Otway Burns and the Snap Dragon will be looked upon as never having had any existence."[1] The author of these lines could not have imagined that in a little more than sixty years Burns would be immortalized by a bronze statue in Burnsville, the county seat of Yancey County in the heart of the Blue Ridge mountains hundreds of miles from the sea; by a simple but imposing tomb surmounted by a cannon from his famed *Snap Dragon* in the colonial cemetery in Beaufort; by the community of Otway in eastern Carteret County; and by a portrait in the North Carolina Museum of History. In our time another bronze statue has been erected in Swansboro, his hometown. The two statues alone are notable, because North Carolinians, whose state motto is "To be rather than to seem," have been justly proud of their reputation as a "vale of humility between two mountains of conceit," and traditionally they have been reluctant to glorify their heroes.

Who was this sea captain who fought for his state and nation in a conflict that within two generations was so overshadowed by the Civil War that it is barely remembered today? Since North Carolina was a minor arena for privateering, how did Otway Burns earn his exalted place in the state's maritime history? Why would a historian compare Burns favorably with the nation's premier naval icon, John Paul Jones, writing that Burns "conducted a campaign on the ocean in the War of 1812 which, in some respects, was on a smaller scale but in other elements was on a larger scale than the brilliant exploits of the great naval hero of the Revolution"?[2] He was not just any privateer, licensed by the government to seize enemy ships and cargoes during wartime; he was the most successful privateer south of Baltimore, taking over forty prizes in three cruises. Through copious news accounts and frequent advertisements of the sale of prize goods, the exploits of Otway Burns were well known to his contemporaries; yet in a remarkably short time the stirring events of 1812–15 were relegated to sea tales related in the taprooms of coastal taverns. Although Burns himself lived to the advanced age of seventy-five, he lost his fortune through numerous business failures. He died in obscurity in 1850 at Portsmouth, North Carolina, and was buried under a modest marker beside his second wife in the colonial cemetery in Beaufort.

The eccentric old privateer was nearly forgotten, and the very next year the state's first popular history, John Hill Wheeler's *Historical Sketches of North Carolina from 1584 to 1851*, made no mention of him. It would be thirty years before Burns entered the state's historical canon in Wheeler's posthumously published *Reminiscences and Memoirs of North Carolina and Eminent North Carolinians*. What had occurred in the thirty-three years between the publication of Wheeler's histories that brought Burns to his attention? The answer lies in a stirring portrait of Burns presented in the *North Carolina University Magazine* (1855–56), which included a narrative purportedly based on the logs of two cruises of the *Snap Dragon* in 1812 and 1813.

By the early twentieth century Burns's grandchildren, especially Walter F. Burns, an investment banker of New York and Chicago, endeavored to ensure a permanent place in history for their illustrious grandfather. From this family initiative came the grave monument, the portrait, the statue in Burnsville, a biographical compilation, and pub-

Captain Otway Burns, as a result of his spectacular success in the War of 1812, became North Carolina's most famous privateer. This painting is a copy of an 1815 portrait. (North Carolina Museum of History, Raleigh)

lished sketches by Chief Justice Walter Clark and University of North Carolina historian Kemp P. Battle. Although these early works on Burns were heavily mythologized and error filled, they became the bases for all subsequent biographies of him. In his portrayal by Walter Burns, Battle, and Clark, there is only a hint of the complex private life that underlay the public side of Otway Burns—sea captain, privateer, war hero, legislator, entrepreneur, merchant, shipbuilder. Little is said about his bankruptcy, his tangled personal life, his three marriages, or the eccentricities of his last years. Among both contemporary observers and modern researchers, however, there is consensus on his iron will, courage, endurance, self-confidence, direct manner, forceful personality, decisive and creative leadership, mastery of seamanship, and colorful character. Leaving aside the legendary Otway Burns, the real man was in fact a larger-than-life individual who well deserves his niche in the pantheon of North Carolina heroes.

Born in 1775 in Onslow County, Otway Burns was drawn to the water as a youth. In the local ports of Swansboro and nearby Beaufort, in Carteret County, he became a seaman, mastering the skills necessary to become a merchant captain and sailing along the east coast as far north as Maine. He married his cousin Joanna Grant, who required him to sign a prenuptial property agreement, on 6 July 1809 and the following year moved to Swansboro, where Joanna gave birth to a son, Owen, who would prove to be Burns's only child.[3] His coastal trading ventures were backed by a partnership with Edward Pasteur, a physician, planter, and well-known political leader in New Bern. When war came in 1812 and Burns decided to become a privateer, he and Pasteur set out to purchase the ship whose speed and maneuverability would respond best to Burns's experienced and superb handling. They found the ideal vessel in New York City in the summer of 1812 and purchased her for $8,000. Originally named the *Zephyr*, she had been built on the West River in Maryland in 1808. A vessel of 147 tons, she was flush decked with two masts and had a length of 85½ feet, a beam of 22½ feet, and a depth of slightly less than 9 feet.[4] Rechristened the *Snap Dragon*, she was commissioned a privateer in New York on 27 August 1812 under Pasteur, who sailed the ship to New Bern, accompanied by Burns. There fifty shares in the ship were sold at $260 per share, and Burns and Pasteur were joined by eight other investors from New Bern, Tarboro, and Edenton.[5]

Her armament varied from six to eight guns, consisting of one pivot gun (a twelve-pounder) and five to seven carriage guns, probably six-pounders, mounted on the sides. At least twice she carried two swivel guns. Other weapons for boarding and hand-to-hand fighting included an array of small arms—as many as sixty cutlasses, forty pistols, sixty muskets, twenty-five boarding pikes, twenty-five pick axes, and three blunderbusses. The crew number on the initial voyage was twenty-five officers and men, but subsequently she carried eighty to a hundred men. Since a vessel the size of the *Snap Dragon* could be sailed by less than ten men, the extra crewmen were for combat and to serve as prize crews.[6]

Under Pasteur's command, the *Snap Dragon*'s first privateering cruise commenced on 14 October 1812 and continued well into 1813. Although Otway Burns traditionally has been credited as the captain of this cruise, the commission and the legal notices concerning the sale of the prizes establish Edward Pasteur as the commander and William Mitchell as the first lieutenant. In addition, there are statements that were executed at sea on 19 December 1812 and 16 January 1813 by prisoners recently captured "by Edward Pasteur commanding the aforesaid Private armed schooner Snap Dragon."[7] Though not the captain of record, Burns was on board the schooner on this first exciting and rewarding privateering venture, probably as a welcome adviser because of his extensive sea experience. It is likely that business partners Pasteur and Burns had been functioning seamlessly at sea for some time, since Burns apparently assumed temporary de facto command of the vessel whenever she was endangered. In the *University Magazine* narrative Burns is portrayed as impetuous, recklessly brave, always right in his instinct for action over the more timid counsel of other officers, and uncannily able to see through the ruses used by the British in an effort to decoy the ship into a trap. Certainly, to a sailor on board the privateer it would have appeared that Burns played a major role in both the success of the voyage and the survival of the ship.

Preparing for this first active cruise in the autumn of 1812, the well-armed and well-stocked *Snap Dragon* rode at anchor in New Bern, lacking only enough crew to man the anticipated prizes. Both Pasteur and Burns were taken aback when they realized that some of the influential political leaders in the little port opposed the war and considered privateering tantamount to piracy. Conspiring to delay the schooner, which was New Bern's first privateer, they persuaded some of the new recruits to borrow money and then sought to arrest them for debt. In two colorful incidents, the crew capsized a boat loaded with constables seeking to board, and, when a local attorney hailed the vessel as "a licensed robber," Burns rowed ashore and tossed him into the river. Doubtless many were relieved when the little man-of-war weighed anchor bound for Norfolk, Virginia, a larger port more familiar with the advantages of privateering. Sailing from there in late October, the *Snap Dragon* headed south accompanied by another privateer, the *Revenge*, but it was soon evident that the swiftly sailing schooner outclassed her consort. In a week's time the two vessels parted ways. On her very first day alone, the *Snap Dragon* demonstrated her speed by outrunning a British frigate and a sloop, and several days later a British merchant ship of fourteen guns was taken as the first prize.[8]

When the privateer arrived in St. Thomas in the Virgin Islands, a boat was manned and sent in at night to determine whether any prizes could be cut out, or captured, but it returned too late to attempt any action.[9] Withdrawing over the horizon, the privateer was disguised as a merchant ship by covering the guns and putting up an old patched set of sails. At dawn the crew were dismayed to find themselves in sight of five British men-of-war—three to the windward and two to the leeward. Although they raised Spanish colors, their ruse failed, for the frigate HMS *Garland,* the only ship in range, fired a shot and signalled a chase to her consorts. With every sail set, the sleek privateer fled toward its escape route, Ship Rock passage, which was nearly forty miles away. Burns laid the course directly for the rock so that the British would not know which side he would take until the last minute. For two hours, the *Garland* fired continually from her bow chasers, drenching the *Snap Dragon* with spray from near misses. At the rock, where two brigs blocked the passage, Burns took the helm and ordered the crew to lie down on the deck. As the American vessel approached the closer brig, the HMS *Sophia,* the British unleashed a broadside of grape and round shot, but the saucy schooner emerged from the smoke unscathed and as night fell was far downwind from her pursuers. Burns could not resist pulling up and hoisting the stars and stripes as he fired a defiant farewell salute. The next sunrise revealed another British man-of-war, the fifteen-gun schooner HMS *Dominica,* which was soon left far astern as the *Snap Dragon* fairly flew over the waves in a fresh breeze.[10]

The *Snap Dragon* had a brief respite around St. Croix in the Virgins, where "several small captures" were taken, presumably coastal traders; but word of her activities reached the ten-gun brig HMS *Netler* on St. Thomas, and the pursuit soon resumed. About forty miles from Tortola the *Netler* flushed her quarry and ran down with the wind, expecting the privateer to flee. In spite of contrary advice from the other officers, Burns, aware of the *Netler*'s armament and concluding that the privateer had a fair chance, chose to fight, so surprising the *Netler*'s commander that he ordered his vessel to come about and reverse course. Now the predator became the prey. Eleven hours later the *Snap Dragon* was closing in, but at dusk the *Netler* made it into Tortola. As darkness fell, Burns hoisted British colors, passed the fort into the harbor, and anchored about a half mile from town. Crewmen familiar with the harbor manned boats for cutting out a prize. Approaching an anchored vessel with their oars muffled, the Americans pulled silently alongside, with "visions of prize money . . . already floating" through their minds, when a hail from the ship was followed by a burst of musketry. They had had the misfortune to come up on the alert *Netler* rather than an unsuspecting merchantman. A confused alarm was raised in port, as skyrockets began to fly in every direction. When a light was hoisted on the *Snap Dragon* to guide her boats to safety, she drew fire from a nearby shore battery. Extinguishing the light, Burns returned fire with the twelve-pound pivot gun. Ready to leave as soon as the boats were aboard, the crew was forced by the absence of any breeze to man the sweeps and row the privateer out of danger. Burns was so piqued over the thwarted operation that the next day he ordered a raid on a coastal plantation, at least garnering fresh meat and vegetables.[11]

After they had spent weeks at sea, with several narrow escapes and only insignificant prizes, fortune finally smiled on the Americans. The day after the Tortola fiasco, the *Snap Dragon* captured a British slaver carrying about fifty "Guinea negroes" to St. Croix. Eighteen valuable slaves who were "very anxious" to go with the Americans, were taken, and the prize was released. Off St. Croix a schooner laden with timber was cut out and burned, the only prize Burns ever destroyed. The *Snap Dragon* slipped into Ponce, a neutral port on the south coast of Puerto Rico, and found the governor there very accommodating. Over a five-day stay he allowed the Americans to replenish their water and to trade for supplies, including a long nine-pound gun.

Now laying a course for the Central American coast, the fabled Spanish Main, the *Snap Dragon* exchanged fire with a British packet, but a rising storm forced her to break off. When a "tremendous gale" hit, the schooner lost her jibboom and hove to under storm sails. Burns took charge of the ship's survival and "never left the deck the whole night, for she wanted watching by such a man as he was, and there was no man on earth that could manage her like him." At four in the morning, when he was below deck for a brief rest, the wind shifted and the *Snap Dragon* was blown into the trough of a wave. When a "tremendous wave knocked her on beam ends, filled the waist with water and set some of the guns adrift, Burns was on deck in an instant and proved himself equal to the crisis." Quickly taking the tiller, he regained control of the vessel and saw to it that the guns were secured. The vessel had three feet of water in the hold, which took two hours to pump out. A crew member wrote, "I am as certain as that I have a soul to be saved that if it had not been for Burns, the Snap and all her brave crew must have gone to the bottom."[12]

Limping into Maracaibo on the Gulf of Venezuela, the *Snap Dragon* anchored off a small fishing village, where her carpenters, aided by the whole crew, completed repairs in four days. The governor visited the vessel and invited the officers to dine with him. When the local fishermen revealed that several British merchantmen were in the gulf trading, the privateer put to sea, scattering five of the traders "like a covey when a hawk darts in among them." The *Snap Dragon* captured the schooner *Rachael* and two sloops, the *Sisters* and the *William and Charles*, and ran another craft aground. After being plundered, two of the vessels were released and one was sent home with a prize crew.[13]

A few days later the *Snap Dragon* encountered four large ships. Running down from the windward, Burns discerned that one of the ships, having topmasts struck and using sails covered with black patches, was probably a disguised man-of-war. It was, in fact, the fast sloop HMS *Fawn*, specially outfitted to lure privateers to their destruction. When Burns ordered the privateer to "haul away," some of the officers, thinking more of the lost prize money than of their own safety, complained, angering Burns, who then turned back to the convoy to teach them a lesson. As the *Snap Dragon* again bore down on the stranger, guns blazing, the decoy withheld fire, hoping that the Americans had swallowed the bait and would come alongside to board. At the last minute, Burns sheered off and the British opened with a broadside of grape and canister, which was aimed too high and merely holed some sails. Their antagonist hurriedly set all sails and began to drive the privateer toward an island. As the breeze freshened, the Americans furled their topgallant sails and single-reefed their mainsail. The narrator who related events in the *University Magazine* wrote, "It was pretty tight times; the wind blowing big guns, the sea breaking over us, and a dangerous looking stranger walking right in our wake." Again Burns sent all but a skeleton crew below and took the helm himself. It was so "tight" that both crewmen and officers were packing their baggage, "certain [they] were ticketed for a free passage to England." Just as the two ships were about to meet, the privateer caught a stray breeze and shot past the British ship at a distance of only 300 yards. When another broadside of grape and canister was fired, the *Snap Dragon* was in a trough and again sustained damage only to her sails. The ships were so close that the Americans could almost hear the British officers shouting commands. By nightfall the privateer was well away, and the crewman recorded, "Nothing saved us that day but the exertions of captain Burns alone, and his skill in sailing manoeavres."[14]

Shortly thereafter, the year 1813 was ushered in with the capture of the sloop *Fillis* out of Curaçao on 18 January. The cargo of mixed dry goods included three thousand goatskins, ten hides, fifty mats, earthenware, twenty kegs of oil, and thirty bushels of yams. The *Snap Dragon*'s crew had a good laugh when the master of the *Fillis* reported that the *Fawn* had claimed in Curaçao to have sunk an American privateer. A prize crew was put aboard, and the *Fillis* successfully ran the mid-Atlantic British blockade into Beaufort, arriving on 23 February with the first news of the privateer in four months.[15]

Sailing west along the Spanish Main, the *Snap Dragon* entered the port of Santa Marta, in Colombia, to accommodate the English prisoners' request that they be put ashore in a neutral port. Because of the history of piracy on this coast, Pasteur was apprehensive that the local Spanish officials might not be as friendly as their counterparts in Puerto Rico and Maracaibo. Anchoring just out of range of the fort, the *Snap Dragon* sent the prisoners ashore in a boat under the command of one of the ship's officers. After tense hours of futile waiting, the privateer sent a second boat bearing a copy of her letter of marque. Both landing parties were immediately imprisoned as pirates. By eight o'clock in the evening, strained "palavering" had resulted in the release of one of the officers, who reported the grim situation. In a bright full moon the *Snap Dragon* left Santa Marta, dropping out of sight over the horizon. Just after dawn, the privateer seized a Spanish military transport ferrying a hundred soldiers from Santa Marta. The Spanish commander was told that unless he secured the release of the Americans in two hours his own troops would be hanged. The *Snap Dragon* returned to the harbor, and in full sight of the Spanish fort but out of range, the Americans rigged nooses on the yardarms. In less than two hours the Americans were reunited and sailed away.[16]

Since water was in short supply on board ship, the *Snap Dragon* was unable to leave this unfriendly coast, and the decision was made to risk resupplying in Cartagena. On the way the Americans sighted three ships which turned out to be two well-armed Spanish "guarda costa" vessels and one British merchant ship. When the Spanish brig fired a warning shot at the privateer, she responded by manning the guns and hailing the brig. The Spanish claimed to be convoying the Englishmen, but Burns replied that as a neutral they had no right to protect either side. Since they were on the high seas, he ordered that the merchant vessel be seized, placing a twenty-one-man crew on board. Some of the cargo was transferred to the privateer, which then entered Cartagena; but the prize was kept offshore to prevent the Spanish from reclaiming it. Burns did not know that the captain of the Spanish brig had falsely reported being fired upon by the *Snap Dragon*, claiming that the Americans had illegally seized the British vessel under his protection. Spanish gunboats were dispatched to locate and retake the ship. Initially, the Spanish were driven off, but they returned with reinforcements and boarded the British ship. The American crew was imprisoned, and this time the privateer was under the fort guns and hemmed in by men-of-war. Three weeks of parley and bribes secured the release of both the prize and the crew members, although two crewmen had died in prison. Not until they were leaving did the Americans learn that the craft had been stripped of a secret cache of 15,000 Spanish dollars, clearly the main reason why the Spanish took such extraordinary measures to recover the prize. The *Snap Dragon* was delayed another week to allow British ships in the harbor to escape. Thereafter, the privateer's crew remained bitter toward the Spanish, and on one occasion some of the recently released prisoners had to be restrained to keep them from hanging a Spanish crewman on a vessel they had stopped.[17]

The *Snap Dragon* paid a short but pleasant visit to the English-settled island of Providence off the coast of what is now Nicaragua. The local "head man" sold the Americans plentiful supplies at reasonable prices. Pasteur allowed the crew liberty. Most returned on time, but one group of Irishmen and marine sergeant Plane, "a saucy scoundrel," got so drunk that they refused to return with First Lieutenant Mitchell, threatening to throw him down the hill and saying that they "had not got their frolic out." The infuriated Burns went ashore alone and approached the rum shop, sword in hand. Sergeant Plane defied him, whereupon Burns "cut him down" and set upon the whole group "until blood ran in streams." In less than an hour he had herded them all back on board.[18]

The privateer sailed north to Cape San Antonio, Cuba, and near Havana took a British vessel from Honduras, which was looted and released. Near Cape Florida, north of the Florida Keys, the *Snap Dragon* engaged the ten-gun British privateer *Providence*, which broke off action after losing three men and sought refuge among the reefs. Approaching home, off Swansboro the crew was amused by a coastal vessel that fled and then pretended to pole frantically as if in shallow water where the privateers knew full well it had seven fathoms, or forty-two feet, under its keel. When the *Snap Dragon* pulled alongside, the crew on the local craft was greatly relieved to find their grinning neighbors on board. That evening the privateer dropped anchor in Beaufort.[19]

The maiden voyage of the *Snap Dragon* had been resoundingly successful. Pasteur and Burns had taken nine prizes and "several small captures." In addition to the *Fillis* and its cargo, which had preceded them to port, they had brought in valuable plunder to sell, including

The western Atlantic

eighteen male slaves, ten boxes of soap, six bales of cotton, leather, cordages, a swivel gun, five muskets, twenty-four cutlasses, twenty-five pounds of powder, and two hundred pounds of indigo.[20] During the six-month cruise, which had been entirely in the Caribbean, there had been a number of "pretty tight times" when the privateer was nearly captured or came close to being lost in heavy weather, and she had been threatened by the corrupt Spanish officials in Santa Marta and Cartagena as much as by British men-of-war. But this cruise established the fame of the *Snap Dragon* as a lucky ship that could make a man's fortune. By this time prizes from other privateers were also coming into the North Carolina ports, which were thought to be so insignificant that the British neglected to blockade them. The influx of wealth ended local opposition to privateering.

On 1 June 1813 a third commission was granted for the *Snap Dragon*, under the command of Otway Burns, with James Brown of New York as first lieutenant. The crew of 127 was made up of 75 locals supplemented by 52 seamen recruited in Norfolk. The privateer now had eleven owners and was armed with eight cannon and two swivel guns.[21] Weighing anchor from Beaufort on 3 June, the racy, diminutive schooner left home for a cruise that would last over two months and be by far her most successful venture of the war. The first stop was to be off Cape Lookout to meet a challenge from the schooner HMS *Highflyer*. An eager crowd had sailed out to the cape from Beaufort to witness the anticipated duel, but the British vessel did not appear. Leaving the coast of North Carolina at Ocracoke, Burns headed north toward the crowded seas off Halifax, Nova Scotia. The military buildup for the defense of Canada kept a steady stream of merchant vessels plying the lanes connecting Britain to the Gulf of St. Lawrence. Over the next two weeks the privateer encountered and boarded several neutral and American vessels. The only incident of interest was the taking of fresh water from a large iceberg just south of Newfoundland's Grand Banks.[22]

On 24 June, after twenty-one days at sea, off Cape Race, Newfoundland, the *Snap Dragon* took three prizes within an hour—the bark *Henrietta* from Liverpool and the brigs *Jane* and *Pandora*. Unfortunately for the privateer, all three vessels were in ballast with no cargo. Burns kept the *Henrietta* and the *Jane*, sending them to Beaufort with prize crews—although the *Jane* did not reach North Carolina, being retaken about two weeks later. The *Pandora* he loaded with the paroled prisoners and released. Two days later, in the early afternoon of 27 June, the *Snap Dragon* began a twenty-six-hour chase that lasted through a foggy night into the next morning, when "a sharp conflict" began. The lifting mist revealed a large convoy of twenty-five to thirty ships protected by several frigates and a seventy-four-gun ship-of-the-line. Burns now could identify his prey as a fourteen-gun brig, which, surprisingly, was fired upon by the frigate, although it was flying the Union Jack. The chase moved toward Burns, but he bore away, suspecting that he was being decoyed into a trap, which was a common tactic employed by war vessels of the era. The next day yielded two more brigs, the *Good Intent* and the *Venus*, again both in ballast. Burns kept the former and sent the *Venus* on with paroled prisoners. Before dark the *Snap Dragon* was able to pull away easily from a nosy British armed brig, the *Ringdove*, but was forced to remain close by to protect the prize. The privateer harried the *Ringdove* with her twelve-pound pivot gun, which could outrange her adversary's carronades. Although the prize escaped that evening, it was retaken three weeks later.[23]

Shortly after this close call, the *Snap Dragon* survived a heavy gale on the Grand Banks. All the yards were struck, as well as the topmast, and the guns were stowed below. With storm sails up, under Burns's skillful handling the schooner rode out the storm as high seas broke constantly over the deck. Taking a quick breather in the midst of the storm, Burns was summoned by a panicked shout from his first officer that the "Snap" was foundering, and he rushed up to find her buried in the waves. Burns took the helm and scudded, or ran before the wind, for eight hours. A crew member remarked that he had "often heard Burns say that if a vessel could scud nine knots, no sea could board her." On that harrowing run the privateer made ten knots.[24]

Near St. Johns, Newfoundland, the *Snap Dragon* stopped several small coasters but found them loaded with timber and let them go. On 30 June, as the privateer approached a strange sail to investigate, Captain Fox, a British prisoner whom Burns had befriended, told him that he recognized the HMS *Adonis*, a schooner of fourteen guns. He advised Burns to pull away while he could. The *Adonis* was well camouflaged as a decoy merchantman, with sails, yards, and mast struck and guns hidden. Now cautious, Burns continued to close with the *Adonis*, which prematurely opened fire with a broadside of grape and canister, and the battle was on. When the cannonading was most intense and the outcome in doubt, Lieutenant Brown lost his nerve and suggested that Burns strike his colors. Burns impulsively broke his speaking trumpet over Brown's head and continued the fight. The privateer was so much faster than the *Adonis* that she darted around her enemy at will; however, the match was so even that after another twenty minutes the *Snap Dragon* withdrew. She suffered light rigging and sail damage and three wounded. Brown was broken in rank to a seaman for cowardice, and Benjamin D. Coakley was raised to first officer. Shortly afterward, a brig laden with salt was stopped and released, and the Americans learned from them that the *Adonis* had suffered three killed and five wounded.[25]

Off Cape St. Francis just north of St. John's, Newfoundland, the *Snap Dragon* found herself in the midst of about ninety fishing boats. Although hoisting British colors did not fool the canny fishermen, they were willing to trade with the Americans, who offered rum for fresh fish. One captain gave them bait, and the privateer fished with them the rest of the day. The Fourth of July was celebrated with the capture of the schooner *Elizabeth*, from which the *Snap Dragon* was resupplied. The *Elizabeth* was sent into St. John's with prisoners, and the privateer headed north to Grates Point, the entrance to Trinity Bay, where the crew relaxed by fishing and taking on fresh water. In a heavy fog at 3:00 A.M. on 7 July the *Snap Dragon* passed close to a ship on the opposite course. Burns tacked and followed in the wake of the ship until noon the next day, when the mist cleared and he saw to his consternation a large frigate bearing down on him. As always, the privateer flitted away quickly, this time into another fog bank, and a deadly game of cat-and-mouse continued for several hours from one fog bank to another until Burns shook off the pursuing frigate. Several other sails appeared, and Burns quickly seized two ships from Cork—the brig *Happy* and the bark *Reprisal*. The *Snap Dragon* was in the process of securing ten additional prizes when her relentless foe, the frigate, suddenly appeared the next morning. Burns hastily released the vessels with paroled prisoners and escaped. That afternoon the privateer, again in heavy fog, blundered onto the brig *Ann* from Liverpool bound for St. John, New Brunswick, with a mixed cargo of domestic merchandise, steel, wire, and crockery, which was invoiced at £83,000 ($368,520). Unwilling to entrust such a rich cargo to anyone else, Burns spent two days transferring it to the hold of the *Snap Dragon* and then in company with the *Ann* turned his bow toward Beaufort. Although a number of neutral and American vessels were again encountered, the privateer saw no more prizes and arrived safely at Beaufort on 10 August.[26]

This voyage made a fortune for the owners and crew of the *Snap Dragon*. In the course of ten weeks at sea, the vessel had taken nine prizes but had been able to keep only four—the bark *Henrietta* and the brigs *Jane*, *Good Intent*, and *Ann*, of which only the *Henrietta* and the *Ann* made port. There were four close encounters with British warships, but only the *Adonis* was ever near enough to exchange fire with the privateer, and even she was too far away to do more than hole a sail and cut a line. The tense twenty-eight-hour chase by the frigate had cost Burns two prizes, but it had also led him to the *Ann*. The *Hen-*

rietta was sold in September, and the *Ann* was condemned by the district court and sold on 11 October at the warehouse of merchant William Shepard, who was one of the owners of the *Snap Dragon*. The cargo consisted of a great number of containers that held an amazing array of textile goods—including all types of cloth, lace, linen, silk, and blankets—25 tons of steel and sheet iron, and 60 casks of card wire estimated to have a value of £2,200. Three hundred buyers, some from as far away as Boston, flocked into New Bern for the auction. The sale of the ship and her cargo brought nearly $500,000, and one source claims that each crewman took home $3,000. Although it cannot be determined with certainty how much Burns made from the cruise, he was entitled to both an owner's share and the captain's share of the proceeds. Needless to say, he was now a wealthy man.[27]

Otway Burns's last cruise on the *Snap Dragon* took place from 20 January to 9 April 1814, a total of eighty days at sea. Leaving Beaufort early in the morning with a crew of one hundred men and officers, the privateer fired a salute as she passed Fort Hampton at the mouth of Topsail Inlet and then turned south toward the Caribbean. Probably to increase the schooner's speed, Burns had reduced her armament to six cannon and two swivel guns. Within two days, during a futile chase, the *Snap Dragon* found herself in a squall that forced Burns to let all sails loose to prevent being capsized by the wind. As the privateer moved south, she stopped several neutral and American vessels. In the Caribbean by 8 February, she was pursued for two days by a ship and a fourteen-gun schooner. On 16 February, the *Snap Dragon* was off the coast of South America, and four days later she labored through another heavy squall. By 23 February the privateer had sailed as far south as 2° north latitude to the Island of Maracá on the coast of Brazil. In need of water, Burns attempted to enter the Araguari River just north of the Amazon, became entangled in a complex of shoals at the mouth, and struck a mud bank. High tide refloated the *Snap Dragon*, which then headed north.[28]

On 3 March, off the coast of Surinam at 6° north latitude, a sail was sighted before dawn. Although it proved to be a British ship of at least twenty-two guns, Burns did not hesitate to attack and engaged her at 7:30 A.M., with both vessels keeping "a regular and constant fire." The adversary turned out to be a match for Burns in seamanship and was able to prevent the Americans from boarding in numbers. With cannon roaring for four hours, at 11:30 Burns maneuvered the *Snap Dragon* close enough for the crew to fire muskets and hoist the red flag to prepare to board, but well-placed shots in the rigging forced the privateer to fall away. During another attempt to board two hours later, the enemy vessel was able to ram the *Snap Dragon* head on, taking the jibboom and bowsprit, and bringing down the foremast. By then, however, the enemy had had enough. A truce was called on the British vessel, whose master allowed those members of the privateer's crew who had boarded to return to their own ship. The British vessel then ran before the wind, leaving behind the crippled *Snap Dragon*, which had been outgunned twenty-two to six. All hands turned out to clear the wreckage. Finding the hull sound below the waterline, Burns rigged a jury mast and set the jib. By late afternoon the privateer was under way. Burns noted in the log that "our sails, rigging and hull is much damaged, and our boat completely ruined." This fiercely fought six-hour action so disabled the *Snap Dragon* that there was little choice but to run for the coast. Burns reported that the enemy "fought desperately," repelling boarders from the privateer with pistols, cutlasses, pikes, hand spikes, and thrown cannon balls, bottles, bricks, and stink pots. He wrote that the enemy's losses were unknown, but that blood ran from her lea scuppers and her hull was damaged by chain and bar shot. American casualties were four killed and seven wounded.[29]

The *Snap Dragon* ran for the coast of South America and entered the Orinoco River in Venezuela on 7 March. She was anchored some twenty miles upriver, and the crew went ashore to cut timber for temporary repairs. Within two days the efforts of the entire crew had put a foremast in place, and with new spars the privateer was rigged as a brig. Officials representing the local commandant visited from Angostura (now Ciudad Bolívar) to inquire about the purpose of the privateer's stay. Burns put them at ease, replying that they would be gone soon. On one hunting expedition, Burns returned with macaws and a fifteen-foot-long snake, probably an anaconda. After a thirteen-day stay on the Orinoco, the *Snap Dragon* headed north for Beaufort. On 24 March, she met an American privateer, the *Saratoga*, which was able to spare a small boat and spars. The only prize of the voyage was taken on 28 March—the Swedish schooner *Eliz*, with a cargo of mahogany, which had been captured by the British and had a four-man prize crew aboard. The *Snap Dragon* sighted Cape Lookout lighthouse on 7 April and made Ocracoke Inlet that afternoon, anchoring at Shell Castle. Two days later she arrived safely at New Bern.[30]

Otway Burns's last cruise on the *Snap Dragon* thus gained only

On 30 June 1814 the *Snap Dragon*, commanded by William R. Graham, was captured by the HMS *Martin* near Halifax, Nova Scotia. (Mariners' Museum, Newport News, Va.)

one prize and endured a severe sea battle that seriously damaged the vessel. Burns realized that the Caribbean, no longer a safe cruising ground, had been virtually swept clean of potential prizes. Although he continued to be an owner of the privateer, he did not go to sea again during the war. Illness, usually described as rheumatism, has been given as the reason he remained at home, but his marriage was breaking up at this time as well. Possibly Burns had a premonition of the future, as the final voyage of the *Snap Dragon* would end in the heretofore lucky schooner's being captured in battle.

The commission for the *Snap Dragon*'s last voyage was issued on 21 May 1814, with William R. Graham as the commander. Leaving port five days later, the privateer headed north for the prime sea lanes off Nova Scotia. The first prize taken was the schooner *Linnet*, with a cargo of fish, oil, and beef tongues. On 30 June, just north of Halifax, Nova Scotia, the *Snap Dragon* encountered the sloop HMS *Martin*, which proved her undoing. Although the *Martin* had to resort to sweeps to catch the *Snap Dragon* in the light breeze, the chase was soon over, and the privateer bowed to superior firepower. The captured ship and crew were taken to Halifax, where the crew was first held in Melville Island prison, later to be transferred to Dartmoor prison in Britain. They were exchanged after the war, which was over by the end of the year. The glory days of the *Snap Dragon* were over.

The privateer was purchased by merchants of St. John, New Brunswick, and sailed briefly under a letter of marque and reprisal. After the war she was bought by a merchant firm in Halifax, and she spent her last months as an island trader between Jamaica and Cuba. She was lost in the Caribbean in March 1816.[31]

In two years, Otway Burns, an obscure coastal trader, had experienced a heady rise to become the first naval hero in the history of his state. Although his exploits won him lasting fame and fortune, his renown was bittersweet, and his life was changed forever. In the summer of 1814 he was nearly forty years old, his health was temporarily impaired, and he had returned from his third cruise to an empty house. His wife Joanna had left him in January and taken his son Owen to live with her relatives in neighboring Jones County. By September she died, leaving their son in the care of her family, and five years passed before father and son were reunited when Burns gained custody through a legal guardianship. In December 1814 Burns married twenty-year-old Jane Hall of Beaufort, and the following April he purchased a lot on Front Street in Beaufort and built a home, which was the Burns residence for the next two decades.[32]

Using his newly acquired fortune, Burns channeled his restless energy into entrepreneurial development, investing in local business and industry. He established shipyards, and in Swansboro in 1818 built the first steamboat in the state, the *Prometheus*, which operated on the Cape Fear River between Wilmington and Smithville (Southport). In Beaufort he built the *Warrior* in 1823 and the brig *Henry* in 1831. During the 1820s he kept a store and taproom on his Front Street lot and was also a partner in a salt works on Taylor Creek. His interest in navigation improvements led to his appointment in 1822 as a commissioner of the Clubfoot and Harlow Creek Canal, which still connects the Neuse River to the Newport River behind Beaufort. Burns was a co-owner of brick kilns that furnished bricks on government contract to build Fort Macon on Bogue Banks. The largest public works project in the region until modern times, the fort was under construction from 1826 to 1834. Burns owned several vessels: the schooner *Venus*, the flat *Elizabeth*, a sailboat, a mullet boat and seine, and a canoe. He also owned eleven slaves, who were involved in his boat building and commercial enterprises and in the operation of his 340-acre plantation on North River in Carteret County.[33]

Burns parlayed his fame into a long legislative career, which began in 1821 with his election from Carteret County to a term in the North

Carolina House of Commons. Over the next fourteen years he served eleven terms—seven in the House and four in the Senate, where he earned a reputation for "enlightened" views and for supporting what he thought was right, regardless of the political consequences. He was an admirer of Andrew Jackson and followed him into the new Democratic Party. The rough-hewn sea captain was praised by a contemporary legislator, William H. Battle, for "his independence and freedom from demagoguery," backed by a "disposition to answer supposed insults with the strong argument of ponderous fists."[34]

The burning issue of the era was long-standing sectional controversy between the eastern and the western portions of the state over democratic representation, which required a constitutional amendment to settle. The overrepresented conservative eastern counties usually blocked legislation for additional counties to the west, for democratic reform, and for internal improvements such as turnpikes and railroads, which would have benefited the western areas. Rising above the prejudices of his region, Burns consistently supported the creation of new western counties, one of which, the mountain county of Yancey, named its county seat Burnsville in his honor. He voted for internal improvements, supported strengthening the newly organized state supreme court, and backed bills encouraging agriculture, manufacturing, local banks, direct election of sheriffs, and election reform. Although he was a slaveowner, his long experience at sea with free black sailors led him to support measures that improved the status of all free blacks. He opposed restrictions on the entry of free blacks into the state and voted for individual emancipation of slaves. He worked for the repeal of acts prohibiting education for slaves and restricting free exercise of religion by slaves and free blacks. His vote for a state constitutional convention in 1835, which passed the Senate by one vote, made possible long-needed democratic constitutional reforms but ended his political career because voters in the eastern section of the state generally opposed the reforms, which would reduce their region's control of the state government.[35]

Coupled with his political ouster was his financial ruin. Traditionally his business failure has been attributed to his generosity and poor management, but the answer more likely lies in the protracted economic depression that began with the Panic of 1837. By the 1830s Burns had borrowed heavily on his property to finance his many enterprises. Overextension of his resources resulted in many mortgages and eventually the sale of most of his property to satisfy his creditors.[36] Reduced to bankruptcy, in 1835 Burns sought and received from the Democratic administration of Andrew Jackson, who had always had his enthusiastic support, an appointment as keeper of the Brant Island Shoal Lightboat near Portsmouth, North Carolina. Even his term as a lightship keeper was not without controversy. In an exposed location in the middle of vast Pamlico Sound, the craft was continually damaged by the gales that battered the Outer Banks. From the onset of his tenure as captain of the lightboat, Burns sought a larger vessel that could better weather the storms, but the appropriation for it never passed Congress. A vicious congressional election in 1843, in which the Democrat Archibald H. Arrington won reelection with Burns's support, led to spurious charges by Whig opponents that Burns had neglected his duties and withheld wages from his crew. Among the Democratic politicians who rallied to his side was Congressman Romulus M. Saunders, who wrote that Burns "is held in great esteem in our State for his brave and meritorious conduct during the late war." The old privateer was cleared after a thorough investigation by his superiors, which revealed that the charges had no foundation and were politically motivated.[37]

Because of the lightboat command, the Burnses moved across the sound from Beaufort to Portsmouth on Core Banks, which was then a port of about four hundred people. Jane Burns died there on 24 October 1839 and was brought back for burial beside her parents in Beaufort. In February 1842 Burns was married a third time, to Jane Smith of Smyrna, who would also predecease him. By 1850 he was living with the family of John L. Hunter of Portsmouth. He died at the Hunter home on 25 October and was buried in Beaufort beside his second wife, Jane.[38]

Edgar S. Maclay, a historian of privateering, wrote in 1916 that Burns on three cruises had captured forty-two prizes with a value of $4 million, had engaged in combat with several men-of-war, and had taken over three hundred prisoners, compiling "a record of astounding audacity and brilliant success that has few parallels."[39] His long experience as a merchant ship captain and owner left Burns with sympathy for those he captured, and he customarily released his prizes or used them as cartel vessels to convey his paroled prisoners to a friendly port. Only once did he mention burning a prize, an uncharacteristic action for him to take. Although Burns was quite willing to make war on Britain and British merchants, he was not comfortable causing suffering to individual merchant seamen or captains. His magnanimity to his prisoners was manifested in several instances where he restored their private property and personal investments in captured cargo.[40] Unlike most privateers, who avoided encounters with men-of-war if possible, Burns readily risked clashes with British privateers and naval vessels when he thought he had an equal chance. He had complete confidence in the speed, agility, and seaworthiness of his beloved *Snap Dragon* and in his own masterful seamanship. Only once did his aggressiveness backfire—in his last engagement with an unknown enemy vessel, which battered both assailants and disabled the *Snap Dragon*.

Without question, in North Carolina and the South the *Snap Dragon* was the preeminent privateer in the War of 1812 and Otway Burns the most famous commander. Through his highly visible role as an entrepreneur and his long career in the legislature, Burns remained on the public stage after the war. To the general populace he personified the colorful privateer who at great risk to himself upheld the nation's honor, enriched his coffers, and shared his wealth by investing in his community's development. Dying a pauper and almost unnoticed, Burns within two generations rose from the ashes to become exalted by his state, memorialized from the Blue Ridge Mountains to the sea and greatly enhancing our maritime heritage.

*During the whole war
no vessel was ever better
manned and commanded
than this daring and
resolute cruiser.*
— *Theodore Roosevelt,
1882*

Johnston Blakeley

The *Wasp* Ravages the English Channel

As the War of 1812 dragged into its third dreary year, the euphoria of the first year had long since dissipated, extinguished by one ignominious defeat after another for the inexperienced United States Army, which was led by incompetent commanders. Considering the conquest of Canada to be unfinished business from the Revolution, the Americans planned thrusts into Canada from Detroit, Niagara, and Lake Champlain in the first six months of the war. The public expected the stalwart militia to rise and rout the despised redcoats as their Revolutionary forebears had done over a generation ago. What the public got instead was an ill-trained, poorly equipped rabble that surrendered Detroit without firing a shot, failed to support American troops who were decimated at Niagara, and refused to cross the border at Lake Champlain, forcing the campaign to be aborted. In the aftermath of the debacle, General William Hull was court-martialed for cowardice at Detroit, other generals were removed or retired, and Secretary of War William Eustis resigned. Fortunately for the country's future, over the next two years capable generals would emerge on the field of battle—the frontier Indian fighter Andrew Jackson in the South and William H. Harrison, Jacob Brown, and Winfield Scott in the North.

Only the nation's little navy had entered the war prepared, with commanders tested in combat in the Mediterranean with the North African corsairs and experienced from years of patrolling the sea lanes. The American navy's secret weapon was its handful of well-designed heavy frigates—the USS *United States*, the USS *Constitution*, and the USS *President*—which were unmatched in single-ship combat. Rated at forty-four guns in an era when British frigates had six to eight fewer guns, the American heavies often carried up to fifty-four guns. Nevertheless, a navy of sixteen ships could hardly challenge the might of the Royal Navy, which deployed a hundred vessels in the western Atlantic and had ruled the oceans throughout a quarter century of world conflict with the Republic of France and Napoleon's empire. What the American navy could do was salve the national morale bruised by the disasters on the Canadian frontier with brilliant victories over their British counterparts. In July, just three days after the surrender of Detroit, in a half-hour duel off the coast of Nova Scotia, the *Constitution* left the HMS *Guerrière* so shattered that she had to be scuttled by the victors. As the fiasco at Niagara wound down in October, the sloop USS *Wasp* defeated the sloop HMS *Frolic*, and the *United States* took the HMS *Macedonian* as a prize. The year ended with news of another lopsided victory by the *Constitution*, this time over the HMS *Java*.

In 1813 the halcyon days of American vessels roaming the high seas in search of enemy merchant and naval ships ended as the British blockade gradually strangled American commerce and bottled up the few remaining frigates. The year saw only occasional naval forays, which were largely unsuccessful. The people's hope had been sustained by the smashing victory of Commodore Perry's fleet on Lake Erie and the continued success of the hundreds of privateers. As 1814 dawned, the future appeared to be bleak for the United States. It was evident that the war in Europe was drawing to a close and that Britain soon would be able to concentrate her vast forces to discipline her upstart former colonies. British fleets and armies gathered to strike from Canada down the ancient invasion route of Lake Champlain, to raid the Chesapeake Bay and attack the country's capital, and to invade the lower Mississippi valley and capture the key port of New Orleans. With the remaining frigates immobilized by the blockade, the

Captain Johnston Blakeley became North Carolina's most famous naval hero in the War of 1812. This restored portrait was painted in 1840 for the Philanthropic Society of the University of North Carolina, Chapel Hill. (North Carolina Collection, Wilson Library, University of North Carolina, Chapel Hill)

navy pinned its hopes on fast, well-armed sloops that could more easily evade the blockaders and take British merchantmen in their home waters. Although rated at eighteen guns, these new sloops carried up to twenty-two cannon.

In the spring of 1814 the newly constructed *Wasp* (the third U.S. naval vessel to bear that name) slipped out of Portsmouth, New Hampshire, into the Atlantic. Emerging weeks later in the English Channel, she astonished the world with a slashing raid into the heart of British commerce, taking fifteen prizes and in separate actions defeating two British sloops in savage combat that panicked British merchants and drove marine insurance rates to new heights. Overnight, a heretofore unknown officer, Johnston Blakeley, became a naval hero to the American people, who were starved for news of any victory, no matter how slight; the sensational news from Britain of the deadly sting of the dangerous *Wasp* boosted the morale of a war-weary public.

Johnston Blakeley had been born in the village of Seaford in County Down, Ireland, in October 1781. When he was two years old, his father, John Blakeley, of Scots-Irish Protestant heritage, emigrated to Charleston, South Carolina. His wife and an infant son died shortly thereafter, and the distraught father took his toddler son north to the port of Wilmington, North Carolina, which had a long-established community of Scots-Irish and Scottish merchants. When the Blake-leys disembarked on the Wilmington waterfront, they found an awak-ening town of about a thousand inhabitants. The little port on the Cape Fear River was just beginning to shake off the effects of the Revolution and a British occupation of nearly a year in 1781. Centered on the courthouse and the wharfside markets, the town was showing signs of a growing prosperity based on a thriving trade with the West Indies and Great Britain, which John Blakeley successfully entered as a merchant. By 1800 the bustling port had a population of nearly 1,700 and was the second largest town in the state.[1]

In 1786 Blakeley became a good friend of Edward Jones, a newly arrived fellow Irish immigrant who soon left trade to become an at-torney. Jones was a natural at law and in 1788 was elected to the state legislature. Three years later he became the state's solicitor general, a position he held for thirty-six years. After Jones's marriage to Mary Mallett in 1790, young Johnston Blakeley was taken into their family as a virtual foster son. The Jones family grew to include two sons, one named for Johnston Blakeley, and four daughters. From all descrip-tions, it was a center of warmth and genteel society. Little else is known of Blakeley's youth except that he attended an academy in Flatbush on Long Island, New York.[2] His foster sister Charlotte Hardin wrote of him that he was "rather small, but well made, with very black hair and eyes; grave and gentlemanly in his deportment, but at the same time cheerful and easy when at home. Among strangers, rather reserved, and when very young rather avoiding than seeking society, he would sit for hours reading and talking with my mother, while the other young people were amusing themselves without."[3]

A letter of 1808 to his foster mother reveals the warm and familiar relationship that Blakeley enjoyed with the Jones family as well as a sprightly sense of humor. Blakeley wrote that the Joneses were "the friends dearest to me on earth" and expressed deep affection for his foster sisters. Mary Jones earlier had warned Blakeley about two young ladies who she thought were pursuing him. He relieved her anxiety, responding that "a cruise in Boston Bay, in the month of October, would cool a passion of more fervor than mine. I was an Ass between two bundles of hay, and had I been willing, neither were disposed to let me *bite them*."[4]

The fortunes of the Blakeley and Jones families depended on the success of the port of Wilmington and its recovery from the privations of war and military occupation. In 1786 a Scottish merchant, Robert

Hunter, wrote that the town was "without exception, the most disagreeable, sandy, barren town I have visited on the continent—consisting of a few scattered wood and brick houses, without any kind of order and regularity."[5] On his presidential tour of the Southern states in 1791, George Washington was entertained royally by the community, with honor guards, artillery salutes, an illumination, and a "grand" ball. The president also found the region to be "the most barren country I ever beheld," but he was impressed with the hospitality of Wilmington.[6] The ten-year-old Blakeley was surely dazzled by the parades, the military exercises, and the generally festive atmosphere of the town during the week of the president's stay.

In 1796 Blakeley's father died, necessitating an abrupt end to his schooling in New York and a return to Wilmington. Since Blakeley was the legal ward of Edward Jones, who hoped that his foster son would become an attorney, the decision was made to send him to North Carolina's newly created state university, which Jones had supported from the outset. His classical academy preparation complete, in 1797 the fifteen-year-old Blakeley made the long journey to Chapel Hill to enter the University of North Carolina, which was then beginning its second year. The university had opened in January 1795 in one building, Old East (then known as North Wing), with one professor, Dr. David Ker, a distinguished, Irish-born classical scholar. The first student, Hinton James of New Hanover County, did not arrive until four weeks later, but by the end of the term there were forty-one students in residence. By the time Blakeley arrived, there were over a hundred students; but, reflecting the woeful lack of academies in the state, about half of them were in the university's preparatory grammar school.[7] As he trudged to the top of the wooded hill, Blakeley reached the little cluster of buildings that he would come to know well—the brick Old East, the plain clapboard president's house, the white-painted steward's hall and kitchen, and the just-completed brick chapel, now known as Person Hall. The students lodged and attended classes in Old East and dined in the steward's hall. The dining fare was meager but cost only $40 for the academic year of ten months. The chapel was used for twice-daily prayers, church services, entertainments, debates of the literary societies, and commencement exercises.

In Blakeley's day, student living conditions were crowded and uncomfortable. Professor Joseph Caldwell, later president of the university, grimly reported: "Here are fifty-six persons huddled together with their trunks, beds, tables, chairs, books, and clothes into fourteen little rooms, which by the excessive heat of summer are enough to stifle them, and in the winter scarcely admit them to sit around the fireplace. When the weather permits they fly to the shade of the trees, where they find a retreat from the burr and hurry and irrepressible conversation of a crowded society."[8]

The letters home of student John Pettigrew confirmed the miserable life that students had to endure in their campus rooms. Although university rules required that rooms be "cleansed" every two weeks, there were numerous infestations of chinches (bedbugs). Pettigrew reported in June 1797 that the chinches had multiplied to such a point that the students had been forced out of their rooms for three weeks. He had made his bed on a table in the hall, which he set up with the legs in pans of water, since the insects were "in general bad swimers."[9] The tiny village of Chapel Hill developing nearby offered the only relief from campus living, and those students who could afford to room in town eagerly sought the few accommodations available.

Such living conditions exacerbated the unruliness of the students, who were subjected to stern disciplinary rules enforced by a young and inexperienced faculty. Although student disturbances and such activities as gambling, drinking, and fighting were reportedly common, Pettigrew wrote, "Students in general have nothing very criminal in their conduct except a vile, and detestable practice of cursing, and swearing, which has become very fashionable here." Of course, it may be that Pettigrew chose not to tell his father about the worst behavior of his fellow students, since he was concerned about "spreading a report which might injure the University."[10]

The student organizations that provided some order amid the chaos were the university's two literary clubs, which were founded in 1795 as the Debating Society and the Concord Society, the next year adopting the more dignified Greek names Dialectic Society and Philanthropic Society. Student life centered on these groups that dominated campus activities well into the twentieth century. In addition to debate and discussion of current political and social topics, the societies provided social interaction for their members and regulated conduct through an officer, the Censor Morum, who levied fines on members who violated society rules and decorum. Blakeley joined the Philanthropic Society on 14 February 1797 and two weeks later delivered his first speech. Thereafter he was a regular participant in debates, speeches, and readings. Officers rotated frequently, and Blakeley held all of the positions, including president.[11]

Onerous university regulations and unpopular faculty members precipitated student protests and disorders in the academic year 1798–99. By the spring term, which a university historian described as "especially stormy," in a week of upheaval the "personally obnoxious" presiding professor James Gillespie was assaulted, another professor was stoned, and still other instructors were threatened. Three of the student leaders were suspended, but a number of students withdrew. The resignation of the offending faculty defused the hostilities on campus, and the university weathered its first serious crisis.[12] Blakeley was among a group of fifty-five students who signed a statement in 1799 pledging to avoid "riotous or disorderly conduct," to obey university rules, and to respect their "Tutors and Professors."[13] One incident that involved the sober-minded Blakeley occurred when presiding professor Caldwell confronted him in his room and questioned him about a particular incident of misconduct. When Blakeley denied knowing anything about the participants in the incident, the overbearing professor lost his temper, questioned Blakeley's honesty, and implied that he might toss him out the window. His honor challenged, Blakeley arose and quietly but firmly said to Caldwell, "I beg, sir, that you will not try it, as it will oblige me to put you out." The stymied Caldwell, chagrined that he was at fault, simply turned away and stormed from the room. Over a decade later, on a visit to his alma mater, Blakeley sought out Caldwell, now the president of the university, and apologized for having, as he said, "once spoken disrespectfully to him."[14]

The studious Blakeley adapted well to university life, excelling in mathematics, navigation, astronomy, and surveying. On the first examinations for which there are records, on 25 March 1798 he achieved a "distinguished" ranking in the class on Virgil, an honor he retained in the annual exams in July. He was present at the university's first graduation ceremony on 10 July 1798, watching as degrees were awarded to seven of his fellow students in the chapel.[15]

Blakeley would certainly have graduated from the university but for a fateful and disastrous fire in Wilmington in 1799 that leveled the uninsured warehouses he had inherited from his father. With the sole source of his income gone, he saw no choice but to withdraw from the university, although his foster father, Edward Jones, readily offered to lend him the funds to complete his studies. Blakeley's sense of honor would not allow him to accept the loan, and he left the university in the fall term of 1799. He did ask Jones to sponsor his application to join the navy as a midshipman. Despite his personal misgivings about his talented ward's chosen career, Jones acquiesced and contacted his friend Congressman William H. Hill from New Hanover County. An appointment as midshipman was issued on 5 February 1800, and on 7 May, in New York, Blakeley reported for duty on the *President*, one of the newly built heavy frigates that were the pride of the navy. The *President* was commanded by Thomas Truxtun, a senior captain and stern disciplinarian. Truxtun, who had served in the Revolutionary navy, had won fame for his brilliant victory over the French frigate *Insurgente*. The *President's* lengthy fitting-out ended in September when she set sail on a four-month cruise in the West Indies.[16]

The United States Navy that accepted midshipman Blakeley in 1800 was less than five years old. During the Revolution the makeshift Continental Navy had been swept from the seas. After the war neither Congress nor the president saw a need to rebuild the fleet, which was out of the question for the poor, debt-burdened new nation. With the restrictions of war lifted, American merchantmen swarmed out onto the high seas, ready to reclaim their niche in the Atlantic trading world. As commerce and accompanying profits soared, the Americans encountered harassment from their former friends, the French, and their former foes, the British, who were locked in a titanic struggle for European supremacy. Triggered by the terrifying French Revolution, the European conflict raged for over two decades, eventually drawing in the United States by 1812. In the Mediterranean, American vessels, now no longer under the protection of the British, became easy prey for the North African corsairs of the states of the Barbary coast— Morocco, Algiers, Tunis, and Tripoli. Thus to a great extent the United States Navy owes its rebirth to the French, the British, and the Barbary pirates.

Less than a month after the last Continental Navy vessel, the frigate *Alliance*, was sold in 1785, corsairs from Algiers took two American merchant ships and enslaved the crews, holding them for ransom. Over the years, more vessels were seized, but the weak U.S. government could neither raise ransom nor afford a navy. The government paid limited tribute, in effect protection money, satisfying the Moroccans, but the rapacious Algerians continued their piratical raiding. Finally in 1794 the long-suffering Congress could no longer bear the humiliation and sanctioned construction of six frigates. The talented Quaker shipbuilders Josiah Fox and Joshua Humphreys of Philadelphia, who envisioned vessels that combined speed and maneuverability with heavier armament than had ever been carried by a frigate, were chosen to develop the design for the new ships. From their collaboration came a revolutionary class of men-of-war—the *Constitution*, the *United States*, the *President*, and the smaller USS *Constellation* and USS *Chesapeake*. Docked in Boston harbor today is the 2,200-ton *Constitution*, which measures 175 feet on her deck and 43½ feet on her beam, and which bears masts that reach aloft over 200 feet. A creation of great beauty that is simultaneously graceful and menacing, the *Constitution* was also a supremely lucky ship, for she survived many years in active service and many battles, outlasting her sister ships and eventually becoming the oldest commissioned warship afloat in the world.

Work on the frigates was well under way when a treaty with Algiers brought a temporary halt to construction in 1795. But almost immediately thereafter French privateers began to take prizes, prompting Congress to pledge to complete at least three of the frigates. The future of the navy was secured when the undeclared Quasi-War with France led to the formation of the Department of the Navy in 1798. The newly built frigates *Constitution*, *United States*, and *Constellation* were launched in 1797, and Congress purchased additional vessels that were converted to men-of-war. Over the next three years the navy expanded to a force of more than fifty ships, which engaged in numerous battles and took about eighty prizes, chiefly in the West Indies.

In the crucible of high seas combat in the Quasi-War, the ships, officers, and men of the fledgling U.S. Navy were forged into an effective fighting force that was, man for man and ship for ship, better than any other navy afloat. Many of the officers measured up to the high performance standards set by John Paul Jones in the Revolution, and several of those who did—Truxtun, Richard Dale, Edward Preble, and John Rodgers—were commanders under whom Blakeley served. Among the many responsibilities of a sea captain was training his midshipmen in seamanship and navigation, and under Truxtun, Blakeley began to learn the art and science of his vocation.

For generations the Barbary Coast corsair states of Morocco, Algiers, Tunis, and Tripoli had engaged in piracy and the kidnapping of hostages for ransom. The European powers had checked them by a combination of force, diplomacy, and tribute. With no navy of its own, the United States negotiated from weakness and had little choice but to pay tribute. The treaty with Algiers in 1795 secured the release of American seamen for a payment of over $500,000, a thirty-six-gun frigate (the *Crescent*), and an annual tribute of naval stores; yet the piracy seemed endless. When the Quasi-War with France concluded, in 1801 the United States was able for the first time to send a fleet to the Mediterranean. Commodore Richard Dale was given command of a four-ship squadron and charged with maintaining the peace with the Barbary corsairs. In his orders Dale was authorized to engage any of the states that committed hostile acts. Upon arriving off North Africa, Dale learned that in fact Tripoli had declared war, and the Barbary Wars of 1801–5 were under way.

When Blakeley reported on board the *President* in New York, the frigate, which had been launched the previous month, was in the midst of the seeming chaos of being prepared for sea. Under the supervision of Captain Truxtun, the fitting-out was an extensive and lengthy process that began with a bare hull and culminated with a fully rigged, fully armed, and fully supplied ship, ready to cruise. Although Blakeley was a newly warranted midshipman, he was involved in all stages of the process. Midshipmen, some of whom went to sea before they were twelve years old, were considered officers-in-training. As a two-year university student who excelled in mathematics and science, the eighteen-year-old, earnest Blakeley was a rarity, and his quick intelligence and education opened up positions of responsibility early in his career. The new warship on which he found himself in the spring of 1800 would be Blakeley's home for the next twenty-two months.

The *President*'s uneventful shakedown cruise in the West Indies in the waning months of the Quasi-War was an ideal training voyage for the ship and its inexperienced crew. In March 1801, under the Peace Establishment Act, the government reduced the navy from a wartime high of about fifty vessels to thirteen frigates. Both the *President* and Blakeley survived the massive cuts.[17] When word arrived in Washington that Barbary pirates were again seizing American merchantmen, a four-ship squadron was formed, consisting of the *President*, the USS *Philadelphia*, the USS *Essex*, and the USS *Enterprise*, to head for the Mediterranean. Commodore Richard Dale selected the *President* as his flagship, and the little fleet set sail in May. Largely as a result of Commodore Dale's caution, this first show of American force in the Mediterranean accomplished little. Dale did establish an intermittent patrol of the little-known three-thousand-mile coast of the Barbary states, which harbored fleets totalling several hundred vessels, although most were lightly armed galleys. Dale and the other American naval commanders were burdened with both military and diplomatic goals, which they were being asked to achieve with a frankly puny force. The *President* cruised on the North African coast from Algiers to Tripoli. In November she struck an uncharted reef off Minorca and was laid up in Toulon, France, for repairs until she was ordered home in early 1802, arriving at Norfolk in April. Dale returned to a dissatisfied government that censured him and accepted his resignation.

Since Blakeley had no assignment, he was given permission to ship out on a merchant vessel, but in August he was ordered to join the twenty-eight-gun frigate USS *John Adams*, which was to be part of the larger Mediterranean Squadron under Commodore Richard Morris. Blakeley's new captain was John Rodgers of Maryland, one of the most capable officers in the navy. Rodgers, who had been the navy's youngest captain, had earned his reputation in the Quasi-War as the executive officer of the *Constellation* and commander of the sloop USS *Maryland*. His biographer considered him noteworthy for "his superior seamanship, his high standards of duty, and his complete mastery of his calling."[18] There could have been no better mentor for Blakeley than Captain Rodgers, who appreciated the dedication and quick mind of his new midshipman. Recognizing Blakeley's potential, Rodgers chose to keep the young North Carolinian with him throughout his assignment in the Barbary Wars and appointed him acting lieutenant a mere four years after Blakeley had entered the navy. Although Blakeley's biographer characterized him as one of "Preble's boys," the record shows that Rodgers had far more to do with molding Blakeley into one of the navy's most promising junior officers.[19]

Morris's vessels sailed when ready, and the *John Adams* was the last to leave the United States, arriving in the Mediterranean in November but not joining the fleet at Malta until January 1803. Unlike his commodore, Rodgers was an aggressive commander, always seeking to close with and engage his enemies. The *John Adams* sailed with the fleet to the North African ports of Tunis, Algiers, and Tripoli and then was detached for convoy duty. Off Tripoli in May Rodgers exchanged fire with gunboats guarding the port and then captured the twenty-gun *Meshouda*. A few days later the *John Adams*, the USS *New York*, and the *Enterprise* engaged Tripolitan gunboats that were protecting merchantmen. Blakeley was in a small-boat raid, commanded by Lieutenant David Porter, to burn the vessels, but the corsairs drove the outnumbered Americans off and put out the fires. The *John Adams* then engaged the Tripolitan gunboat fleet, inflicting some damage on them. In June Rodgers, now in command of the blockade off Tripoli, intercepted a sortie by the Tripolitans and fought a twenty-two-gun vessel.

After forty-five minutes of pounding, the Tripolitan polacre disintegrated in a "tremendous explosion, which burnt the hull to pieces and forced the main and mizzen masts one hundred and fifty or one hundred and sixty feet perpendicularly into the air."[20]

In September Morris was relieved of command, and Rodgers was appointed in his place. At Gibraltar Commodore Edward Preble arrived with a third squadron and with orders for Rodgers to return to the United States. Because Morocco was veering toward hostilities, the two commodores combined their squadrons to visit Tangier. The show of force convinced the Moroccans to reaffirm their 1786 treaty with the United States, whereupon Rodgers sailed the *John Adams* to Washington, arriving in December.

On furlough in Wilmington in April 1804, Blakeley received orders to report for duty on the frigate USS *Congress*. Commanded by Captain Rodgers, the *Congress* was part of a squadron under Commodore Samuel Barron that was being sent to the Mediterranean in response to the shocking news that the *Philadelphia* had been captured at Tripoli. Before Barron's fleet arrived, Captain Stephen Decatur had destroyed the *Philadelphia* in a brilliant night raid, but the new fleet brought significant American naval power to the Mediterranean.

While the *Congress* was being fitted out in the Washington Navy Yard, Captain Rodgers appointed Blakeley an acting lieutenant as of 18 May. The *Congress* joined Commodore Barron's three other vessels at Hampton Roads in July and then sailed for the Mediterranean. Once in the Mediterranean, Captain Rodgers was ordered to cruise the North African coast in company with the *Essex*. When Commodore Barron fell ill, Rodgers was given command of the blockade at Tripoli for a month. Blakeley was one of three lieutenants commanding a small-boat raid that attempted to cut out a wheat-laden coastal supply vessel near Tripoli, but the raid was foiled by overwhelming numbers of armed Arabs on shore.[21]

As a reward for his initiative and success, on 1 November Rodgers succeeded to command of the frigate *Constitution*. He took Blakeley along with him to his new command of some four hundred officers and men. Rodgers was then named acting commodore by the ailing Barron. At the beginning of 1805 Barron commanded a dozen vessels, including five frigates, and Rodgers had the most powerful fleet element on station blockading Tripoli. In May Rodgers succeeded Barron as commodore of the Mediterranean Squadron. Meanwhile, a force of Arab rebels, Greek mercenaries, and a few U.S. Marines led by

General William Eaton marched overland and took the Tripolitan port of Derna. The threat of Eaton's army and the blockade brought the bashaw of Tripoli to sue for peace in late May. The negotiations were handled by old friends Tobias Lear and Commodore Rodgers. Peace with Tripoli, which had been the main antagonist, brought the Barbary Wars to a close. Commodore Barron returned to the United States on the *President*, accompanied by a group of officers that included Blakeley.

Upon arrival in Hampton Roads in September, Blakeley was ordered to report to the new eighteen-gun brig USS *Hornet*, which sailed to join the Mediterranean fleet. With the war over, the fleet was radically reduced again early in 1806, and Blakeley was fortunate to be on one of the three ships remaining in the Mediterranean—the *Constitution* and her consorts, the brigs *Hornet* and *Wasp*.[22] In March 1806 Blakeley was furloughed from the *Hornet* and ordered to Washington, where he was assigned temporarily to the *Chesapeake*, which was being decommissioned. With no place left in the now-diminished navy, Blakeley followed the course of many of his brother officers in the summer and shipped out on a merchant vessel, the *Bashaw*, which was bound for South America.

Blakeley's commission as a lieutenant was finally confirmed by the United States Senate on 8 January 1807, although Blakeley remained in South America until the fall of that year.[23] Once again the British came to the rescue of the shrunken U.S. Navy when on 7 June the frigate HMS *Leopard* fired on the *Chesapeake* in Chesapeake Bay, forcing her to surrender and give up four alleged deserters. The public cried out for war to avenge this outrage, but the Jefferson administration, realizing that because of its own miserly fiscal policy the country was not prepared to defend itself, did not go that far, instead passing a controversial trade embargo and increasing military appropriations. Commodore Rodgers, now commanding the New York station, had his protégé transferred to his command in 1808. From the brig USS *Argus* in November Blakeley wrote to his foster mother, reporting an illness and the premature graying of his black hair.[24] The next year, after two brief assignments, Blakeley was placed again on the *John Adams*, which was to be refitted in Charleston, South Carolina. Blakeley was given temporary command to sail the frigate to Charleston.[25]

As the country moved inexorably toward war with Britain, Blakeley was furloughed from the *John Adams* in November 1810 and then on 4 March 1811 took command of the brig *Enterprise* as an acting master commandant. A workhorse of the navy since 1799, the *Enterprise* had been built as a twelve-gun schooner but had just been rebuilt in the Washington Navy Yard as a fourteen-gun brig.[26] Constructed in Maryland to a pilot-boat design, she was swift and maneuverable, although she no longer sailed as well after being altered into a brig. She was launched during the Quasi-War and had served throughout the Mediterranean conflict, taking several prizes.

Blakeley and the *Enterprise* were first stationed at Charleston, South Carolina. Upon the outbreak of war, Blakeley's first important mission was to ferry General James Wilkinson to New Orleans. In part because of its disease-ridden and debilitating climate, New Orleans was considered a professional dead end by ambitious naval officers. Fearful that he would be relegated to this obscure station on the Gulf coast while his peers on the Atlantic seaboard would have opportunities to distinguish themselves in combat, Blakeley requested permission to return to "any Atlantic port."[27] Secretary of the Navy Paul Hamilton clearly agreed that the *Enterprise* was more useful on the east coast and ordered her back to St. Mary's, Georgia. By the time Blakeley's orders arrived, the pestilential climate of the lower Mississippi had stricken the officers and men of the *Enterprise* with yellow fever, sending to the navy hospital both of the ship's lieutenants, two of her four midshipmen, and about a third of her crew. To enable Blakeley to leave, the station commander reluctantly drafted crewmen from his harbor defense gunboats to serve on the *Enterprise*, but before she could depart, on 19 August a hurricane struck and drove the brig ashore. Luckily the damage was minor and quickly repaired. Blakeley finally sailed in January 1813, glad to be rid of a port that had offered "nothing, but delay, disappointment and disaster."[28]

The *Enterprise* arrived at St. Mary's in January 1813. Again Blakeley found himself in a backwater, consigned to ferrying supplies to Florida. In frustration he wrote to the secretary of the navy in April, pleading that he be allowed to cruise for prizes, saying that he wished only "to enjoy in common with the rest of the Navy an opportunity to go against the Enemy." Shortly thereafter he went to sea, but he encountered no British vessels. The time was well spent, however, in training his crew and sharpening their gunnery skills. The need to bolster defenses in New England caused the *Enterprise* to be ordered to Portsmouth, New Hampshire, where she arrived in June. Blakeley's commission as master commandant or commander was issued on 24 July. With his ship in a high state of readiness, Blakeley finally saw action on 19 August when the *Enterprise* intercepted the British privateer schooner *Fly* and captured it after an eight-hour chase.[29]

Blakeley felt that good fortune had finally turned his way, but two days later he was ordered to Newburyport, Massachusetts, to oversee construction of a new sloop, the *Wasp*. He was relieved on the *Enterprise* by his executive officer, Lieutenant William Burrows, who just sixteen days later won lasting fame and death in taking the HMS *Boxer* off Portland, Maine. Blakeley mourned his fellow officer but had to swallow his disappointment at so narrowly missing such an opportunity. He did have the satisfaction of knowing that the battle was won by his well-trained crew, but the fame and promotion that he sought eluded him still.

The *Wasp* and her sister ships, the *Peacock* and the *Frolic*, were a new class of sloops being built as swift commerce raiders to aid privateers in their costly marauding among the British merchantmen. Designed by William Doughty, naval constructor of the Washington Navy Yard, these ship sloops were faster and more heavily armed than their British counterparts and were so successful in service that they had a lasting influence on American naval architecture. Blakeley's pent-up frustration surely faded when he reported to the shipyard and saw the graceful *Wasp* taking shape—a lean hull, 118 feet in length on the gundeck and 31½ feet on her beam. Rated at 509 tons and eighteen guns, she would carry two long twelve-pounders and twenty of the stubby but murderous thirty-two-pound carronades. She would have a crew of up to 173 men. Blakeley was soon joined by his lieutenant from the *Enterprise*, Thomas Tillinghast, and the two officers, eager to get back to sea, prodded the builders to keep up their pace. Launched in the fall, the *Wasp* moved to Portsmouth, New Hampshire, early in 1814 for her final fitting-out for sea.[30]

Early 1814 was a significant time in Blakeley's life for other reasons as well. It is not known when Blakeley became acquainted with his future wife, Jane Anne Hoope, the daughter of New York merchant John Hoope, who apparently had done business with his father. Blakeley may have known the family when, as a youth, he was in school in New York. More likely, Jane Anne—who was described by one contemporary as "a very interesting and amiable woman"—caught his eye, and returned his interest, in 1808 or 1809 when he was serving on the New York station with Commodore Rodgers. Once Blakeley took command of the *Enterprise* in 1811, he had little spare time until he was given his assignment to complete the construction of the *Wasp*. Since it was obvious to the young couple in the winter of 1813–14 that Blakeley's forthcoming cruise would mean a lengthy separation, they married late in 1813, sharing little more than four months together before Blakeley sailed away in the service of his country.[31]

The day finally arrived when the *Wasp* was ready for sea. Having no idea when he would see his bride again, Blakeley nonetheless was determined to seek the fame that had eluded him so far, and that he feared might elude him further, during the war. Before embarking from Portsmouth he had written that if he had remained on the *Enterprise*, his "name might be classed with those who stand so high. . . . The *Peacock* had ere this spread her plumage to the winds and the *Frolic* will soon take her revels on the ocean, but the *Wasp* will, I fear, remain for some time a dull, harmless drone in the waters of her own country."[32] Despite his misgivings at leaving Jane, his spirits soared when he gave the order to weigh anchor. To the cheers of the crew of the frigate USS *Congress* and the fort garrison, the *Wasp* departed Portsmouth on 1 May at four o'clock in the afternoon, cleared the harbor at dusk, and set off into the Atlantic under a fresh breeze.[33]

On the month-long voyage across the Atlantic the monotony was broken by sighting and chasing an occasional strange sail, calling the crew to general quarters, exercising them with their cannon and muskets, and coping with stormy weather.[34] Blakeley's goal was the English Channel, where British ships, presumably safe in home waters, formed their convoys for outgoing voyages and scattered upon their return for their various home ports. Traffic in the Channel was consequently enormous. American privateers were reaping a rich harvest on this cruising ground, and Blakeley set out to join them with high hopes. The *Wasp* arrived on station in late May and on 2 June took and burned her first prize, the bark *Neptune*. Unlike privateers, who expected to seize property for profit, Blakeley was a commerce raider who had orders to destroy his prizes after looting them for needed supplies and provisions. Over the following weeks the *Wasp* seized another four ships—the brig *William*, the brig *Pallas*, the galliot *Henrietta*, and the 325-ton ship *Orange Boven*. The outclassed *Orange Boven*, armed with eight guns, surrendered quickly after a single broadside was fired. All of these prizes were burned or scuttled, except the *Henrietta*, whose cargo was thrown overboard so that she could be used as a cartel ship to convey paroled prisoners to England.[35]

On 28 June, just after four o'clock in the morning, Blakeley sighted two sails. The *Wasp* began the chase but almost immediately detected another ship bearing down on them. By midmorning the Americans were able to identify the strange vessel as a brig flying the Union Jack. Their adversary was the HMS *Reindeer*, armed with sixteen twenty-four-pound carronades, two long six-pounders, and a twelve-pound carronade. She was commanded by William Manners, an experienced seaman. In light air and a flat sea the two ships slowly closed the distance until at 1:15 in the afternoon Blakeley ordered the drummer to "beat to quarters," preparing the ship for action. After another hour passed, the *Reindeer* began to gain on the *Wasp* and made her final approach. At 3:15, having closed to sixty yards, Manners commenced firing with round and grape shot from the twelve-pounder. The Americans stood to their guns, taking five rounds without being able to reply. After an agonizing nine minutes under fire, Blakeley ordered his helmsman to luff, turning the *Wasp* into the wind. As his ship came around, Blakeley fired a running broadside. The *Reindeer* matched the maneuver and the two brigs crept along side by side, pounding each other with broadsides at a distance of twenty yards. Captain Manners, now wounded in both legs and realizing that the heavier fire from the *Wasp* was ravaging his vessel, turned the *Reindeer* toward the *Wasp*, crashing into her port side. The British swarmed to the rail to board the *Wasp* but were repeatedly beaten back by the "cool and deliberate" American musket fire. Leading the van, Manners was shot down. Summoning his remaining strength, he pulled himself up into the shrouds, urging his men forward, until he was hit in the head by a marine sharpshooter. Blakeley ordered, "Boarders away," and the Americans stormed onto the *Reindeer*, quickly carrying the deck.

Within nineteen minutes from the time the *Wasp* had opened fire, the *Reindeer* was a bloody wreck. Midshipman David Geisinger reported that her decks were "an awful and shocking spectacle." The bulwarks and boats were smashed; over half her crewmen were casualties, a total of twenty-five killed and forty-two wounded; and the next day her weakened foremast fell. Blakeley had the prisoners and the twelve-pounders removed and ordered the drifting hulk burned. The *Wasp* too was damaged and suffered five killed and twenty-one wounded, four of whom died later. Burdened with badly wounded American and British crewmen and over seventy prisoners, Blakeley set a course for the nearest neutral port, L'Orient in France, gathering en route two more British merchantmen. Independence Day was celebrated by burning the brig *Regulator*, laden with port wine, and two days later the schooner *Jenny* was scuttled. Blakeley's first appearance

THE WASP AND AVON

THE WASP AND REINDEER.

The USS *Wasp* was victorious over the British warships HMS *Reindeer*, on 28 June 1814, and HMS *Avon*, on the evening of 1 September 1814. (North Carolina Division of Archives and History, Raleigh)

in the Channel had been spectacular, yielding seven prizes and the defeat of a comparable man-of-war. In his dispatches to Washington, Blakeley praised his crew, especially noting the "cool and patient conduct of every officer and man, while exposed to the fire of the shifting gun of the enemy, and without an opportunity of returning it," and their ardor and courage in repulsing boarders and taking the prize. The news of Blakeley's victory was published widely, electrifying the war-weary home front and alarming the British public.[36]

During a three-week interlude in hospitable L'Orient, which Blakeley found "protracted and tedious," the wounded were taken to a hospital on shore, and extensive repairs were completed on the hull, sails, and rigging of the *Wasp*. Seventy-nine prisoners were sent to England on a cartel ship. On 27 August the resupplied *Wasp* headed back to her former cruising ground in the English Channel. Blakeley was elated to be back at sea, reporting, "We are now off this place with a fair wind and favourable prospect." Blakeley destroyed two prizes in the first two days on station, the brigs *Lettice* and *Bon Accord*. On 1 September he encountered a Gibraltar-bound convoy of ten merchantmen protected by the seventy-four-gun *Armada*. The swift *Wasp* easily outsailed and outmaneuvered the lumbering ship-of-the-line, darting in and cutting out and burning the brig *Mary*, which carried a valuable cargo of cannon and military stores.

Continuing south toward Gibraltar, the *Wasp* sighted four sails in the late afternoon. Blakeley immediately ordered pursuit of the nearest vessel. By seven o'clock the prey was clearly identified as an armed brig, which began to signal her consorts with lanterns, guns, and rockets. Another two hours of chase brought the *Wasp* in range, and at 9:26 P.M. Blakeley ordered his shifting twelve-pounder to open fire. To prevent his prey from escaping, Blakeley sailed the *Wasp* across the stern of his enemy to the lee side, placing his vessel between his victim and its support. The *Wasp* began pouring broadsides into the stranger. Although the gunners contended with a stiff breeze, high seas, and the darkness of night, the ships were so close that the *Wasp*'s well-trained cannoneers were deadly effective. After nearly forty minutes of precision firing on a shadowy silhouette defined only by a foamy bow wave and flashes of cannon, the Americans observed one of the ship's masts tumble over, followed by a noticeable slackening of fire. Blakeley's hail asking if his adversary had surrendered was answered with cannon shot. A renewed fusilade of broadsides issued from the *Wasp*, and within just two minutes came a frantic plea to cease fire and a surrender. As a boat was being lowered for a boarding party, the belated enemy consorts began to appear. Two vessels came on the scene, firing signal rockets and guns, and a third was close behind them. The *Wasp* had suffered superficial damage and only three casualties, but Blakeley decided that the risk was too great to take on three more unknown antagonists in a night battle. He slipped away in the gloom, taking a parting broadside, mostly in the rigging, from his new enemy.

The vanquished but rescued British vessel was the brig HMS *Avon*, armed with sixteen thirty-two-pound carronades and two long nine-pounders. She was left in sinking condition by the *Wasp*'s gunnery, which had shot away the shrouds and main boom, destroyed the tiller, dismounted five guns, and damaged the hull so gravely that the casualties, ten killed and thirty-two wounded, were hastily evacuated before she went down. The vessels that came to her aid were the HMS *Castilian* of eighteen guns and the HMS *Tartarus* of twenty guns. Upon seeing the ravaged *Avon*, their commanders decided to stay close in support.[37]

The *Wasp* continued south, taking and scuttling two more brigs, the *Three Brothers* and the *Bacchus*. By 21 September the *Wasp* was about seventy-five miles east of the Madeira Islands when she captured the brig *Atalanta*, armed with eight guns. The valuable cargo of wine, brandy, and silk induced Blakeley to keep the prize for the first time on the cruise. He entrusted the command to Midshipman David Geisinger, who had gallantly led the boarding party onto the *Reindeer*. Geisinger was ordered to take the prize to the United States, and the two ships parted company near the island of Porto Santo. The *Wasp* sailed before the trade winds, on 9 October intercepting a neutral Swedish brig, the *Adonis*, about 225 miles southwest of the Madeiras. Two American officers, passengers on the *Adonis*, transferred to the *Wasp*, which sailed into the vast central Atlantic toward home by way of the West Indies.[38]

The first authentic news of the *Wasp* since Blakeley's departure in late August arrived with Midshipman Geisinger, who made port at Savannah, Georgia, on 4 November. Blakeley's record of his battle with the *Avon* was received with both excitement and relief by a public eager for news of more exploits of their new hero but distressed by reports in the British papers that the *Wasp* had gone down with the *Avon*. None could have felt more relieved than his young wife, who was well along in her first pregnancy. Accounts of the dramatic night action in the Channel were interspersed with commentary that labeled the *Wasp* "one of the most successful of our cruizers" and claimed that she had destroyed an estimated £200,000 worth of British shipping. An officer's letter was quoted, saying that "the *Wasp* is a beautiful ship, and the finest seaboat, I believe in the world" and that "Captain Blakeley is a brave and discreet officer—as cool and collected in action as at table."[39] Only two other naval officers of the War of 1812 came close to matching Blakeley's record—Charles Stewart, who achieved two single-ship victories over the British, and William H. Allen, who

Udney Maria Blakeley (1815–42), the only child of Johnston Blakeley, was educated at the expense of North Carolina in recognition of her father's service to the state. This portrait was painted by the noted American artist Thomas Sully in 1830. (North Carolina Museum of Art, Raleigh)

successfully raided British shipping in the English Channel. Blakeley, however, was unique in accomplishing both feats.[40]

Already under way in Congress was a move to recognize the victory over the *Reindeer*. In mid-October Secretary of the Navy William Jones wrote to the Naval Committee that the battle had been a "brilliant action of nineteen minutes, which was terminated by *boarding*, in gallant and decisive style, having repulsed the enemy in repeated and vigorous attempts to board the Wasp." A resolution passed on 3 November commemorated the victory by awarding a gold medal to Blakeley, silver medals to his lieutenants, and swords to the midshipmen and the sailing master. On 24 November Blakeley was meritoriously promoted to captain.[41]

Meanwhile, weeks stretched into months, and the *Wasp* was long overdue. When she failed to return, unfounded stories of ships purported to have sighted her began to circulate in Southern ports. Most compelling was the report of her involvement in a sea battle off Edisto Island, South Carolina, but the British made no claims of destroying the *Wasp*. The ship simply vanished mysteriously in the central Atlantic and was never seen again. It was difficult, however, for the public to

This silver coffee and tea service was a gift from the state of North Carolina to Udney Maria Blakeley in honor of her father's service in the War of 1812. It was made by Anthony Rasch in 1818. (North Carolina Museum of Art, Raleigh)

accept that their hero had been swallowed by the sea and denied a glorious death in battle. As time went by, it became undeniable that the *Wasp* had been claimed by the sea, and the poignancy of the loss was preserved in the words of a popular ballad:

> No more shall Blakeley's thunders roar
> Upon the stormy deep;
> Far distant from Columbia's shore
> His tombless ruins sleep;
> But long Columbia's song shall tell
> How Blakeley fought, how Blakeley fell.[42]

What of his anxious wife and his daughter, born in January 1815 in Boston and christened Udney Maria? Jane was left with memories of spending only a few months with her now-famous husband, who was missing in action. After months of uncertainty, the realization crept over her that she must face the future without him. The loss that the state of North Carolina and the nation felt was partly assuaged by aiding the fatherless child and her mother. By January 1816 Jane Blakeley, who had little property of her own, had accepted her husband's loss and petitioned Congress for support through her representative from Massachusetts, Artemus Ward. Her appeal and appeals from the families of lost crewmen moved Congress in April to authorize the awarding of twelve months' pay to surviving relatives and the distribution of $50,000 in prize money for the destruction of the *Reindeer* and the *Avon*. Jane Blakeley received $900 in back pay and $7,500 as her share of the prize money, nearly 20 percent of which was taken by the distribution agent. Another $600 in prize money came from the condemnation and sale of the *Atalanta*. As a naval officer's widow, she also qualified for a pension of $50 a month for five years, commencing on 20 April 1815. When she was remarried in Boston on 22 June 1819 to Dr. Robert Abbott of Christiansted, St. Croix, in the Danish West Indies, the pension was granted to her daughter and was paid until 1830.[43]

Meanwhile, the state of North Carolina had moved to honor its native son. In 1815 the legislature voted to award a sword to Blakeley in recognition of his victory over the *Reindeer*, but no action was taken. Again in December 1816 the legislature reauthorized the sword but also took the unusual step of adopting Blakeley's daughter, Maria, assuming the obligation to pay for her education. Governor William Miller sent the adoption resolution to Jane Blakeley in January 1817, eloquently expressing the wishes of the legislature, telling her of "the high regard in which the memory of your much lamented husband is held by his native state, to assure you of the deep interest which the legislature will always take in your happiness and welfare, and to request, on their behalf that you will do the State of North Carolina the honor of educating your infant daughter."[44] She gratefully accepted the state's offer, writing that the gift "is an act of such noble, and unexpected generosity that it deprives me of all power to express what I feel on the occasion."[45] She applied for $600 a year and ultimately received some $8,000 from the state, a significant appropriation for that era. In regard to the sword, she suggested that a silver tea service would be more appropriate for her daughter, and an inscribed service was delivered to Maria Blakeley on her sixteenth birthday.[46]

Jane Blakeley Abbott and her husband moved to Christiansted, and Maria was sent to a school in Philadelphia. When she finished her education in 1828, Maria returned to St. Croix, a bright and beautiful young woman, to join her family. There she met and fell in love with Baron Joseph von Bretton, a local physician, whom she married on 19 May 1841 in St. John's Episcopal Church. The next year she died in childbirth, and she was laid to rest in the parish cemetery on 2 March. Johnston Blakeley's only grandchild died with her.[47]

When aroused to action
Cooke was one of the most
industrious and indefati-
gable officers in the navy.
—*Commander John N.*
Maffitt, CSN, *1880*

James W. Cooke

The *Albemarle* Clears the Roanoke

The Union occupation of northeastern North Carolina's fertile Roanoke River valley in 1862 deprived the Confederacy of badly needed provisions and manpower, and over the next two years the region was pillaged repeatedly by the Union army, deserters, and sympathetic guerrillas. Federal forces in New Bern, Washington, and Plymouth lurked within easy striking distance of the Wilmington and Weldon Railroad, "the life line of the Confederacy," which funneled essential war materials to the Virginia battlefields and which had been threatened by recent raids. By 1864 editorials calling for peace written by the disgruntled and influential Raleigh editor William W. Holden appealed to a growing audience in a war-weary state that had contributed more soldiers to the conflict than any other in the Confederacy. Also rampant in North Carolina was a keen sense of having been neglected by the Richmond authorities, who had made such paltry provisions for the region's defense two years earlier and had repeatedly failed in half-hearted attempts to recover the occupied territory. The double risk of losing the general support of North Carolinians and jeopardizing the most vital supply line in the Confederacy motivated President Jefferson Davis, at the suggestion of General Robert E. Lee, to authorize yet another campaign in North Carolina during the winter lull of 1864.

An earlier effort to retake New Bern in March 1863 had been foiled chiefly by the accurate fire of Union gunboats; but by 1864 Southern leaders believed for the first time that the Confederate navy would soon be able to neutralize the gunboats' effect, as construction was nearing completion on two ironclad warships—the css *Neuse*, being built on the Neuse River, and the css *Albemarle*, on the Roanoke River. In January Lee dispatched a force of some thirteen thousand troops under the ineffectual General George E. Pickett, whose campaign plan had been developed by his second-in-command, the able Brigadier General Robert F. Hoke, a native North Carolinian. A naval commando contingent led by Commander John Taylor Wood was charged with capturing a Union gunboat to use in taking the port. The attack on New Bern in early February fell just short of success, primarily as a result of poor coordination of the various Confederate columns, and Pickett returned to Virginia, leaving Hoke in command at Kinston, North Carolina.

Determined to try again to force the Federals out but realizing that he had to act before his troops were recalled to Virginia in the spring, Hoke was convinced that he must have one of the ironclads to support his operation. Upon learning that the *Albemarle* was further along, he chose Plymouth on the Roanoke as his objective and paid a call on Commander James W. Cooke at Hamilton, North Carolina, to see how soon the ironclad would be ready. Hoke found the vessel afloat but lacking most of her armor, with Cooke driving his workforce to finish the outfitting. When Hoke told him he needed the warship by mid-April, Cooke hesitated, knowing how much more had to be done; but the general persuaded him to have the *Albemarle* at Plymouth in two weeks. Hoke opened his attack on 17 April, and that evening the *Albemarle* cast off on her shakedown cruise, towing a portable forge, with workmen still clambering over the deckhouse, applying the iron armor. Few if any other warships in history have gone into battle unfinished and manned by a crew of mostly landsmen who had never fired the cannon on board. So much was being demanded of Commander Cooke and the untried *Albemarle*. Hoke's initial attack had been stymied by the Union's extensive fortifications and heavy gun-

Located near the mouth of the Roanoke River, the town of Plymouth, North Carolina, was the key to controlling the important valley beyond and thus the scene of fierce fighting during the Civil War. (North Carolina Collection, Wilson Library, University of North Carolina, Chapel Hill)

boat fire. Plymouth would fall to the South only if the *Albemarle* made it down the winding channel, over the obstructions, past the batteries, and through the squadron of waiting Federal warships.

What was Commander Cooke thinking on the two-and-a-half-day voyage downriver? Despite Union fears of his ironclad, he knew the weaknesses of the jerry-built vessel. He may have been fatalistic about the outcome, but he resolved to do his duty, to make do, and to accomplish the best he could with what he had. Possibly in his few spare moments over those two days his thoughts returned to scenes of his boyhood on the North Carolina coast in Beaufort, days of fishing and sailing under a bright blue sky, visiting the offshore Shackleford and Bogue Banks, and avidly listening to sea stories told in his uncle's tavern on the waterfront. His early years had been filled with hearing local yarns of the pirates Stede Bonnet and Blackbeard and tales of daring escapades told by a family friend, the colorful, famed privateer from the War of 1812, Captain Otway Burns.

If ever a North Carolinian was destined for the sea, it was James Wallace Cooke. Cooke was named for his grandfather, Captain James Wallace of Beaufort. His great-grandfather was John Wallace of Portsmouth, who as "governor" ruled Shell Castle Island in Ocracoke Inlet, developing it into one of North Carolina's most important ports. Owned by John Gray Blount, Shell Castle had by the beginning of the nineteenth century become the gateway for all seaborne traffic into Ocracoke Inlet, which was the key opening to world trade for all of the ports on the treacherous North Carolina sounds. As a center of lightering, or the transfer of cargo from oceangoing to smaller vessels, Shell

Castle grew from a desolate sandbar to a busy settlement with residences, warehouses, taverns, ship's stores, and a lighthouse.

In 1810 Esther Wallace married Thomas Cooke, a merchant whose seafaring forebears had migrated from Rhode Island to New Bern. Thomas and his brother, Henry Marchant Cooke, moved to Beaufort about the time of Thomas's marriage. Esther and Thomas Cooke had two children, James, born on 13 August 1812, and Harriet, born on 26 August 1814. While returning by schooner from New York, where he customarily restocked his merchandise, Thomas Cooke was lost at sea near Beaufort when a fierce hurricane claimed all on board the ship on 15 August 1815. The next year Esther died in October. The orphaned Cooke children were kept by their relatives, with James joining the growing family of his father's brother, Henry, the collector of the port of Beaufort, and infant Harriet going to live with her uncle Joseph Borden.[1]

Surveyed in 1713 and chartered in 1723, Beaufort is one of the oldest towns in North Carolina. Situated on Taylor Creek about a mile and a half from the inlet, then called Old Topsail, the town had grown by 1810 to have a population of 585. In Cooke's youth the inlet was guarded by a new eight-gun, semicircular brick fort, Fort Hampton, which would be replaced in 1834 by Fort Macon. Bustling Front Street was lined with docks, warehouses, fish houses, ship's chandlers, taverns, and stores. The lone church in town was built by the Episcopalians but was used by all denominations. The townspeople's principal occupations—shipbuilding, trade, and fishing—were derived from the sea. Surrounded by great stands of live oak and cedar, the port had a reputation as a shipbuilding center, crafting "some of the swiftest sailers & best built Vessels in the United States." The fisheries produced whale and porpoise oil, salt mullet, and shellfish. In the nineteenth century the little port, sited so close to the ocean and swept by fresh breezes, was considered uncommonly healthful and touted as a vacation spot where inlanders who sought "amusement connected with the water may here receive full gratification; whilst bathing in the surf and walking on the beach."[2]

It was through his uncle's political connections as port collector that fifteen-year-old James Cooke received a midshipman's appointment in the United States Navy on 1 April 1828. He was initially assigned to the training ship *Guerrière*, a forty-four-gun frigate. Other frigates on which he served were the *Constitution* (1835–37) and the *Macedonian* (1840–41). John N. Maffitt, a fellow North Carolinian and lifelong friend who entered the navy four years after Cooke, served with him on the *Constitution* and *Macedonian* cruises. Maffitt described Cooke as an excellent officer and a gentleman of "the highest order of Merit," who in his career personified "perseverance, energy and Knightly valor."[3] Another contemporary, Mrs. Catherine Edmondston, described him as "a plain sensible unaffected man," who was "gentlemanly, well informed, & eminently practical."[4] Cooke was promoted to passed midshipman on 14 June 1834. Facing the prospect of going to sea for a long time, he set up a trust for his sister, Harriet, including the houses and lots he owned in Beaufort, his property on Portsmouth Island, and nine slaves.[5]

Over the following thirty-two years in the U.S. Navy, Cooke compiled a solid but undistinguished career, with extensive sea duty. He spent most of his time at sea in newly designed ship sloops or corvettes, which were somewhat larger and more heavily armed than sloops built in the early years of the century. The new class was not altogether satisfactory at first, the vessels being described as sluggish sailers lacking grace. In later versions, rebuilt along the lines of the *Wasp* of 1814 fame and carrying reduced armament, the redesigned corvettes earned a reputation for fast sailing. While a midshipman, Cooke served on the *Natchez* and the *John Adams*. Later he did tours of duty on the *Ontario*, the *Germantown*, and the *Decatur*.[6] During his cruise on the *Macedonian*, on 25 February 1841 Cooke was promoted to lieutenant. His next assignment was on the receiving ship *Ontario* in New Orleans, followed by another voyage on the *Constitution*. While serving again on the *John Adams*, he had a nearly fatal bout with yellow fever, and on recuperation leave arrived in Norfolk in the spring of 1848.[7]

Awaiting orders in Norfolk, on 5 July 1848 he married Mary Elizabeth Ann Watts of Portsmouth, Virginia. The Cookes began their married life at Pensacola Navy Yard, where he was assigned as executive officer and also served in the Gulf Squadron. On 18 February 1853 Cooke began a three-year stint at the U.S. Naval Observatory with the noted oceanographer, Lieutenant Matthew Fontaine Maury. During this tour the Cookes bought a farm in Fairfax County, Virginia, near Washington, D.C. They planted a large peach orchard, eventually consisting of some five hundred trees, and began raising their only child, a son, Lechmere Rittenhouse Cooke. In 1856 Cooke was separated from his family for a year when he took command of the store ship USS *Relief*, which made two voyages to South America to supply

Captain James W. Cooke became North Carolina's highest ranking Confederate naval officer. Unassuming in appearance, the indomitable Cooke won fame as the commander of the css *Albemarle*. (Southern Historical Collection, University of North Carolina, Chapel Hill)

the Brazil Squadron.[8] The next year he returned to his farm and was looking ahead to his future retirement from the navy, anticipating a bucolic life of farming and tending his orchard.

Even as he looked forward to his own future with satisfaction, Cooke was troubled by the escalating sectional crisis that threatened the very existence of his country. He may have been relieved that—unlike South Carolina and six other Southern states, which had chosen to leave the Union by the beginning of 1861—his native North Carolina narrowly rejected secession in January of that year. The seven seceded states met in Montgomery, Alabama, in early February to form the Confederate States of America. For Lieutenant Cooke, already wrestling with the issue of what, ultimately, would be the honorable thing for him to do, waiting was the only course, since both North Carolina and his adopted state of Virginia remained in the Union. The firing on Fort Sumter on 12 April settled the question for Cooke. Virginia seceded five days later, and a second referendum elected a majority of secession delegates to a North Carolina convention that met in Raleigh on 20 May. North Carolina became the eleventh and last state to leave the Union and join the Confederacy.

On 2 May Cooke sent his resignation to Secretary of the Navy Gideon Welles and then traveled to Richmond to seek a commission in the Confederate States Navy. Since it was obvious that northern Virginia soon would be a war zone, the Cooke family left their farm, heading south to Portsmouth. Shortly thereafter, Union soldiers vandalized their former home and cut down the prized orchard.[9] As the former senior lieutenant in the United States Navy, Cooke hoped to receive a promotion to commander despite the Confederate naval policy of offering a rank equal to that previously held. A further complication for Cooke was that the Confederate navy was literally inundated with hundreds of officers and possessed few if any ships, naval yards, or naval stations. Cooke also had been preceded by numbers of officers from the states that had seceded earlier than North Carolina.

After consulting with the Navy Department, Cooke reluctantly accepted a commission as a lieutenant in the Virginia navy on 4 May. He was assigned immediately to the construction of a battery on the James River at old Fort Powhatan, one component in what eventually became an impregnable complex preventing the Union fleet from ascending the river to Richmond. On 11 June 1861 Cooke was commissioned a lieutenant in the Confederate States Navy and was then sent to northern Virginia to superintend placement of obstacles in the Potomac River at the batteries near Aquia Creek, which were commanded by Captain William F. Lynch. While there, Cooke received his baptism of fire when the batteries were attacked by Union gunboats on 31 May and 1 June. In his report of the action Captain Lynch commended Cooke for his "spirit and alacrity." Here also Cooke requested that the Navy Department reconsider him for a higher rank, but Secretary Stephen R. Mallory replied that he must be content with his lieutenancy.[10] On 18 July Cooke was detached from Aquia Creek and ordered to Norfolk to take command of the steamer css *Weldon N. Edwards*, which was then sent to augment the defenses of North Carolina.[11]

The firing on Fort Sumter back in mid-April had prompted North Carolina governor John W. Ellis to prepare the state for defense, and by the time the state seceded in May, existing coastal forts had been seized and garrisoned and new batteries were under construction at the unprotected inlets of Oregon, Hatteras, and Ocracoke. The state also acquired and armed a small navy of river steamers and canal tugboats—the *Warren Winslow*, the *Raleigh*, the *Beaufort*, the *John W.*

Ellis, and the *Weldon N. Edwards*—called somewhat wryly the "mosquito fleet." Extinguishing the lighthouse lanterns enabled the tower at Hatteras to be used as a lookout to sight Union warships and potential prizes for state cruisers and Confederate privateers, which gathered chiefly at Hatteras but also at Ocracoke. Before long, Hatteras Inlet was crowded with shipping. In early August a detained merchant captain observed that riding at anchor inside the inlet were twelve prizes, including three lightships used for storage, three brigs, and six schooners. Most of these ships had been taken by the *Winslow*, the fastest of the raiders, which was at Hatteras along with two privateers, the *Gordon* and the *Mariner*. Despite a Union blockade, the isolated inlet, which was now the gateway to most of North Carolina's ports, was doing a brisk trade with ships regularly calling at Halifax, Nova Scotia, the West Indies, and Europe. Officials of major insurance companies in Philadelphia, alarmed over the rise in rates resulting from privateering, pressured Secretary of the Navy Gideon Welles to send an expedition to end "piracy" on the North Carolina coast. During August Cooke and the *Edwards* were stationed at Ocracoke Inlet, primarily to transport supplies. Cooke was not happy with his command, describing the ship as "entirely worthless, the boilers worn out and the timbers . . . rotten."[12]

The humiliating defeat of the Federal army at Manassas on 21 July prompted Washington authorities to plan a counteraction that would nullify the loss's dampening effect on Northern morale. The privateering and trade at Hatteras Inlet was a thorn in the side of the U.S. Navy, which had concentrated on major ports in its initial blockade of the vast Southern coast. The navy responded to the "nest of pirates" at Hatteras with a joint army-navy expeditionary force. In late August a fleet of seven men-of-war, mounting 143 guns, under Commodore Silas H. Stringham, appeared off Hatteras, accompanied by transports bearing a small army contingent commanded by General Benjamin F. Butler. Over two days, 28–29 August, Commodore Stringham's fleet, which possessed overwhelming superiority in guns, bombarded the fortifications at Hatteras, forcing their surrender while incurring little damage from the outranged Confederate cannon. On the first day, exposed Fort Clark was abandoned as Butler's troops were landed with difficulty in the high surf. The next day, despite reinforcements and the arrival of the Confederate fleet, Fort Hatteras was pounded in a three-and-a-half-hour shelling. When fire threatened the powder magazine, Commodore Samuel Barron reluctantly surrendered his command, giving the North its first victory of the war and ending Confederate privateering on the Outer Banks. Cooke's *Edwards* and the rest of the Confederate fleet evacuated the batteries at Ocracoke and Oregon Inlets as well as the military dependents at Portsmouth.

The former North Carolina navy had been turned over to the Confederacy in late July and was under Commodore Barron's command. Once in Confederate service, the vessels were used not only to protect North Carolina waters but also as dispatch and supply vessels in Virginia. When Barron surrendered at Fort Hatteras, all of his naval vessels escaped. Captain Lynch, fresh from success on the Potomac, replaced the captured Barron and took command of the North Carolina squadron. Cooke and the *Edwards* were sent back to Norfolk for refitting after the withdrawal from the inlets, and in September Captain Lynch ordered Cooke to Roanoke Island. On 30 October, at New Bern, Cooke took command of the css *Ellis*, a one-hundred-ton sidewheel steamer that mounted two guns. Throughout the fall and winter, the *Ellis* was involved in the Confederate defense buildup undertaken in anticipation of a second Union expedition to the region. Meanwhile, after extensive refitting, the *Edwards* was rechristened the css *Forrest*.[13]

On 3 November the fleet, consisting of the flagship *Sea Bird*, the *Ellis*, the *Curlew*, the *Forrest*, and the former Union gunboat *Fanny*, left the Neuse River below New Bern and steamed across the sound to test Union vigilance at Hatteras. The *Sea Bird* fired two rounds at Fort Hatteras, but the foray was cut short by the breakdown of the wheezy vessels *Fanny* and *Forrest*, both of which had to be towed away. Three days later, while reconnoitering Ocracoke Inlet, the squadron discovered a disabled French naval vessel, the *Prony*, which had run aground, and the Confederates rescued her crew. The next day, the *Winslow* struck a wreck in the inlet and was lost. The *Ellis* participated in rescuing the crew and salvaging equipment, and then burning the vessel. For over a month the *Ellis* was in Norfolk under repair, returning to Roanoke Island on 26 December. During January the *Ellis* was engaged primarily in construction of a line of obstacles to prevent enemy incursion into Albemarle Sound. Cooke kept his crew busy towing and sinking coastal vessels and driving piles across Croatan Sound from Roanoke Island to the mainland.[14]

In mid-January a "major amphibious force" commanded by General Ambrose E. Burnside arrived at Hatteras Inlet to complete the Union's conquest of the sound country. Burnside commandeered a ragtag fleet of transports, ferry boats, barges, tugboats, passenger steamers, and sailboats all along the northeastern coast to ferry some 13,000 troops to the rendezvous at Fortress Monroe in Virginia. Under the command of Flag Officer Louis M. Goldsborough, the flotilla of more than 120 ships, including seventeen naval vessels mounting forty-three guns, embarked from Chesapeake Bay in January 1862. After weathering a severe storm at Cape Hatteras, the Union squadron lost several transports in a series of gales at Hatteras Inlet. Once in Pamlico Sound, in early February, the expedition moved north to attack Roanoke Island, the key to subjugating northeastern North Carolina.[15]

The island was defended by batteries, redoubts manned by some 2,500 soldiers, channel obstructions, and the Confederate "mosquito fleet." Over the winter Commodore Lynch had augmented his squadron and now had ready for battle eight river steamers or canal tugboats and a schooner. Each of the eight steamships was armed with one thirty-two-pound pivot-mounted cannon, and the schooner carried two guns. The *Sea Bird* was Lynch's flagship; Cooke was on the *Ellis*; and the *Curlew*, the *Forrest*, the *Appomattox*, the *Beaufort*, the *Raleigh*, the *Fanny*, and the schooner *Black Warrior* rounded out the fleet. Not only were the Confederates facing a four-to-one disparity in cannon, but the Union guns were also of heavier caliber. Lynch arranged his squadron in battle formation across Croatan Sound behind the obstructions, anchored at either end by shore batteries on Roanoke Island and the mainland.

Late in the morning on 6 February, while the Confederates were driving additional piles, distant black smudges above the water signaled the approach of the enemy. The *Appomattox* was sent down to reconnoiter and hurriedly returned with a report that more than fifty enemy vessels were closing on them.[16] Throughout the tense day and all during the night Northern ships converged on the lower end of Roanoke Island. The following morning both fleets opened fire. Despite being outranged by the heavier Union cannon, the rebel flotilla remained on station behind the obstructions, returning fire throughout the day. Most of the Yankee shelling was concentrated on Fort Bartow, the closer of the Confederate batteries. Although at the height of the bombardment the fort appeared to be "enveloped in the sand and dust thrown up by shot and shell," casualties were light.[17]

Cooke kept the *Ellis* in the middle of the fray, replenishing his ammunition first from the sinking *Curlew* and then from the disabled *Forrest*. Late in the afternoon, as the bombardment was tapering off, Cooke's executive officer, Midshipman Camm, was seriously wounded, losing his left arm.[18] That night Lynch ordered the remainder of the Confederate fleet, having completely exhausted its powder and shot, to retire to Elizabeth City, hoping to be resupplied and to return to the battle immediately. Thinking that the island forts were secure, the commodore had no inkling that over ten thousand Union soldiers had landed and would overwhelm the meager Confederate garrison and outflank the forts, forcing the island's surrender on 8 February.

With little ammunition available in Elizabeth City, Lynch sent the *Raleigh* to Norfolk with an emergency plea for powder and shot. As the southern terminus of the Dismal Swamp Canal, the river port was too valuable to give up without a fight. Enough powder and fuel were scraped together for the *Sea Bird* and the *Appomattox* to return to Roanoke Island the following day. En route, Lynch encountered a boat that brought the shocking news of the island's surrender. When the Confederates sighted Union ships steadily approaching, Lynch ordered a hasty retreat to the Pasquotank River. At Elizabeth City Lynch distributed the meager supply of ammunition among his vessels. That afternoon, the five remaining ships—the *Sea Bird*, the *Ellis*, the *Appomattox*, the *Beaufort*, and the *Fanny*—formed a battle line diagonally across the river, flanked by a four-gun militia battery at Cobb's Point on the east side and the *Black Warrior* on the west bank. Knowing that his fleet would be sacrificed, Lynch ordered his captains to fight as long as possible and then destroy their vessels.[19]

The Union gunboats anchored for the night about ten miles downriver from Elizabeth City. The next morning, 10 February, they were spotted just after daybreak steaming upstream. Lynch landed at the battery for a final consultation with the local militia commander and was horrified to find that the battery was virtually deserted, with only a civilian and seven militiamen remaining. He sent word to Lieutenant William H. Parker of the *Beaufort* to garrison the battery, and he remained on shore to command it. A skeleton crew was ordered to take the *Beaufort* up the canal to Norfolk. Lynch expected the Federal gunboats to form a line and shell the battery; however, the bold Union leader, Commander Stephen C. Rowan, was well aware of the weaknesses of his foes and determined to close rapidly and engage them. His fourteen heavily armed ships could, he felt, easily overwhelm his enemy, and he also had too little ammunition for a lengthy bombardment. Rowan arranged ten of his vessels into two columns and kept four ships in reserve.[20]

When the enemy squadron came in range, Lynch ordered his battle line to open fire. The Yankee gunboats plowed relentlessly upstream with "shot and shell passing over the vessels in advance and falling thick and fast among vessels in the main columns." At less than a mile Rowan ran up the signal, "Dash at the enemy," and then opened fire. The Union columns rapidly passed the fort and closed on the rebel fleet in disastrous chaos. The *Black Warrior* was set on fire by her panic-stricken crew. The USS *Perry* rammed the *Sea Bird*, sinking the Confederate flagship. The *Fanny* was run aground, abandoned, and burned. The *Appomattox* temporarily escaped up the canal, while the *Forrest*, on shore for repairs, was burned by her own officers, along with a gunboat under construction.[21] Only the *Ellis* put up any real fight. As the USS *Ceres* came alongside her and boarders clambered over her rail, the fearless Cooke met them, "cutlass in hand," and was shot and bayoneted in the swirling combat. He "fought with the fierceness of a tiger, refusing to surrender or haul down his flag." The seriously wounded Cooke was overpowered and taken as a prisoner to Rowan's flagship, the USS *Delaware*. Some of his crew escaped by wading ashore in the swamp, but several were shot down in the water. Cooke had given the order to blow up the *Ellis*, but a black coal-heaver, deserting to the Union sailors, informed them of the order, and they cut the fuse before the explosives discharged.[22] Within minutes the Confederate fleet ceased to exist and Elizabeth City was occupied. Lynch and about fifty of his men escaped to Norfolk.

Although it would appear that resistance was futile for the hopelessly outgunned Confederate squadron, its "boldness and unflinching attitude . . . in defying immense odds" won the admiration of friend and foe alike. Commander Maffitt wrote of the naval battles at Roanoke Island and Elizabeth City that they "reflected much credit upon the personal courage of all the Confederate officers therein engaged. With mere abortions for gunboats, badly armed and sparse of ammunition, they confronted without hesitation the well-equipped and powerful vessels of the North."[23]

Cooke's life had been saved by one of his acquaintances from the old navy, who saw that he received proper medical treatment on the *Delaware*. The Confederate wounded and prisoners were transported to the Union base at Roanoke Island and on 12 February were released on parole until exchanged.[24] As soon as he was able to travel, Cooke crossed the lines to return to Portsmouth for recuperation. During the interlude at home with his wife and children, Cooke must have witnessed the momentous appearance of the ironclad CSS *Virginia*, which had been constructed on the burned-out hull of the USS *Merrimack*. Launched on 13 February at Gosport Navy Yard, the *Virginia* debuted on 8 March by attacking the U.S. Navy's largest men-of-war anchored in Hampton Roads. Accompanied by the gunboats *Raleigh* and *Beaufort*, two survivors of the North Carolina squadron, the *Virginia* rammed and sank the USS *Cumberland* and left the USS *Congress* burning and sinking. The next morning the *Virginia* was confronted by the ironclad USS *Monitor*, a revolutionary design incorporating a revolving gun turret. Although the first battle in world history between armored ships ended in a draw, naval warfare was changed forever. Cooke must have been impressed with the new men-of-war, but he could have had no idea that an ironclad would figure prominently in his own future.

The *Virginia* alone could do no more than she had already done, and she was too powerful for the Union fleet to contain. With the naval balance of power stalemated, the North finally decided that the only way to eliminate the *Virginia* was to send an expedition to take Norfolk and destroy the lair of the dreaded iron monster. As rumors of a forthcoming Union invasion arose, Cooke moved his family away from the war zone to his native North Carolina. By April he and his family were living in Warrenton, where he continued to recover from his wounds.[25] On 10 May the Gosport Navy Yard was once again wracked by fire and explosions as the Confederates withdrew before a superior Union thrust. An attempt to move the deep-draft *Virginia* up the James River failed, and the next day she was set afire and disintegrated when the flames reached her magazine.

In August Cooke received word at Warrenton that he had been exchanged, and on the nineteenth he was ordered to proceed to Drewry's Bluff, the extensive battery complex on the James River, where he was to take command of the *Beaufort*. When he arrived at naval headquarters on 25 August, he was handed a commission as commander with a date of rank of 17 May.[26] For the next month Cooke and the *Beaufort* settled into the routine of carrying dispatches and scouting on the upper James River. His destiny was not, however, to languish in a minor command in a naval backwater, and once again events in North Carolina intervened to project him onto center stage in the conflict.

The first Federal victories in North Carolina, which had so bolstered Northern morale, were later overshadowed as Union and Confederate forces locked in a titanic struggle for the Confederate capital of Richmond. Consequently, the Union failed to capitalize on the strategic importance of cutting the rail lifeline running from Wilmington to Virginia, and North Carolina slipped into the background, with both sides content with the status quo there. Confederate authorities, always rankled by the barrage of criticism from the press in North Carolina and Richmond for virtually handing the northeastern region of the state to the enemy, were prodded from time to time to undertake a reconquest. Occasionally, troops had been spared from Virginia and assigned the task of retaking the area. But timid commanders, too few men and guns, and the lack of naval support doomed all of these efforts except one—that of General Hoke early in 1864.

The key element in the Union stranglehold on the region was the extensive flotilla of shallow-draft, well-armed gunboats that dominated the North Carolina sounds. Compared to the vanquished Confederate "mosquito fleet," whose nine small vessels had mounted but ten guns, the Yankee gunboat horde, many of which were converted ferries or passenger steamers, were bigger, faster, and armed with numerous large-caliber cannon. By 1864 in Albemarle Sound alone, the North concentrated eight ships, mounting a total of fifty-two heavy guns; moreover, other vessels were stationed at fortified enclaves at Washington, New Bern, Beaufort, and the inlets. Since naval gunfire was murderous to unprotected infantry, the Confederates' only hope of wresting control of the region from the North lay in building a new fleet. There was neither time nor the industrial infrastructure to construct conventional gunboats in numbers that could match the Union's, but a few ironclads built especially for shallow waters might successfully challenge Federal superiority. Among the innovations sponsored by the energetic Secretary Mallory was the creation of an ironclad fleet, particularly shallow-draft vessels for defense of the interior waters. Fortunately, the Confederacy's chief naval constructor was the talented John L. Porter, who had shared responsibility with ordnance expert John M. Brooke in the construction of the css *Virginia*. For river defense, Porter designed a class of flat-bottomed, armored rams, 150 feet long and about 40 feet wide, that would draw less than ten feet. They would mount newly cast, heavy-caliber Brooke rifles.

This new type of vessel was ideally suited for the torpid rivers of the North Carolina coastal plain, and by the fall of 1862 the Navy Department let three contracts to private shipbuilding firms for construction of armed rams. Howard and Ellis of New Bern would build a vessel at Whitehall on the Neuse River above New Bern. Martin and Elliott of Elizabeth City would construct one vessel at Tarboro on the Tar River upstream from Washington and another at Tillery on the Roanoke River above Plymouth. The Navy Department transferred Flag Officer Lynch from Mississippi to North Carolina to superintend and expedite work on the projects. Although Lynch had more command and combat experience on the North Carolina sounds than any other high-ranking naval officer, he was faced with a nearly impossible task—overseeing the simultaneous construction and outfitting of all of the vessels in the state, plus recruiting and training their crews. Ship construction in the agrarian South, which had few experienced engineers, mechanics, or foundries, was always difficult. Furthermore, Lynch was deficient in the tact and diplomacy needed to dampen interservice rivalry and maintain good relations with the testy North Carolina state government.[27]

The agent for Martin and Elliott was Gilbert Elliott, a talented genius who, at the age of nineteen, took on construction of an ironclad ram and an armored battery. Despite his youth, he already had extensive experience in the Elizabeth City shipyard, which had been destroyed by the Union invasion back in February. After that debacle, Elliott had enlisted in the army as a first lieutenant and was serving as regimental adjutant when he was sought out by the Navy Department for a new construction project. A furlough from the army was secured, and Elliott set up a shipyard near Tillery on the Roanoke River seven miles below Halifax to begin work on a four-gun armored floating battery designed for river defense as well as on the steam-powered ironclad ram.

Ship armor was more precious than gold in the Confederacy, and in October Secretary Mallory ordered Commander Cooke to expedite the accumulation of the plating. Cooke was then living in Warrenton and would be based out of the Halifax Navy Yard. This initial assignment evolved into Cooke's becoming the official liaison from the navy to the contractors responsible for all four of the ironclad vessels being built on the Neuse, Tar, and Roanoke Rivers. Cooke and Elliott, who were kindred spirits, met in October and formed an unshakable bond of friendship that made possible a close collaboration for the next two and a half years, through three construction projects and shared combat. Elliott wrote of Cooke that he "made every effort to hasten the completion of the boat. He was a bold and gallant officer. . . . Of him it was said that 'he would fight a powder magazine with a coal of fire.' "[28]

By March 1863, with the floating battery well under way, Elliott decided to move his shipyard downstream to a cornfield at Edwards

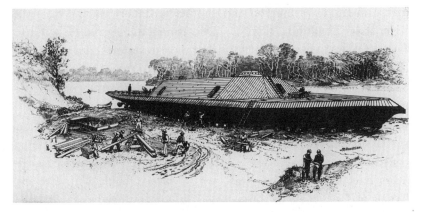

The css *Albemarle* was built in a makeshift shipyard at Edwards Ferry on the banks of the Roanoke River. (North Carolina Division of Archives and History, Raleigh)

Ferry near Scotland Neck in Halifax County. Fortuitously, a close neighbor to the new site was Peter Evans Smith, a man with a local reputation as a "mechanical wizard" who had a fully equipped forge on his farm. Also nearby were the two plantations of Patrick and Catherine Edmondston, who became intimately acquainted with the gunboat and its builders. Elliott scoured the countryside for forges, portable sawmills, tools, and laborers. The keel was laid for the iron-clad in April, and when the yellow pine frame began to rise, the country folk came to gawk, never before having seen such a huge vessel on their riverbank. Small by seagoing standards, she was 35 feet wide on her beam and 158 feet in overall length, including the ram, a beak of solid oak covered with two inches of iron plate. The sixty-foot-long casemate that housed the gun deck was sloped at an angle of thirty-five degrees. With headroom of seven feet, the top of the casemate was a sixteen-foot-wide open steel grate that allowed light and ventilation— and rain—into the gunboat. The casemate was armored with layers of pine and oak onto which four inches of iron was bolted. The deck was covered with one inch of armor, and the sides of the hull were plated with two inches of iron to two feet below the waterline. The vessel would be armed with two pivot-mounted 6.4-inch Brooke rifled cannon and would be powered by two two-hundred-horsepower engines driving two propellers. Completely outfitted and armored, the gunboat would weigh 376 tons and draw only eight feet of water.[29]

From the outset, Elliott said, "no vessel was ever constructed under more adverse circumstances." The energy, drive, and creative talents of Elliott and Smith were concentrated on the vessel, and almost by the sheer force of their will she began to take shape. With a half dozen ironclads simultaneously under construction in North Carolina, there was intense competition for skilled laborers, machinery, timber, iron, and armament. Cooke's role in the project expanded from administrative oversight to actually procuring iron for the armor plating. He personally searched the countryside, scrounging every bit of iron that he could find to be shipped to the Confederacy's foundries, chiefly Tredegar Iron Works in Richmond, which rolled the iron into armor plates. His friend Commander Maffitt wrote that "his greed for iron became amusingly notorious." The workmen at the Tredegar Works in Richmond and the Clarendon Foundry at Wilmington rather enjoyed the periodic visits of this single-minded officer whom they labeled the "Ironmonger Captain."[30]

Worn-out railroad rails were the most valued form of scrap iron, and there was constant bickering among the Navy Department, the state government, and rival naval officers for the precious commodity. Cooke's chief problem was Wilmington-based Commodore Lynch, whose priority was the Cape Fear River ironclads, even though he had official administration over all of the North Carolina vessels. After Lynch interfered by ordering a premature launching of the Roanoke River ironclad and delaying shipment of armor plating, Cooke was detached from his command. In January 1864 Cooke was assigned to the Navy Department, taking his orders directly from Secretary Mallory and charged with completing the Roanoke River ironclad.[31]

Rumors and reports were soon circulating down the rivers to the Federal navy, which, possessing no ironclads, was alarmed at the prospect of facing several of the powerful craft at once. Since Elliott was building a floating battery and an ironclad at the same time, the Roanoke River intelligence reports were the most garbled. The Federals could do little about the Roanoke vessels because of elaborate obstructions, mines, and the massive battery at Fort Branch on Rainbow Bluff about forty miles downstream. A Union cavalry raid launched up the Tar River in July 1863 did, however, destroy the Tarboro ram and several railroad bridges, and punitive thrusts up the Roanoke several times came within a few miles of Edwards Ferry. These Yankee successes forced Captain Lynch to order that Cooke launch his vessel early so that it could be moved upriver to be finished at the more secure Halifax Navy Yard. Fortunately, the river rose enough to make a launch possible. On 5 October Catherine Edmondston and many of her still-skeptical neighbors gathered to watch Mary Spottswood break a bottle of wine over the prow and christen the vessel CSS *Albemarle*. Dozens of horses, mules, and oxen strained to haul the great vessel down the greased log ways over a six-foot drop into the river. Hours after the crowd drifted away, at 3:00 A.M. on 6 October the iron leviathan finally gave way and slid into the water.[32]

A few days later both the *Albemarle* and the floating battery were towed upstream to Halifax. At the naval yard Cooke took over the final work on the ironclad, installing the shafts and propellers forged at the Charlotte Naval Yard and the twin steam engines. Over the next several months workmen began applying the armor plate that was on hand, using a faster twist drill designed by Peter Smith; but armor sufficient to complete the vessel continued to elude Cooke.[33] Plans laid in Richmond to use the ironclads to retake eastern North Carolina gave a new sense of urgency to the project, and Secretary Mallory intervened to establish the highest priority for the *Albemarle* and her sister ship the *Neuse*. Neither vessel was ready for General Pickett's half-hearted demonstration at New Bern in early February, but the remaining troops in North Carolina were left in the capable hands of General Hoke, who was confident that with the aid of the *Albemarle* he could retake Plymouth.

About 1 April the *Albemarle* had been moved downriver to Hamilton, where she awaited the last of her armor plate. There Hoke pleaded urgently for the ironclad's participation in the coming attempt on Plymouth. Despite his misgivings, Cooke agreed to have her at Plymouth on the eighteenth. Opening his campaign on 17 April, Hoke advanced to within five miles of the town. Artillery fire was exchanged that day, and the next morning Confederate guns bombarded the Federal earthworks, also striking the transport *Bombshell*, which sank at the dock. Although the *Albemarle* had not arrived, nor had the anxious Hoke heard from Cooke, an assault was ordered in the afternoon against the outlying redoubt. The day ended with the Confederates in good position to resume the attack, if only the ironclad would appear. But the question remained, where was the *Albemarle*? On the afternoon of the seventeenth, Cooke commissioned the *Albemarle* and cast off from Hamilton, headed downstream stern first, dragging heavy chains to slow the ship down. Portable forges were manned by blacksmiths, and workmen scrambled over the vessel busily applying the last of the plate armor. The green crew ran through gun drill to the sound of hammering and the shouts of mechanics.[34]

At Williamston a large crowd gave the ram a gala welcome, complete with a band playing on the riverbank. The *Albemarle* stopped briefly for the ceremony and offloaded extra workmen and equipment. During the night two breakdowns delayed her a total of ten hours, but by mid-morning of the eighteenth she was under way again. At ten o'clock that evening the ironclad was three miles upstream from Plymouth, above the Union river obstructions. Initial reconnaissance by one of the officers reported that she could not pass the obstacles, but Gilbert Elliott, who was aboard as a volunteer, personally reconnoitered the pilings and found that there was indeed just sufficient depth for the ram to proceed. At 2:30 on the morning of the nineteenth the *Albemarle* cleared for action and silently passed the Union batteries, which opened fire that sounded to the crew like "pebbles thrown against an empty barrel." Under a setting moon, the *Albemarle* steamed about one mile below Plymouth and encountered the six-gun USS *Southfield* and the eight-gun USS *Miami*. The Yankee gunboats were chained together to entrap the ram, but Cooke turned into the starboard bow of the *Southfield* and drove the massive ram some ten feet into the side of the enemy vessel. He reversed engines, but the *Southfield* sank so quickly that she dragged the forward deck of the ironclad under. As water poured into the forward ports, the shaken crew was poised to abandon ship. At the last moment, the *Southfield* struck bottom, rolled slightly, and released her mortal foe. The *Miami*, under the valiant Commander Charles W. Flusser, came alongside and opened fire at point-blank range. Fearing boarders, Cooke ordered his marines topside to engage the enemy with rifle fire. Suddenly, Commander Flusser was killed at his bow gun, apparently the victim of one of his own shells ricocheting off the sloping casemate of the ram and exploding over his gun. The battered *Miami* fled downstream into the darkness, leaving the *Albemarle* as uncontested ruler of the river.[35]

While the ram lay offshore below Plymouth in the predawn, Elliott established personal contact with Hoke, and the *Albemarle* moved in to pound the Union fortifications from the rear while Hoke's men attacked. Hoke accepted the surrender of the town on 20 April, capturing over 2,400 prisoners, tons of supplies, forty guns, and, most important to Cooke, some two hundred tons of coal. Hoke received a meritorious promotion to major general, and the Confederate Congress voted a joint resolution of thanks to Hoke and Cooke for the "brilliant victory." For the beleaguered South, awaiting the onslaught of General Grant, the victory in North Carolina was welcome news indeed. By the end of the month, Federal forces evacuated Washington after pillaging and burning much of the town.[36] The reoccupation of Plymouth and Washington, North Carolina, was a rare instance of Confederates recovering territory that had previously been taken by Union forces.

After the victory at Plymouth, Cooke and the *Albemarle* ventured down to Albemarle Sound, but the Union picket boats always kept their distance. Continuing his reconquest, General Hoke moved south to threaten New Bern. With the hapless *Neuse* aground in the low Neuse River since 22 April, Hoke once again had to rely on the *Albemarle*. This time she would have to steam two days through hostile waters, running a gauntlet of Union gunboats that were being concentrated in Albemarle Sound to destroy her. Uneasy about the hazards of the voyage, Cooke nevertheless responded that he and the ironclad were ready. As Hoke advanced on New Bern in the first week of May, Cooke prepared the *Albemarle*, the steamer *Cotton Plant*, and the *Bombshell*, the former Union transport, which had been raised by the Confederates, for the momentous voyage.[37]

On 5 May the Confederate flotilla cast off, entering Albemarle Sound by mid-afternoon. The Union vessels guarding the river mouth fled down the sound for ten miles. When Cooke sighted larger gunboats approaching, he signaled his consorts to retreat. The *Cotton Plant*, laden with troops, responded immediately, but the better-armed *Bombshell* continued in company. Forming his fleet of seven ships into two battle lines, the able commander of the Union squadron, Captain Melancton Smith, was eager to avenge the loss of the *Southfield*. Smith's fleet carried a total of fifty heavy guns, but he expected the brunt of the fight to be borne by the USS *Sassacus* (ten guns), the USS *Miami* (eight guns), the USS *Wyalusing* (eight guns), and the flagship USS *Mettabesett* (ten guns). His captains had orders to unleash broadsides as they passed, to attempt to ram, and to ensnare the ironclad in a net to foul its propellers.

At 4:40 P.M. the *Albemarle* opened fire as she turned to the starboard, and as the Yankee battle lines passed they replied. An early shot struck the ironclad's after cannon, shattering about twenty inches of the muzzle, but the close range of the battle meant that its accuracy was not affected. Leading the battle line, the *Mettabesett* steamed past the

The USS *Sassacus* rams the *Albemarle* in the Battle of Albemarle Sound on 5 May 1864. Heavily damaged, the *Sassacus* was put out of action, while the *Albemarle* continued to fight. (Naval Historical Center, Washington, D.C.)

ram and engaged the lightly armed *Bombshell*, which maneuvered away. The *Albemarle* was soon surrounded and being pummeled unmercifully by the *Sassacus*, the *Wyalusing*, and the *Mettabesett*, but the shot from the Union gunboats was seen to "bound away in the air like rubber balls" off the slanting casemate. Returning to the battle, the *Bombshell* peppered the *Sassacus* with her twenty-pound Parrott gun and her three howitzers. A broadside from the Yankee gunboat quickly compelled the *Bombshell* to strike her colors. The *Sassacus*, now some distance away, turned and at full steam charged back into the battle, ramming the *Albemarle* and riding up on her after deck. As the *Sassacus* struck, the ironclad's damaged stern gun was fired point-blank into the bow of the Union vessel. The *Albemarle* heeled over, taking water through the aft gun port, and, as a crewman later reported, there "was a good deal of confusion," with some terrified men running about. Although Cooke was knocked down by the collision, he was able to steady the crew, commanding, "Stand to your guns, and if we must sink let us go down like brave men."[38] The redoubtable Commander Francis A. Roe of the *Sassacus* drove his vessel harder against the ram, hoping to force her under. His crew, ordered to throw grenades and powder charges toward the *Albemarle*'s hatches and smokestack, endured galling fire from rebel marksmen. Cooke ordered his helmsman to swing the ram to port, and she broke free from the *Sassacus*, firing another shot, which crippled the enemy gunboat, striking the boiler and filling the engine room with steam that horribly scalded many of the crew. The *Sassacus* ground across the rear deck of the *Albemarle* and drifted off, apparently sinking. The *Miami* came up, attempting to explode a spar torpedo under the ironclad, but was foiled by Cooke's maneuvering. The hail of heavy shot and shell striking the *Albemarle* created a hellish din, causing concussions among most of the crew, who were bleeding from nose and ears. About 6:30 P.M. the *Commodore Hull* attempted to ensnare the ram in a net but failed. Now the smokestack of the ironclad was so riddled that she began to lose power as the boiler fires faded. With the ship's coal nearly gone, Cooke ordered the furniture and bulkheads dismantled and burned to keep his vessel moving. The fires finally began to blaze, raising steam pressure, when the ship's lard, ham, and bacon were tossed into the furnaces. Cooke fired a last shot at his antagonists as they slowly retreated down the sound, and the *Albemarle* steamed laboriously back to Plymouth.[39]

In the nearly three-hour engagement, the *Albemarle* had fired twenty-seven rounds, many of which had struck home, and had been the target of 557 rounds, most of which missed her low profile. Except for damage to the after gun and the smokestack, she was in good shape. Most of the Union gunboats suffered damage, and the *Sassacus*, which Cooke thought he had sunk, was severely disabled. There were no Confederate casualties, but thirty-seven men from the *Bombshell* were taken prisoner. The Union suffered a total of eight killed and twenty-one wounded, with the *Sassacus* losing five killed and fifteen wounded.[40] The Confederates could claim a tactical victory over great odds, but the Union gunboats had achieved their strategic objective of stopping the *Albemarle*, forcing her to return to her river haven. Hoke's troops, on the verge of taking New Bern, were ordered back to Virginia, and the liberation of eastern North Carolina was again left unaccomplished. In retrospect it would seem that had the *Albemarle* and the *Neuse* been able to act together to support the aggressive Hoke, eastern North Carolina could have been completely cleared of Union forces in a short time; however, it was not to be.

The superficial damage to the *Albemarle* was quickly repaired, after which Cooke made several appearances at the mouth of the Roanoke. But the intense strain he had been under for months now began to take

The *Albemarle*'s most dangerous moment came when the *Sassacus* temporarily forced her under and water poured through the gun ports. The shaken aft gun crew rallied and fired a point-blank round into the *Sassacus* that severely damaged her. (North Carolina Division of Archives and History, Raleigh)

its toll, causing his health to deteriorate. His request to be relieved of duty was granted, and Commander Maffitt was named to replace him on the *Albemarle*.[41] On 10 June Cooke received a meritorious promotion to captain for his conduct in the Battles of Plymouth and Albemarle Sound. He returned to his family at Warrenton, but three months later he was summoned to take charge of the inland naval defense of North Carolina, with headquarters at Halifax. His most pressing assignment was to superintend construction of another ironclad at Edwards Ferry by Gilbert Elliott and Peter Smith, who had just two weeks earlier been granted a contract.[42]

The whole region was shaken on 28 October by the disastrous news that the *Albemarle*, by this time under the command of Lieutenant Alexander F. Warley, had been sunk at her moorings by a torpedo launch in one of the most daring naval raids of the war. During the night Lieutenant William B. Cushing, who had earned a reputation for audacious commando action, succeeded in driving his boat over the *Albemarle*'s protective log boom and detonating a charge under the hull. Cushing escaped, rejoining the Union navy, and three days later a flotilla dashed upriver and recaptured Plymouth after a short bombardment. At least temporarily, Confederate mines, river obstructions, and the formidable battery at Fort Branch kept the Union navy confined to Plymouth.[43]

Cooke remained in Halifax into the early months of 1865, attempting to keep the new gunboat's construction on schedule. Although Catherine Edmondston reported on 20 February that the vessel was nearing completion, the Confederacy had little more than six weeks left. With Confederate armies melting away through desertion in April, Federal columns entered the upper Roanoke valley. On the evening of 7 April Cooke received orders to evacuate Halifax, and he personally set fire to the boats at Edwards Ferry. Viewed from the Edmondstons' home, "at dark the whole hemisphere was suddenly lighted up with lurid flames whose origin none could be blind to. It was the gunboat! Silently & solemnly it burned on, whilst we stood an excited group."[44]

Cooke was paroled in Raleigh on 12 May 1865. Ironically, the *Albemarle* was raised and taken to the Norfolk Navy Yard, where she was purchased by the U.S. Navy and moored on a back wharf until 1867. By then the unprotected hull was unsound, and she was sold for scrap. Both Cooke and his wife visited the derelict ship prior to the sale. Cooke lived quietly in Portsmouth until his death on 21 June 1869. Of the intrepid ironclad captain, a contemporary wrote, "He was as bold and gallant a Sailor as ever 'walked the quarter deck.' "[45]

He lighted the seas with a
track of fire, wherever he
passed, and sent conster-
nation and alarm among
the enemy's shipping.
—*Admiral Raphael Semmes,*
CSN, 1868

John N. Maffitt

The *Florida* Ranges the Atlantic

The USS *Constitution* rode easily at anchor on a bright June day in 1837 in the ancient harbor of Piraeus, Greece, in sight of the distant Acropolis of Athens, the seat of Western culture. The crew had diligently scraped, painted, and polished, preparing the frigate for a visit from the youthful King Otho, who had been a prince of Bavaria, and his bride, Queen Amalia. Promptly at ten o'clock in the morning, Commodore Jesse D. Elliot's aide, Midshipman John N. Maffitt, just eighteen years old, gave orders for the ship's barge to pick up the royal party at the dock. Shortly after the barge tied up at the landing, a carriage arrived, escorted by Bavarian cavalry. The king, arrayed in a general's uniform, stepped out first and then helped the "young and beautiful" queen, who was adorned in a brightly colored native costume, to step down. As she climbed into the barge, Maffitt steadied the queen with his arm. On the trip out to the ship, the sea breeze kicked up a spray, whereupon the midshipman "gallantly threw his cloak around her majesty."

As the royals entered the reception on the quarter deck, the marine honor guard presented arms while the ship's band played the Greek national anthem. Commodore Elliot was informed that after the king and queen had inspected the ship, they desired to waltz. He replied that although he himself was no dancer, he had many young men on board who were fine dancers. At his command, the band struck up a rousing tune that "electrified" the queen, to whom the commodore presented his charming aide as a partner. They were quickly joined by the king and others, and soon about twenty couples were twirling about the deck. When dusk fell, the *Constitution*'s crew erected an awning and created a grand ballroom chandelier by arranging muskets with candles in their muzzles around the capstan. Finally, at two o'clock in the morning the dance ended. As the royal couple was being rowed to shore, they looked back on a ship completely illuminated on the yards and masts, while a twenty-one-gun salute boomed out. Maffitt again enfolded the queen in his cloak for the passage across the harbor, and he cherished that cloak for the rest of his life.[1] Such romantic scenes as this made a deep impression on the teenaged midshipman and were never forgotten. Maffitt later incorporated them in a novel, *Nautilus, or Cruising Under Canvas*, published in 1871, about his experiences sailing aboard that ship of the old navy, which has become an icon of American history.

John Newland Maffitt was, as he put it, "a son of old Neptune," born at sea on 22 February 1819 to John Newland and Ann Carnic Maffitt. John Newland Maffitt Sr. of Dublin, Ireland, and a graduate of Trinity College, Dublin, had been converted to Methodism and chose to become a minister. He followed his physician brother, William, to America and settled in Connecticut. When he decided to become an itinerant preacher in the New England Conference, pursuing a calling that would provide little income, his family dissolved. In 1824 Dr. William Maffitt adopted his five-year-old nephew, John Jr., and took him to his plantation near Fayetteville, North Carolina. Ann Maffitt kept her other children with her and moved to Galveston, Texas, where she successfully ran first a boardinghouse and then a hotel.

John Jr. had little if any contact with his father after the separation, so one can only speculate on how much John Sr. influenced his son. John Maffitt Sr. became one of the most famous evangelists of the Second Great Awakening, a period of intense religious revivalism that swept the United States in the antebellum era. Known as the "Methodist Meteor" and the "Prince of the Pulpit," Maffitt on stage exuded religious zeal, flowery oratory, and a thinly disguised animal magnetism that stirred the emotions of thousands who attended his revival meetings, especially young women. His most lasting achievement was helping to found the *Christian Advocate*, the national Methodist newspaper, but his career peaked with election as chaplain of the House of Representatives in 1841. Another failed marriage to a much younger woman late in life disillusioned his followers, and he died in obscurity in Mobile, Alabama, in 1850.[2]

John Jr. seemed to have inherited his father's attractiveness, his literary bent, and his passionate nature, tempered by his mother's practicality. Looking back years later, he wrote of his boyhood home, Ellerslie near Fayetteville, that he loved "every blade of grass in the dear old place." A childhood friend, Duncan McRae, related that Maffitt was "a born leader." He was very close to his first cousin Eliza Maffitt, who was like a sister to him, and fondly wrote to her of their youth together, remembering himself as that "wild cousin of yours who used to run about the woods like a Mohawk Indian." When he was nine, his uncle sent him to White Plains, New York, to attend a Methodist classical academy for the next four years.[3]

In his thirteenth year, on 25 February 1832, Maffitt was appointed a midshipman in the navy, and in September he reported to the USS *St. Louis*, an eighteen-gun sloop of war, which embarked on a cruise to the West Indies from Pensacola, Florida.[4] After an extended leave in early 1834 taken at home in North Carolina, Maffitt attended a naval school at the Boston Navy Yard from which he was assigned in February 1835 to the frigate *Constitution* for a three-year cruise in the Mediterranean.[5] On this voyage he formed a lifelong friendship with another midshipman from North Carolina, James W. Cooke. The *Constitution* was the flagship of Commodore Elliot, who played such a prominent role in the royal ball at Piraeus. From Elliot's account of the royal entertainment, it is obvious that the fame of Maffitt's father had influenced his appointment as the commodore's aide. The Mediterranean Fleet, then as now, was charged with protecting American shipping and interests in the region, paying diplomatic and social calls in many of the fabled ports of the Mediterranean.

While the *Constitution* was back in Port Mahon in the Balearic Islands for refitting, Maffitt was assigned to the USS *Shark*, a twelve-gun schooner, which returned to Norfolk in March 1838. There he was granted ninety days' leave to prepare for his examinations. He wrote a vivid portrait of leave in Norfolk after months at sea: "High in spirits,

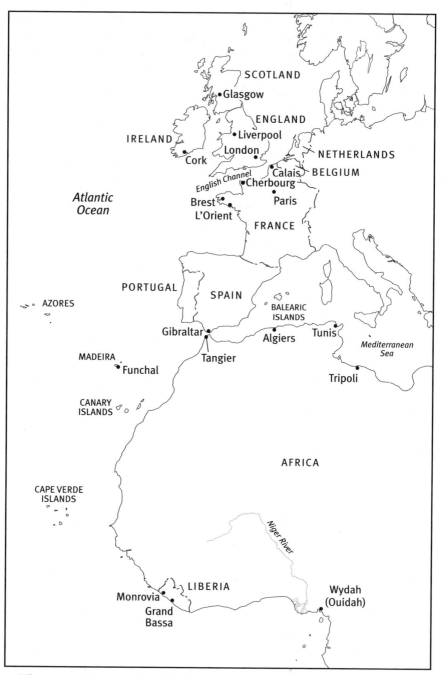

The eastern Atlantic and the Mediterranean

the reefers disentangled themselves from their crowded lair. The sight of oysters in every style of cookery brought to memory scenes of old delights, beautiful maidens versed in naval lore, picnics to the Dismal Swamp, and those genial flirtations so often ending in partnership for life."[6] Maffitt traveled to Baltimore, where he rented a single room and devoted himself to intensive study. At the Exchange Hotel, on 8 June, carrying with him his journals and letters of recommendation from his commanding officers, he went before a board of senior officers to stand a rigorous oral exam on seamanship and navigation. He handled himself superbly before the intimidating board and was rated passed midshipman from 23 June. Granted another leave, he saw his cousin Eliza in Portsmouth, Virginia, and then went on to Texas to become better acquainted with his sisters.[7]

In October he joined the packet *Woodbury* for a month and then was ordered on 20 November 1838 to the eighteen-gun sloop, USS *Vandalia*, which was operating out of Pensacola in the Gulf of Mexico. Several cruises took him to the coast of Mexico, which was undergoing another of its many revolutions and coping with a French incursion at Veracruz, where Maffitt wandered through deserted streets, observing how the buildings had been shattered by a naval bombardment. At Matamoros, Maffitt narrowly escaped death when the ship's boat was capsized in a rough inlet. He swam ashore and rode out the gale in a fisherman's hut. From 11 March 1839 he was appointed acting lieutenant to replace an officer who was washed overboard and drowned in a storm.[8] His next assignment, beginning in October, was a year's service as an acting master on the USS *Macedonian*, a thirty-six-gun frigate. By May 1840 Maffitt was in Veracruz, where yellow fever raged, forcing him to remain on board ship. Commenting on the current civil war, he wrote, "The whole country is in a wretched state, nothing but anarchy and confusion."[9]

Returning to Pensacola in August, Maffitt met Mary Florence Murrell, who was visiting from Mobile, Alabama, and fell in love. He had written to Eliza the year before that in regard to a future wife he would "not be over-particular" and "should like an amiable disposition and a fine mind. Riches would be *no objection*."[10] From a prominent Mobile family, Mary Murrell was attractive and amiable enough to captivate the romantically inclined Maffitt. In October he was granted three months' leave from the *Macedonian*, and he and Mary were married in Mobile on 17 November 1840. Coming back off leave in February 1841, he was assigned to shore duty at Pensacola Navy Yard. The next

October he returned to the *Macedonian* as acting master and rejoined his friend Cooke. While he was at sea in February 1842, his wife gave birth to a daughter Mary Frances, who would be called Florie. Once in port, Maffitt had Florie baptized on the *Macedonian*. He remained with the frigate until he was detached to the U.S. Coast Survey on 20 April 1842.[11]

Accurate charts being essential for navigation at sea, the U.S. Coast Survey was a long-term, cooperative program of scientists and the navy to map the entire coastline of the United States. At the time Maffitt joined the survey, it was under the administration of the Treasury Department. Usually, talented naval officers served a tour with the survey and then returned to sea duty; but Maffitt, having an affinity for mathematics and navigation, was so skilled and efficient that the survey director, Professor Alexander D. Bache, especially requested that his tour be extended. To the detriment of his naval career, Maffitt remained in the program for fourteen years.

Maffitt's specialty became hydrography, the field analysis of coastal waters. Over the years he took tens of thousands of sightings, triangulations, depth soundings, tide and current velocity measurements, and bottom samples. His field work began in May 1843. On 3 February of the next year he received his commission as lieutenant, with a date of rank of 25 June 1843.[12] When the Mexican War began, Maffitt requested transfer to active duty in the navy, but Bache, who considered him irreplaceable, denied his wish. He later summarized Maffitt's particular importance to the survey by stating, "As a surveying officer he has not been excelled by any one. . . . The quantity and quality of his work has been remarkable indeed. His vessel has always been a model of efficiency and neatness . . . his work has been upon the most dangerous parts of the coast, and he has encountered the dangers without shirking."[13]

As chief of a hydrographic survey party, Maffitt commanded several different vessels over the years. The first was the schooner *Gallatin* at Nantucket and Boston in 1848. The next year he had the schooner *Morris*. By 1850 Maffitt had been appointed an assistant of the survey and had moved to work on the southern coast from Virginia to Georgia. Among his major projects were mapping a harbor of refuge below Cape Hatteras, charting Georgetown and Beaufort Inlets, and discovering a new entrance to Charleston harbor that would be named Maffitt's Channel.[14]

When the survey duty began, Maffitt moved his family to Baltimore.

Because he would be away so much, he hired a longtime acquaintance to attend to his business affairs and all the needs of his family. His first son, Eugene Anderson, was born in Baltimore in November 1844. Sometime during his work at Nantucket and Martha's Vineyard, his marriage was compromised, possibly by the man hired to look after his business. He and Mary separated, but Maffitt retained custody of the children.[15]

In the summer of 1851 Maffitt and the *Gallatin* were based at Fort Johnston in Smithville (now Southport) at the mouth of the Cape Fear River. Not too far upriver was his boyhood home at Fayetteville, which he visited frequently. For entertainment Maffitt managed a theatrical troupe in the village, which provided a focal point for the summer society of parties and dances. The next year Maffitt worked around Charleston in a new command, the schooner *Crawford*. At Charleston he met Mrs. Caroline Laurens Read, a naval officer's widow and a scion of one of South Carolina's most distinguished families, which included John Laurens of Revolutionary War fame. The couple was married in Charleston on 3 August 1852. While they were on their honeymoon, the new Mrs. Maffitt's youngest child, Caroline Read, burned to death in an accident while staying at Ellerslie. The tragedy scarred both of the Maffitts so deeply that each time they moved, the child's casket was shipped with them and reburied, finally remaining in Washington, D.C., where they last resided. John and Caroline Maffitt set up housekeeping in Smithville with Florie and Eugene Maffitt and Mary and Laurens Read. During their marriage the pair had two sons, John Laurens, born at Smithville, and Alexander Colden Rhind, born in Virginia. As a result of lengthy survey work on the James River in 1854, Maffitt purchased a home on the lower river, which he named Carrieville for his wife. The Maffitts lived there four years, until the fevers prevalent in the river bottoms began to debilitate Caroline Maffitt.[16]

Maffitt's extraordinary contributions to the coast survey, while appreciated by those in the scientific community, were not so well understood by older naval officers, who viewed the survey as an obligatory tour that in Maffitt's case had sidetracked him far too long from line service. In response to the need to remove supernumerary, or superfluous, officers from the navy list, in 1855 Maffitt was placed on furlough, which could lead to involuntary retirement. Maffitt appealed to Secretary of the Navy James L. Dobbin, a family friend from Fayetteville, and he was allowed to remain on active duty.

Preparing to contest retirement, Maffitt secured testimonials and endorsements from peers and former commanding officers. In the summer of 1857 he defended himself before a naval court of inquiry. Maffitt's parade of supportive testimony from a distinguished group of naval officers, both in person and by depositions, in addition to his "masterful defense," won him restoration to active duty and a vindication for his many years of service in the coastal survey. On 29 January 1858 he was commissioned a lieutenant on the active list, dating from his original commission in 1843. He remained with the survey for several weeks, completing his reports.[17]

Then in May he was detached from the coast survey and given command of the USS *Dolphin*, a four-gun brig that would cruise off Cuba to interdict the illegal slave trade and suppress piracy. He took command on 1 June. The *Dolphin* was cruising off the north coast of Cuba in late August when a suspicious brig was sighted. Coming in range, Maffitt hoisted British colors and fired two blanks with no results. When he then fired two shots across the vessel's bow, she ran up American colors. Maffitt responded with the United States flag and fired a high round that struck the topsail, which brought the unknown brig to a standstill. The ship bore the name *Echo*, but the master had no proof of nationality. The boarding party sent over by Maffitt found 360 slaves crouched on a temporary deck with less than four feet of clearance. A prize crew sailed the *Echo* to Charleston, and the district admiralty court, determining that the slaver was from New Orleans, condemned it. Because it was the first seizure of a slaver in the late 1850s, the *Echo* made national headlines. A month later, the rescued Africans were embarked on the steam frigate USS *Niagara* for a voyage to Liberia, which had been colonized from the United States by former slaves.[18]

Upon his return to the United States in September, Maffitt was again assigned temporarily to the coast survey and stationed in Washington, D.C. He sold his home in Virginia and moved his family to Washington. Domestic happiness was short-lived, for Caroline Maffitt died in March 1859 after a long illness. Florie Maffitt wrote: "Our beloved, our noble, beautiful Mamma—died in Papa's arms surrounded by fond friends and loving children—to Papa she was *everything*, and their mutual love, and devotion, to each other, was beautiful. . . . Poor Papa's misery does not abate."[19] Maffitt's consolation was his children. He kept Florie and Mary Read in school in Washington at Mrs. Kingford's Seminary, while Eugene and Laurens Read were tutored in

Georgetown, and the younger children were sent to Ellerslie to his beloved cousin, Mrs. Eliza Maffitt Hybart.[20]

On 14 June 1859 Maffitt was ordered to take command of the USS *Crusader*, a new five-gun, steam-powered, three-masted bark. Again he was ordered to the Caribbean to suppress piracy and capture slavers. For the next twenty months Maffitt alternated between his station off Cuba and calling at the Gulf ports of Key West, Pensacola, and New Orleans. After months of fruitless cruising, on 23 May 1860 the *Crusader* approached a bark that attempted to run. Maffitt quickly overhauled her and fired a shot across the bow that brought out a French flag. When Maffitt displayed the American colors and sent over a boarding party, the master hauled down his flag and cast it and his papers into the sea. The characteristic stench and closed hatches convinced the boarding party that the vessel was a slaver even before they set foot on her deck. As they neared the ship, they heard a "suppressed moaning" and then the "unmistakable murmur of many voices." As the Americans boarded, the hatches flew open and "with a tremendous shout . . . out burst hundreds, the self-liberated slaves," a total of 426 men, to be exact. When the men saw the "Stars and Stripes . . . like a bright rainbow of promise—they became perfectly frantic with joy." In contrast, a group of more than a hundred women stood apart from the noisy men. "Entirely nude, but innocently unabashed, they sat or knelt in tearful and silent thankfulness. Several of them held infants in their arms, and through their tears, like sunshine behind a cloud, beamed an expression of the deepest gratitude and happiness."[21]

Once the Africans were clothed in spare canvas and fed, the slaver *Bogata* was towed to Key West. The marine detachment and prize crew saw that the slaves were fed well and had adequate exercise and time in the fresh air on deck. The Africans had been prisoners of war taken by the King of Dahomey and sold to slave traders at Wydah. Surprisingly, they were in good health; only seven had died on the voyage from Africa. At Key West they were housed by the government until they could be returned to Africa. Maffitt's last captures came in July and August—the *William R. Kilby*, which had been abandoned by her crew and had only three African boys on board, and the *Young Antonio*, which had no slaves but which Maffitt suspected to be a pirate ship. In all, Maffitt had been responsible for liberating 789 slaves.[22]

While Maffitt was serving his country on the high seas, the victory of Abraham Lincoln in the election of 1860 precipitated South Carolina's secession on 20 December 1860, and the nation began to dissolve. By the time Maffitt brought the *Crusader* into Mobile on 3 January 1861, Alabama was on the verge of secession. To continue operating the ship, Maffitt cashed a draft on the reluctant port collector for prize money. The agitation over Alabama's secession emboldened a "band of desperadoes" who attempted to board the *Crusader*, but the unruffled Maffitt—in counsel with the local newspaper editor and his former father-in-law, both prominent citizens—let it be known that he would fire on anyone who threatened his ship. He sailed for Havana, where he resupplied the vessel out of his own funds, and then went to New York. He was detached from duty on 1 March and joined his family in Washington.[23] By that time the Confederate States of America had been formed, with its temporary capital in Montgomery, Alabama.

Although Maffitt had returned his ship to the government, he was not reimbursed for the personal funds he had spent keeping the vessel at sea. The attack on Fort Sumter on 12 April forced a decision among Southern naval officers who still remained in Federal service. Just six days later, Maffitt sent his children south to his brother-in-law, John Laurens, in Charleston and from there to his cousin at Ellerslie in North Carolina. Surrounded by war preparations in the capital and watching his Southern friends leaving, Maffitt submitted his resignation on 28 April. Discovering that his name was on a list of suspects to be arrested, on 2 May, the day his resignation was accepted, he left his home and considerable personal property, crossed the Potomac, and headed for Montgomery, arriving there on the seventh.[24]

Maffitt met with an indifferent President Davis, who was convinced there would be no war and therefore felt no need for a navy. Even more disconcerting was Maffitt's awkward interview with Secretary of the Navy Stephen R. Mallory who as a U.S. Senator in the 1850s had supported the naval efficiency board that had nearly retired Maffitt. Discouraged, Maffitt finally let himself be persuaded by Secretary of State Robert Toombs and other friends in the government not to leave the capital. On 8 May he was commissioned a lieutenant and ordered to report to Commodore Josiah Tattnall at Savannah, which he did on the following day. Tattnall's "mosquito fleet" of tug boats and river steamers consisted of the flagship *Savannah*, the *Sampson*, the *Resolute*, the *Huntress*, and the *Lady Davis*. Maffitt was appointed flag captain of the css *Savannah*, but he was appalled by the whole squadron, as was his commodore, who made "holy vows that he will yet sink . . . those d—d old tubs off the bar." Maffitt himself described his new

A jaunty John N.
Maffitt, in a portrait
probably made in 1862.
His Confederate naval
officer's cap bears the
insignia of a lieutenant.
(North Carolina Divi-
sion of Archives and
History, Raleigh)

command as an "absurd abortion for a man of war." Also with Maffitt
as midshipmen were his son Eugene and his stepson, Laurens Read.[25]

That summer, work proceeded on the fortifications to protect Port
Royal Sound in South Carolina, the finest anchorage on the southeastern coast. A Union expedition to wrest control of the sound from
the Confederates and establish a base for the South Atlantic Blockading Squadron was organized by Flag Officer Samuel F. DuPont and
General Thomas W. Sherman. On 29 October the Union fleet, carrying over two hundred guns and some twelve thousand soldiers, left
Hampton Roads. Off Cape Hatteras the expedition weathered a severe
storm, arriving off Port Royal in early November. The Confederate fortifications faced the invaders with only one-fifth as much armament—a
total of thirty-five guns at Fort Walker on Hilton Head and Fort Beauregard on Bay Point, and only eight guns in Tattnall's diminutive
squadron.[26] The Federal ships began rendezvousing off the bar on
4 November. While Union ships were marking the channel at the
entrance of the bay near sunset the next day, the aggressive Tattnall

ordered his squadron into battle, exchanging fire with the invaders at long range for about forty minutes. On the sixth, while Tattnall was on shore, Maffitt took the *Savannah* out and engaged in a short duel with the enemy gunboats, sustaining minor damage. Tattnall was furious at the risk taken and suspended Maffitt from command. The next day a destructive four-hour bombardment forced the surrender of the Confederate forts and the withdrawal of the "mosquito fleet" to Savannah and Charleston. Maffitt's son and stepson, assigned to guns at Fort Beauregard, were cited by their commander for "coolness and courage" under fire. Despite his disagreement with Tattnall, Maffitt wrote that Tattnall had "boldly engaged the overwhelming force of the enemy with a gallantry that was unprecedented."[27] In Savannah the two men settled their dispute, which was a result of misunderstood orders. At the request of General Robert E. Lee, who was the newly appointed departmental commander, Maffitt was named as naval aide to Lee's staff. Maffitt began a "very agreeable association" with Lee at his headquarters at Coosawhatchie, South Carolina, where he was assigned for the purpose of mapping roads, building forts, and obstructing the Coosaw River.[28]

Maffitt's many years on the coast survey were a decided asset to his engineering work in South Carolina, but neither he nor General Lee was destined to sit out the war in that backwater department of coastal swamps and rivers. By 1862 it had become obvious to the more prescient Confederate leaders that their agrarian nation must purchase arms and technology abroad to compete successfully with the industrial North. Increasingly, therefore, blockade running was considered crucial to the survival of the Confederacy. At the same time, the Union was effectively sealing the South's major ports, enhancing the strategic importance of obscure inlets and secondary ports. No other officer in the Confederate navy could approach Maffitt's encyclopedic knowledge of the southeastern coast. Furthermore, Maffitt was well known to the influential George A. Trenholm, head of Fraser, Trenholm and Company of Charleston and Liverpool, one of the South's largest overseas trading companies and the leader in private blockade running.[29]

A cargo of Confederate arms stranded in Nassau provided the occasion for Maffitt's introduction to blockade running. Trenholm, who had already recommended Maffitt to the government as an agent to oversee the trade, now offered him the command of the *Cecile*, which was to be used with the *Kate* to run the badly needed arms into the South. Probably at Maffitt's suggestion, a little-known inlet at New

The rakish css *Florida* at anchor in the harbor of Brest, France, in the fall of 1863. (Cape Fear Museum, Wilmington, N.C.)

Smyrna, Florida, became the destination. On 7 January Maffitt took command of the *Cecile*. He left Charleston in late February and reached Florida a little over a week later. By early spring, however, Union forces occupied the Florida coast, leaving only Wilmington and Charleston open on the Atlantic seaboard.[30]

In April Maffitt received his appointment as administrative agent in charge of blockade running, stationed at Nassau in the Bahamas. Leaving from Wilmington and accompanied by his daughter, Florie, Maffitt arrived in Nassau on 4 May and checked into the Royal Victoria Hotel. The talk of the port was the recent arrival from Liverpool of the *Oreto*, reported to be a Confederate cruiser. Sailing Master John Low approached Maffitt that very night with orders from Commander James D. Bulloch, who directed Confederate naval operations in Europe, for the command of the new vessel. Bulloch stressed the importance of Maffitt's mission, saying, "Two small ships can do but little in the way of materially turning the tide of war, but we can do something to illustrate the spirit and energy of our people, and [we] . . . may yet repay upon the enemy some of the injuries his vastly superior force alone has enabled him to inflict upon the States of the Confederacy."[31] The machinations of the U.S. consul led to the *Oreto*'s being detained as being in violation of neutrality and to an admiralty court hearing.

The *Oreto* marked the first success of Commander Bulloch, who had been sent to Liverpool to acquire or build warships for the Confederate States Navy. Using local attorneys and financing arranged through Fraser, Trenholm and Company, Bulloch had been unable to buy appropriate ships; accordingly, in June 1861 a contract was let with William Miller and Sons to build a vessel based on a modified design of Royal Navy fast dispatch boats. Under the ruse that the *Oreto* was being furnished for an Italian firm in Palermo, the vessel began to take shape. Rated at seven hundred tons, her wooden hull 191 feet long, she was three-masted and sloop-rigged. Her distinctive twin funnels served two powerful engines that drove the screw propellers. Under sail and steam she could make better than twelve knots. Despite the best efforts of U.S. minister Charles Francis Adams and his minion, Consul Thomas H. Dudley in Liverpool, to prove that the *Oreto* was in fact a Confederate warship in violation of British neutrality, construction proceeded, and she was launched in January 1862. To foil Adams's spies, the *Oreto* left Liverpool under command of an English captain on 22 March, ostensibly for another sea trial, carrying ladies and gentlemen apparently enjoying a day's outing. All of the passengers except John Low, a sailing master of the Confederate navy, were promptly set ashore, and the *Oreto* left Liverpool bound not for Palermo but for Nassau.[32]

Maffitt kept his new command a secret and entered into the society of Nassau as if he would be there for a long time. Captain Raphael Semmes, later the famed commander of the css *Alabama*, recorded a vivid portrait of Maffitt's part in the Confederate community at the Royal Victoria, saying, "Maffitt in particular, was the life of our household. . . . Being a jaunty, handsome fellow, young enough, in appearance, to pass for the elder brother of his son, a midshipman who was to go with me to the *Alabama*, he was a great favorite of the ladies. . . . Social, gay, and convivial, he was much courted and flattered, and there was scarcely ever a dining or an evening party, at which he was not present. But this was the mere outside glitter of the metal. Beneath all this *bagatelle* and *dolce far niente*, Maffitt was a remarkable man."[33]

Since Maffitt could do nothing that would connect him with the *Oreto*, all transactions involving the controversial ship had to be handled through intermediaries. The armament acquired by Commander Bulloch, four seven-inch rifles, arrived on the steamer *Bahama* and was stored pending the outcome of the hearing. Maffitt's plea to the Navy Department for officers brought a master who proved to be incompetent and a midshipman whose first view of the sea was his voyage to Nassau. Fortunately, the experienced Lieutenant John N. Stribling arrived on the *Bahama*. Stribling had served on the css *Sumter* under Semmes and readily volunteered to join Maffitt. Secretary Mallory's instructions simply told Maffitt to "cruize at discretion" and "do the Enemy's commerce the greatest injury in the shortest time." In the midst of the complicated preparations to get away from Nassau, virulent yellow fever struck the port.[34]

At noon on 2 August the admiralty judge declared the *Oreto* free to leave Nassau, and the next day she steamed to the outer anchorage under the nominal command of Maffitt's stepson, Laurens Read, who actually held the position of paymaster. Late in the afternoon Maffitt and his officers went aboard with the rest of the crew, a total of eighteen. With twelve Union men-of-war in the area and several close at hand, Maffitt escaped around midnight on the fourth. He rendezvoused with Stribling, whose schooner carried the arms and equipment, and the next day the two vessels anchored off Green Cay.

Both officers and men pitched in to work around the clock in the tropical summer heat at the "physically exhausting" task of hoisting the guns aboard and mounting them. Yellow fever brought on board by one of the men began to pass through the crew, claiming the steward's life in mid-month. With no surgeon on board, Maffitt wrote, "Nearly my whole time, day & night was devoted to the sick." Nevertheless, by 17 August the armed vessel was commissioned the css *Florida* and the Confederate flag was hoisted to the crew's lusty cheers.[35]

The *Florida* was a cruiser in name only because, through a packing error, her guns lacked the necessary fittings to be trained and fired. With most of the crew ill or debilitated, she was in an "absolute helpless condition." Maffitt set a course for Cárdenas, Cuba, where the ship was received cordially by Spanish authorities and a physician was immediately located. Maffitt himself fell ill on 22 August and was delirious for nine days. As he began to recover, he was distressed to learn that Laurens was seriously ill. On 30 August Laurens died, and in anguish Maffitt wrote that the "blow came like the raven wings of fate, darkening my very soul to nearly producing a relapse." Four more men were buried with Laurens at Cárdenas. The *Florida* sailed to Havana, but because of the fever season Maffitt found it impossible to recruit a crew. He reluctantly decided to leave Havana for a Confederate port, choosing Mobile because it was closest and was at that time only lightly guarded by blockaders.[36]

On 4 September, late in the afternoon of a bright, cloudless day, the *Florida* arrived off the Mobile bar. The blockade at Mobile was maintained by Commander George H. Preble, an old friend of Maffitt, in the ten-gun USS *Oneida* with two smaller consorts, the USS *Winona* and the schooner USS *Rachael Seaman*. The *Oneida* and *Winona* headed out to intercept the stranger, which appeared to be British and was flying the British red ensign. Nearly too weak to stand, Maffitt was brought on deck, where he ordered full speed ahead, aiming for the *Oneida*. As Maffitt had hoped, to Commander Preble the stranger approaching with "confident boldness" appeared to be a Royal Navy vessel testing the alertness of the blockaders. At eighty yards, the *Oneida* fired a warning shot and ordered the stranger to heave to. When a second shot across the bow brought no response, it was closely followed by a broadside that, fortunately, was aimed high and blew away rigging and hammocks. All of the Yankee vessels then opened fire at will. Maffitt wrote, "In truth, so terrible became the bombardment, every hope of escape fled from my mind."[37] To gain some speed Maffitt sent men aloft to set the topsails, and the enemy gunners switched to shrapnel that devastated the rigging and caused several casualties. Maffitt sent all of the crew below except the officers and the helmsman. To the resolute captain the half hour under fire seemed an eternity. The Union vessels fired fifty rounds, many of them striking their target. Maffitt wrote, "The loud explosions, roar of shot and shell, crashing spars and rigging, mingled with the moans of our sick and wounded, instead of intimidating, only increased our determination to enter the destined harbor."[38] At the critical moment, a light southeast breeze nudged the *Florida* ahead, and she came to rest under the protective guns and cheering garrison of Fort Morgan. Maffitt's adversary, Commander Preble, recorded that the rebel cruiser's escape was due to "superior speed and unparalleled audacity." Colonel William L. Powell of the fort commented that "the scene was brilliant . . . one of the most dashing feats of the war."[39]

With the *Florida* safely at anchor in the bay, Maffitt attended to the needs of his ship and crew. Many crewmen remained ill with fever, and two had been killed and eleven wounded by enemy fire. Described by Maffitt as "a perfect wreck," the cruiser had been riddled with shot and shell and required extensive repairs. Since the fever-ridden ship was quarantined, Admiral Franklin Buchanan, the station commander and the South's foremost naval hero, sent down a steamer to serve as a hospital ship. A few days later he visited the cruiser, bringing his personal congratulations to the plucky crew and praising their "gallan-try" and "cool determined bravery."[40] Secretary Mallory put aside his personal misgivings about Maffitt and wrote, "The escape of your defenseless vessel from an overwhelming force . . . was alone due to the handsome manner in which she was handled, and I do not remember that the union of thorough professional skill, coolness, and daring have ever been better exhibited in a naval dash of a single ship."[41] Maffitt himself was so completely exhausted from his multiple ordeals that he suffered a relapse.

Maffitt's friend, Commander Preble, had not fared so well. His hesitation to open fire on what he believed to be a British ship had allowed a rebel man-of-war to escape, and he became the scapegoat. On orders from President Lincoln he was summarily dismissed from the service. While acknowledging his error, Preble defended his sub-sequent actions to the extent of writing to the president and gathering the support of his commander, Admiral David Farragut. He was rein-stated the next year by the president's order.[42]

The tasks of repairing, arming, and resupplying the *Florida* and recruiting a crew stretched out over three months. The most valuable officer to arrive was the dauntless Lieutenant Charles W. Read, whom Maffitt requested because of the mettle he had demonstrated in the battle for New Orleans. Frustrated by the *Florida*'s lengthy layover and unable to comprehend the difficulties of outfitting in the local situation, Secretary Mallory impetuously removed Maffitt from com-mand in December. Fortunately, President Davis was on a timely visit to Mobile, and with the strong recommendation of Admiral Buchanan, the president responded to Mallory that "Capt. Maffitt brought her in gallantly & *he* will take her out."[43] Early in the new year the rebel raider at last was ready to join her sister ship, the CSS *Alabama*, in her intended career of commerce destruction on the high seas.

Armed with a nine-gun battery of six six-inch rifles, two seven-inch rifles, and a twelve-pound howitzer, the deadly raider, now painted a camouflage gray, was poised at the entrance of the bay as 1863 began, waiting night after night for a stormy cover to help her evade the twelve blockaders gathered to intercept her. The right moment came early on the morning of 16 January. In a stiff wind, bitter cold, and a light mist that turned into rain, the *Florida* made her break for the open sea. The nearly invisible cruiser slipped past the first two blockaders, but while she was passing the third, coal dust flared in the funnel, revealing her position, and touching off pandemonium. With the alarm raised throughout the fleet by drumbeats and flashing lights, the Union ships gave chase. At daybreak six pursuers trailed out behind the swift raider, which was making more than fourteen knots on rugged seas, and as the day passed all but two dropped out of sight. A change of course after dark brought at dawn the relief of an empty horizon between a "foamy sea and black clouds."[44]

On 19 January the *Florida* halted her first prize, the brig *Estelle*, valued at $130,000. With no way to return prizes to blockaded ports, Confederate cruisers had little choice but to destroy them. The *Estelle*'s officers and crew were treated with "generosity and courtesy" and allowed to keep their personal possessions. The brig, with its cargo of sugar and molasses, was torched. The next day the cruiser entered Havana to secure cash and clothing for the crew. The drum and fife entertained the crowds of visitors with "Dixie" and "Bonnie Blue Flag."[45] Two days later the *Florida* cleared Havana and burned the bark *Windward* and the brig *Corris Ann*. When the Havana coal was found to be defective, Maffitt ran up to Nassau to refuel. At both Caribbean ports the cruiser received friendly welcomes and attracted crowds of Southern sympathizers. To Maffitt Nassau was "decidedly a Confederate strong hold," experiencing a boom from the heavy blockade runner traffic to and from Southern destinations. Upon leaving Nassau, the raider picked up a shadow for two days, the USS *Sonoma*, a steamer of nine guns. After shaking her, Maffitt headed north to raid the New England coast but was turned back by a gale off Cape Hatteras. On 12 February the *Florida* intercepted and burned the 1,300-ton clipper ship *Jacob Bell* of New York, just back from a voyage to China and laden with sixteen thousand chests of tea, ten thousand boxes of fireworks, and camphor. The cargo and vessel were valued at $1.5 million, making the *Jacob Bell* the most valuable prize taken by any raider during the entire war. Forty-one passengers and crew were aboard, including two women, for whose comfort Maffitt gave up his cabin. Within four days the prisoners were transferred to a neutral Danish ship.[46]

The *Florida* arrived at Bridgetown, Barbados, on 25 February. The first Confederate vessel to visit the island, she received an enthusiastic greeting, and Governor James Walker invited Maffitt to an official dinner at Government House that night with officers from the island's regiment. The next day the ship entertained a stream of pro-Southern visitors from the city. Maffitt appointed a Confederate agent and then left the island that evening, somewhat befuddled by his overindul-

The css *Florida* burned the rich prize ship *Jacob Bell* on 12 February 1863. *Harper's Weekly* described the *Florida* as "the British pirate." (Naval Historical Center, Washington, D.C.)

gence in the island's legendary rum. After the *Florida* ran afoul of a merchantman as she "bulled among the shipping" while leaving the harbor, the chagrined Maffitt vowed to "abstain entirely hereafter." He was bemused at being "lionized quite extensively—a kind of wondrous curiosity—a Rebel Pirate!"[47] Not until 6 March did the raider garner another prize, the one-hundred-ton clipper ship *Star of Peace* from Calcutta, which carried saltpeter for the Federal army. After the prize was set on fire, she was used as a target for gunnery practice. The raider steamed away late in the afternoon, and when she was about twenty miles away, the saltpeter ignited with high and brilliant flames that "illumined" her sails.[48]

Out on the high seas, striding the deck of a rakish ship, Maffitt captured his exhilaration in a letter to his children, saying, "I am now in the middle of the broad Atlantic—the Sea is running to a great height, & our little Steamer is dashed from billow to billow, like a Race Horse, as if she knew how much was expected of her." Pierced by the poignancy of a long separation from his beloved family, he concluded, "You will not hear from me in a long, *long* time, as our pathway is far, far away from Dixie . . . , but if it *is possible* I will write, so do not be uneasy about me. I have a large work before me, & shall *endeavor* to do it well. . . . And now God bless you my darling children, be true, & good, & let me find you united & very affectionate. My love to all."[49]

After taking and burning the schooner *Aldabaran*, on 28 March Maffitt kept as a tender the bark *Lapwing*, which carried 260 tons of anthracite coal. Lieutenant Samuel W. Averett and a crew of eighteen were placed on board with a twelve-pound howitzer for armament. Commissioned the *Oreto*, the ship was ordered to cruise in tandem some six to eight miles out. Maffitt gave Averett rendezvous points in case they became separated. Two days later the bark *M. J. Colcord* was captured and burned, but the *Florida* lost sight of the *Oreto*. Maffitt did not see the tender until two weeks later when she was sighted just as the *Florida*, which could carry coal for only nine days' steaming, had nearly run out of fuel. Three valuable prizes were burned in late April—the 1,300-ton ship *Commonwealth*, the bark *Henrietta*, and the clipper ship *Oneida* from Shanghai with a $1 million cargo of tea and silks. The *Florida* then anchored at the island of Fernando de Noronha, a Brazilian penal colony, awaiting the arrival of the *Oreto*. Faced with an unfriendly commandant, Maffitt left the island and on 3 May located the *Oreto*, which had captured and bonded for $40,000 the ship *Kate Dyer*. Having determined that the slow *Oreto* was unsuitable to serve as auxiliary, Maffitt decommissioned and stripped the vessel and sent it to Rocas Island to finish coaling later.[50]

On 6 May when the *Florida* stopped the brig *Clarence*, which was carrying a cargo of coffee, Lieutenant Read requested that he be allowed to arm the prize and cruise with her. His daring proposal was to attack Union merchant ships at Hampton Roads. Maffitt provided him with a twelve-pound howitzer, small arms, and twenty men, including an assistant engineer. Read and the new auxiliary cruiser *Clarence* embarked on a phenomenal voyage up the east coast of the United States, burning or bonding a total of twenty prizes in twenty-one days during June and ending with an audacious exploit on the coast of Maine. With only the one howitzer, Read increased his armament by mounting "Quaker guns," wooden spars painted black to resemble cannon. Off Chesapeake Bay he learned from captives that only thoroughly inspected government supply ships were allowed in the well-guarded harbor that had been his primary destination. His alternative was to work his way up the New England coast, destroying as many prizes as he could. The news that a rebel cruiser was on the coast stunned the United States; at home Catherine Edmondston wrote, "Our little Navy has carried dismay & destruction into the heart of

Abolition Commerce." Twice Read changed vessels, first to the bark *Tacony*, which made most of the captures, and then on 24 June to the fishing schooner *Archer*. Two days later, at sunset, he sailed boldly into the harbor of Portland, Maine, with plans to cut out a prize. After midnight Read and his men boarded the two-gun revenue cutter *Caleb Cushing* and sailed her out under a light breeze. The next day two fast steamers loaded with troops caught the Confederates, who were becalmed offshore. After firing the few shot available, Read torched the vessel and abandoned her before she exploded. The *Archer* was recaptured, and Read and his men were imprisoned at Fort Warren in Boston harbor for about a year before being exchanged. The "rebel pirates" had alarmed the eastern seaboard and forced the navy to detach about three dozen ships, which had scurried about aimlessly in search of them.[51]

While Read and his cruisers were wreaking havoc on the Atlantic coast, the *Florida* experienced continued success as well, taking an additional eleven prizes through the summer of 1863. At Recife, the port of Pernambuco, Brazil, Maffitt negotiated a four-day layover for engine repair, although the nervous Brazilian officials were strongly pressured by the United States. At sea, after burning the ship *Crown Point*, the *Florida* sojourned near Rocas Island, hoping the *Lapwing* would appear. Maffitt then headed north toward the Atlantic coastal sea lanes in June, sweeping up the clipper ships *Southern Cross*, *Red Gauntlet*, and *Benjamin F. Hoxie* and the whaler *Varnum H. Hill*. Near New York on 7 July the packet *Sunrise* was bonded. At noon the next day Maffitt sighted the U.S. side-wheel steamer *Ericsson*, which had been chartered to hunt the *Tacony*. Knowing that his armament was superior, Maffitt kept on course until in range, then fired a shot that struck the foretop of the steamer and followed with a broadside. The *Ericsson* narrowly escaped by plunging into a timely fog bank and changing course. When she cleared the fog, the *Florida* was some four miles distant. The chase continued until five o'clock when the raider broke off to investigate another sail nearby. That evening Maffitt took two prizes, the brig *William B. Nash* and the whaling schooner *Rienzi*.[52]

Almost out of coal, Maffitt headed toward Bermuda, docking there on 15 July. The British garrison commander notified Maffitt that he would respond in kind to a salute, so on the morning of the sixteenth the *Florida* gave and received a twenty-one gun salute. The gesture was more a courtesy to the popular Maffitt than a recognition of the

Confederacy. Although the war was not going well, the enormous impact of blockade running on Bermuda's economy ensured the island's continued support of the South. Having been out of touch with the Navy Department since leaving Mobile seven months earlier, Maffitt took the opportunity to catch up on his reports and sent home captured navigation equipment as well as a gift from the crew of tea, coffee, and shoes to the hospitals of Richmond.[53]

The pleasant twelve days of nearly constant socializing, parties, dinners, and conducting tours of the ship came to an end on 27 July when the *Florida*, decked with flowers brought as an island farewell, nosed out of the harbor, whose quays were lined with admiring spectators. Setting a course toward Europe, the raider soon captured and bonded the ship *Francis B. Cutting*. Not long thereafter the engineers noted that long months at sea had begun to take a toll. The propeller shaft was out of line and the engines needed overhauling; furthermore, the copper sheathing of the hull was obviously deteriorating. Since such extensive repairs required that the *Florida* be hauled out in dry dock, Maffitt chose to head for Brest, France. The cruiser paused on the Irish coast to send Lieutenant Averett ahead to make the necessary arrangements with John Slidell, the Confederate commissioner in Paris. In the last two days before docking at Brest the raider burned the ship *Anglo-Saxon* and bonded the packet *Southern Rights*.[54] Nearing the end of her voyage under Maffitt, the *Florida* had taken twenty-three prizes and had outfitted two auxiliary cruisers that captured another twenty-two. Of Maffitt's prizes, nineteen were destroyed, causing millions of dollars in direct losses and in increased insurance costs. An additional toll borne by the United States was the considerable cost of sending dozens of her warships on fruitless searches for the Southern raiders.

When the *Florida* entered the harbor at Brest on 23 August, the French port admiral granted Maffitt permission to remain, although authority for use of the government repair facilities had to come from Paris. After much diplomatic discussion, the cruiser was allowed into the dry dock on 11 September. To dispel the notion promulgated by U.S. agents that the *Florida* was a pirate ship, Maffitt opened his vessel to unlimited visitation. The French were won over by his personal charm and gentlemanly air as well as by the sharp observance of naval routine on the ship.

When correspondence from Richmond finally caught up with him at Brest, Maffitt was gratified to learn that he had been promoted to

commander, dating from 29 April, for "gallant and meritorious conduct" in his exploits at Mobile Bay and on the high seas. Mallory
offered his personal congratulations on "the brilliant success" of Maffitt's cruise and on his "skill, courage, and coolness."[55] Maffitt's health,
however, had finally failed him. The lingering effects of his bout with
yellow fever and the stress of the voyage had affected his heart, and he
requested that he be relieved from duty for reasons of health. On
17 September he was granted medical leave and detached from his
command. With deep regret and bittersweet memories, he left the
vessel that had been his home for fourteen months and on which he
had experienced so much excitement, renown, and pleasure, but also
tragedy and pain. Maffitt and the *Florida* had reached their pinnacle of
fame. The ship would go to sea again and take a dozen more prizes;
Maffitt would have more to do for his country; but the Confederacy
had less than a year and a half left.[56]

On the recommendation of a physician in Paris, Maffitt took a
recuperative trip to Sweden, after which he went to London, where he
learned from Commander Bulloch that he was to be assigned duty on
blockade runners. He and Bulloch traveled to Greenock, Scotland, on
the Clyde River to inspect two swift steamers that had been designed
especially for blockade running. Bulloch had named one of them
Florie, for Maffitt's daughter, and the other *Lilian*. Bearing a low
silhouette, these long, narrow vessels could achieve fourteen knots.
Near the end of the year Maffitt was assigned the *Florie*, which was
under contract to the state of Georgia, and he left for Nassau. Rough
weather apparently damaged the vessel, for she sailed instead to Halifax, Nova Scotia, where she underwent repairs, and thence to Bermuda, where Maffitt switched to the *Lilian* for a race to Wilmington
with the *Florie*. Leaving on 1 June on a bright cloudless day, the sister ships fairly flew over the water. Briefly distracted by a vessel he
thought was on fire, Maffitt arrived near Fort Fisher about dawn on the
fourth day out. Since the fort's lights were not visible, the gray camouflaged *Lilian* lay offshore most of the day. In the afternoon a blockader
sighted her, and the chase was on. After shaking her pursuer in two
hours, the *Lilian* circled back toward the coast at dusk. Although she
nearly ran into another blockader, the *Lilian* anchored safely under
the fort's guns that night, beating the *Florie* by a day.[57]

Maffitt's 1864 homecoming to the booming port of Wilmington,
which was jammed with blockade runners, was his first visit to the
Confederacy in eighteen months. He reported immediately to the

The *Lilian* outruns a blockader near Wilmington. Maffitt is pictured on the paddle wheel, at the left, in a dark suit. (North Carolina Division of Archives and History, Raleigh)

Navy Department in Richmond and was given command of the celebrated ironclad css *Albemarle* at Plymouth, North Carolina, replacing his friend, Commander James W. Cooke. Under Cooke the *Albemarle* had earned her reputation as one of the South's most formidable ironclads, winning a clear-cut naval victory at Plymouth, which enabled the port to be retaken by Confederate forces, and battling a vastly superior Union gunboat fleet to a tactical draw on Albemarle Sound. True to his reputation for audacity, Maffitt was eager to get into action and was happy to have verbal orders to attack the enemy. The local army commander, however, was so afraid to risk the *Albemarle* that requests for caution quickly flowed up the chain of command to the secretary of war and thence to Secretary Mallory. To his credit, Mallory responded that the decision for the best use of the ironclad rested with its commander. Maffitt made a few forays to the mouth of the Roanoke, but the Union fleet kept its distance. His only offensive action was to plan a small-boat commando raid for some of his men, who burned the mail boat on the Dismal Swamp Canal.[58]

Occasional river cruises and a mail boat raid were pathetic achievements for the former commander of the *Florida*. Upon hearing of his appointment, a local diarist had written, "Poor gentleman, I pity him! How he will chafe cooped up in this narrow crooked river after roaming at will the broad bosom of the sea in search of Yankee commerce."[59] Well aware that the talented Maffitt's skill and experience were being wasted in static river defense, on 9 September Secretary Mallory ordered Maffitt to Wilmington to take command of one of the new class of blockade runners that would be operated by the government.

Upon his arrival in Wilmington, Maffitt learned that he would command the *Owl*, which was due in port soon. While waiting for her, Maffitt had time to submit reports on the *Florida* and visit his family in Fayetteville. The *Owl* arrived on 1 December, enabling Maffitt to leave port before Christmas and deliver 780 bales of cotton to Bermuda. There the blockade runners anxiously awaited news of the outcome of the Federal attack on Fort Fisher. When word came that the fort had survived a major bombardment, the *Owl* and five other blockade runners left immediately for Cape Fear. Unbeknown to them, a second expedition hurled another massive bombardment and landed troops that took the fort on 15 January 1865 in a day of bloody hand-to-hand fighting. That night Maffitt brought the *Owl* into Old Inlet from the south and anchored near Fort Caswell. An officer from the fort confirmed that Fort Fisher had fallen and that Federal vessels were anchored close at hand across the river. Fort Caswell was being evacuated and would be blown up. Maffitt quickly retraced his route, although he was pursued for a time by the sole blockader in the inlet. Of his five companions from Bermuda, three were decoyed into the inlet by signals from the fort, and only the wily Captain John Wilkinson escaped. Maffitt reached Bermuda on 21 January and was able to prevent more runners' departure and almost certain capture.[60]

Since Charleston was now the only major east coast port still open, Maffitt set a course for South Carolina on 26 January. Attempting to enter Charleston through Maffitt's Channel in a mist, the *Owl* nearly collided with a blockader and had to sheer off. The startled enemy fired a broadside that was high but ripped into the bulwarks and the engine room, wounding twelve men. As the *Owl* disappeared into the night, she left the blockaders in total confusion, firing into each other. The unflappable Maffitt headed to Nassau to repair his ship.[61]

From Nassau, Maffitt decided to reach the last open Confederate port, Galveston, Texas. En route he first stopped in North Carolina to drop off a dispatch bearer from Europe and then steamed to Havana. Finally arriving at Galveston, he ran aground at the harbor entrance.

Under fire from blockaders but aided by a local gunboat, the *Owl* made port and delivered her cargo on 5 May. Maffitt returned to Havana, where as senior officer in the region he was joined by Lieutenant J. Pembroke Jones, who brought him his last orders and dispatches from Richmond. Maffitt abandoned any thought of running further cargoes into what was left of the collapsing Confederacy and sailed for Liverpool to turn over his command to Fraser, Trenholm and Company. There in a ceremony on board the *Owl* on 14 July, Maffitt thanked his crew, dismissed them from the service, and lowered the Confederate colors for the last time.[62]

Maffitt himself, "deeply depressed" over the failure of the Confederacy, simply was not ready to ask for pardon from his former enemies. For the time being, he and Eugene remained in Liverpool, where Maffitt studied for and passed the examination leading to a British master's license. On 7 March 1866 he secured a position as captain of the merchant steamer *Widgeon*, sailing to South American ports. Over the next year the *Widgeon* was leased to Brazil as a transport in its war with Paraguay. Some of Maffitt's most vivid nightmares of the Civil War were reenacted when smallpox broke out among the troops he was ferrying. Despite the high pay, he was so sickened by the savagery of the conflict that he resigned in March 1867.[63]

Returning at last to New York, the apprehensive Maffitt was pleased to be received cordially by his former comrades in the U.S. Navy at the Brooklyn Navy Yard. He sought the support of his navy friends for a presidential pardon, which was eventually granted. As predicted by his longtime friend George Preble, it took time because he had done the "merchant marine too much damage."[64] Maffitt continued on to Wilmington, joining his daughter, Florie, now Mrs. Joshua G. Wright, and his son Eugene. Purchasing a 212-acre farm on Wrightsville Sound, which he dubbed the Moorings, Maffitt brought together his stepdaughter, Mary Read; his son Colden Rhind; and Eugene and his new bride, Catherine Martin.

At the time of Eugene's engagement, Maffitt had been charmed by his future daughter-in-law's sister, Emma Martin. In January 1869 Eugene's wife invited Emma to the Moorings for a prolonged visit. On the six-mile carriage drive from town, Maffitt and Emma were beset by a severe rainstorm, in the course of which he wrapped her in his faded naval cloak. Emma remarked that the cloak surely had a romantic past, to which Maffitt replied that indeed it had shielded the Queen of Greece and had been to Europe, Palestine, and "among the Pyramids." Emma challenged him to "become its historian," citing the enthralling stories of naval life with which he entertained family and friends. Maffitt replied that he might attempt it if she would be his "amanuensis," or secretary. Much to her surprise, the next day he handed her the beginning of what would become *Nautilus, or Cruising Under Canvas* (1871), Maffitt's novel about his early voyage as a midshipman on the *Constitution*. Thus began a literary partnership that resulted in their marriage on 23 November 1870.[65] His friend John McIntosh Kell, first lieutenant on the *Alabama*, wrote to Maffitt that Emma had inspired his pen "with the fire of poetry and romance."[66] Despite their age difference of twenty-eight years and the initial opposition of both families, the marriage was a perfect match, and it produced three children—Mary Read, Clarence Dudley, and Robert Strange.

The Maffitts lived a rich, full life at the Moorings, raising their new family, farming, and writing. Theirs was always an active and interesting household, with the Maffitt youngsters, the various older children and their spouses, and frequent guests, including former colleagues from the navies of both the United States and the Confederate States. Among Maffitt's farming ventures were peanuts, a vineyard of scuppernong grapes, an extensive orchard, and fields of strawberries, blackberries, and raspberries. Family outings centered on the nearby sound, with frequent sailing and fishing trips. Maffitt kept up an extensive correspondence and continued to write, publishing reminiscences of Confederate naval life and blockade running, as well as sketches of Raphael Semmes and James W. Cooke. His unpublished manuscripts included a novel about West Indian piracy during the War of 1812.[67]

Only twice did Maffitt become involved in public affairs after the war. In October 1869 the controversial armed steamer *Hornet* or *Cuba*, owned by the New York Cuban junta, which promoted Cuban independence, sailed into Wilmington seeking coal to continue a voyage south. The federal government seized the vessel for violating U.S. neutrality. After prolonged court wrangling, the ship was ordered back to New York. Maffitt readily agreed to go to sea one last time for this New York voyage. If he entertained any thoughts of another adventure on the high seas, they were dispelled in the futile negotiations with the junta.[68] A more pleasant break in his agricultural and literary routine was a journey to Washington to give testimony on behalf of his lifelong friend George H. Preble at a court of inquiry looking into the *Florida*'s brilliant run through the Mobile blockade. Preble, who had been so unjustly dismissed from the navy, had been reinstated, but in 1872 he sought to have the blemish completely removed from his record. Maffitt's detailed testimony of the heavy damage to the *Florida* by the blockaders was a major factor in Preble's exoneration and eventual promotion to rear admiral.[69]

Maffitt's last years were punctuated with personal loss, injury, and impecunity. His beloved daughter Florie, who of all of his children seemed to be most like him, died in 1883. Democrat Grover Cleveland's election as president the next year led to Maffitt's being nominated locally to the U.S. Customs House, but he was turned down. Suffering from Bright's disease, a chronic inflammation of the kidneys, he became unable to manage the farm. To cut expenses, the family moved into a modest house in Wilmington in 1885. Maffitt's physical deterioration brought on such deep depression that he spent three months in the state mental hospital in Raleigh. His son Eugene died in January 1886, about a month before the captain returned home for the last time. A few days before his death on 15 May, the now frail captain sat up, wrapped in his fabled cloak, and told his family, "The ship is ready, the sails are set, and the wind is favorable; all we are waiting for is Mr. Lambert to come and ask God's blessing upon us; then we will heave anchor and away on the billows."[70]

*An officer of
extraordinary
ability and enterprise.*
—*Jefferson Davis,
1881*

John Taylor Wood

The Night Raider Seizes the *Underwriter*

From the opening guns of the Civil War the Chesapeake Bay had been the setting for intermittent naval raids and sabotage of navigational aids, but on the dark night of 7 October 1862 Lieutenant John Taylor Wood introduced a Confederate naval tactic, "partisan warfare at sea," that would evolve into modern amphibious commando warfare.[1] Wood had conceived his operations out of the maritime tradition of cutting-out, or using small boats to take a ship by means of a surprise night assault. Long practiced by pirates, privateers, and navies, cutting-out was perfected by the Royal Navy in the Napoleonic Wars and used by the U.S. Navy in the North African Barbary Wars. The tactic was ideally suited to the Confederate navy, which lacked both money and time to build a fleet capable of matching the vastly superior one of its foe. Wood's proposal for shore-based small-boat raids in the Chesapeake appealed to Secretary of the Navy Stephen R. Mallory's instinct to take the war to the enemy and provided an excellent stopgap measure until the construction of Confederate ironclad fleets could be finished. To Wood's specifications, ships' boats were built in the Richmond Navy Yard, and wagons were especially outfitted to carry the boats overland, creating a navy on wheels that could be moved to any of the many peninsulas in the Chesapeake region.

On the evening of 1 October Wood and his well-trained contingent left Richmond with the Potomac River as their destination. Arriving on the south bank of the river, Wood sent out search parties to locate a potential target. After a frustrating wait, on the afternoon of 7 October the schooner *Frances Elmore* was spotted at anchor off Pope's Creek on the Maryland shore. At dusk the boats quickly crossed the river, glided silently alongside the unsuspecting schooner, and made fast with grappling hooks over the bulwark. With pistols and cutlasses in hand, the rebel sailors spilled over the rail, quickly overwhelming the crew of seven. Finding the schooner loaded with hay for the military, the raiders set fire to the vessel, bundled the prisoners into their boats, and vanished into the night, leaving Union rescuers to puzzle out what had happened to the transport and her crew.[2]

John Taylor Wood, one of the most charismatic and creative naval commanders of the war, was born 13 August 1830 at Fort Snelling, Iowa Territory, near present St. Paul, Minnesota, the son of army surgeon Robert C. Wood and Anne M. Taylor. Through his mother, Wood had powerful political connections. She was the daughter of General Zachary Taylor, Mexican War hero and president of the United States from 1849 to 1850, and the sister of Sarah K. Taylor, the first wife of Jefferson Davis. Wood's mother was born in Louisiana, while his father was from New England. Like most military families, the Woods moved about the country, developing no particular allegiance to any section but retaining strong feelings for the nation as a whole. The state in which Wood spent most time as a youth was Louisiana, from which his family moved to Washington, D.C., when his grandfather was elected president and Wood's father, a colonel, became the nation's assistant surgeon general.[3]

Pursuing a military career was a family tradition, although Wood was the first in his family to choose the navy over the army. His younger brother, Robert C. Wood Jr., attended West Point and was a lieutenant in the Second United States Cavalry.[4] Unlike his older contemporaries who learned seamanship through time-honored service as an apprentice midshipman on a man-of-war, Wood attended the naval school at Annapolis, which had been established in 1845 under Commandant Franklin Buchanan. Upon application to the navy, he was notified on 7 April 1847 that he should report to Annapolis for an examination. He qualified for entrance to the naval school and an appointment as acting midshipman in July. Barely seventeen, he was assigned the next month to sea duty on the forty-four-gun frigate USS *Brandywine*, which sailed to Brazil. There he was ordered to the ship-of-the-line USS *Ohio* for a nearly three-year cruise in the Pacific. When the *Ohio* returned to Boston in the spring of 1850, the twenty-year-old Wood established his residence in Baltimore and then received orders to report to Annapolis for further study.[5]

After five months of schooling, Wood went aboard the modern sloop USS *Germantown*, cruising off Africa to suppress the slave trade. From the *Germantown* Wood was assigned to the ten-gun brig USS *Porpoise*, which engaged in a joint patrol with the British schooner HMS *Bright*. The importation of slaves was outlawed in the United States, but demand in Brazil, Cuba, and the Spanish West Indies fueled the trade, for which slavers used swift schooners manned by Spanish and Portuguese crews. While sailing off Liberia, the *Porpoise* was sent to the Gulf of Guinea to monitor the vast Niger River delta. On patrol the *Porpoise* sighted a brigantine at dawn and began a day-long chase in fickle wind, which ended when continual firing of the bow chaser brought down enough of the slaver's rigging to cripple her. Wood commanded the second of two boats sent over to board the vessel. After a scuffle that prevented the captain from destroying the ship's papers and possibly the vessel itself, Wood took charge of the prize, his first command. Responding to dreadful "moans, cries, and rumblings" below decks, he ordered the hatches opened and was nearly overwhelmed by the "sickening and overpowering" stench of almost 400 desperate men, women, and children, "gasping, struggling for breath, . . . all expressing terrible suffering." The unfortunate captives were quickly brought on deck, and with the aid of the *Porpoise*'s doctor, some water, and a little whiskey, all but seventeen were revived.

Ordered to sail to Monrovia, the capital of Liberia, which had been colonized by freed American slaves, Wood was directed to leave the Africans under the protection of the local authorities. He gained the confidence of his passengers by taking excellent care of the ill and providing plenty of rice and yams, fresh air, and exercise for all of them. Through an interpreter he learned that the slaves had come from the interior and had been sold by their kings, chiefs, or families to Arab traders, who had brought them to the coast to be bought by the slave ship captain.

After weathering a severe gale, Wood brought his vessel into Monrovia. Initially relieved at safely making port, he was stymied by the local bureaucracy, which he circumvented by meeting face to face with President Joseph Roberts. In time, Wood received directions to deliver his charges to the governor of Grand Bassa, about 150 miles down the coast. There, after much palavering with the governor and the more powerful tribal chief King George, he landed his reluctant passengers, who were convinced, with some justification, that they would be reenslaved by the king and refused at first to leave the ship. Although it was a "painful" experience, Wood had his orders. He, too, believed that his charges would not long remain free, but the best he could do for them was to hold the king accountable for their freedom and threaten action by the navy if they were not protected.[6]

Returning to New York on the *Porpoise* in July 1852, Wood was ordered on 1 October to the Annapolis school, which was now called the U.S. Naval Academy. He completed his academy training with a warrant as passed midshipman, dating from 10 June 1853. Following a three-month leave, he reported in December to the Mediterranean Squadron under Commodore Silas H. Stringham, a forty-year veteran and a stern disciplinarian, and was assigned to the sloop USS *Cumberland* in Genoa, Italy. His eighteen-month tour of duty in the Mediterranean ended with his return to Boston in July 1855, after which he served as assistant commandant of midshipmen at the naval academy. Subsequently he was commissioned a lieutenant with a date of rank of 16 September 1855.[7]

It is not known when Wood began to court Lola Mackubin, the daughter of George and Eleanor Mackubin of Annapolis, but he was in Annapolis, attending the naval school, on three different occasions between 1847 and 1853. Lola's father had been state treasurer of Maryland for many years, and the family had some prominence in the society of Annapolis, the state capital. It is likely that Wood's posting to the academy in 1855 and his rapid promotion influenced their decision to marry. Their wedding took place on 2 November 1856, when Lola was twenty-one years old. As a young naval couple the Woods were fortunate to be together on shore the first year and a half of their marriage. In September 1857 their first child, Anne Mackall, was born.[8]

John Taylor Wood,
photographed in 1861,
when he was on the fac-
ulty of the U.S. Naval
Academy at Annapolis.
His uniform is that of a
lieutenant in the U.S.
Navy. (Nimitz Library,
United States Naval
Academy, Annapolis,
Md.)

Since no promising naval officer wanted to be left ashore too long, at
his request Wood received orders for sea duty as gunnery officer under
Captain Samuel Barron on the new forty-gun steam frigate USS *Wabash*, the flagship of the Mediterranean Squadron. Lola traveled to
New York to be with her husband the last few weeks before the
Wabash departed on 1 June 1858. The voyage began in the West
Indies, with visits to Haiti and Port Royal, Jamaica, followed by an
extended stay at Key West. By late August the *Wabash* was at Gibraltar, from where the squadron moved on to Marseilles and Genoa. The
separation from his family was harder than Wood had anticipated, and
he began to think about leaving the navy, writing to Lola, "As things
stand at present in the Navy, there is little chance for advancement, I
am a Lt. now & will be nothing else for 20 years certainly, should I
remain."[9]

While sailing down the coast to Naples in 1858, Wood took the
opportunity to visit the great marble quarries at Carrara and found in a
sculptor's workshop a bust of his grandfather, Zachary Taylor, which
he purchased and sent home.[10] From Naples the squadron visited
many of the ports of southern Europe and the Middle East before
returning to Italy. At Leghorn (Livorno) on the Tuscan coast, Wood

received on 8 August a letter from Lola that indicated all was well at home. He wrote to her about a rigorous and highly successful gunnery practice on the ninth in which he endeavored to perfect his craft, saying, "I never saw anything like it on board ship, the tar[get] was knocked away completely three times, my Division struck it six times, my large Pivot gun fired like a rifle. I can almost knock a man over at the distance of a mile."[11]

The next letter from home, however, contained the dreadful news that their little Anne had died on 18 July. Devastated, Wood replied to Lola, "I thought I never would be reconciled to this world again. I felt ready to die"; but Lola's strength and courage bolstered him, giving him, as he told her, "new life[,] for I did not think you would be able to stand this blow." The experience deepened Wood's religious faith, which sustained him throughout his life, and upon his return home he was confirmed in the Episcopal Church. At first Lola considered joining him in the Mediterranean, but he finally discouraged her coming since he would be home within a few months anyway. Leaving for the United States in November, the *Wabash* arrived in New York on 16 December 1859, and Wood sent a telegram the same day to summon Lola to the Astor House for a reunion.[12]

Now firmly committed to staying at home, Wood sought a teaching position at the naval academy, using his father's influence as well as that of his other political contacts in Washington. Throughout January he moved back and forth between Washington and Maryland. Amid shopping trips with Lola in Washington, he accompanied his father in paying a call on President James Buchanan. He also observed in Congress "the fractious speeches on the sectional issue" and "a disgraceful scene of a brawl" in which a congressman drew a pistol. He sadly mused, "I do not know what will become of the Country. I have great fears that its days are numbered." The only member of Congress whose speeches favorably impressed him was his uncle Jefferson Davis from Mississippi, whom Wood characterized as "the ablest man in the Senate."[13] Anticipating that he would secure the appointment to the academy staff, Wood purchased a farm just outside Annapolis, which he named Woodland. Also thinking of a possible future outside the navy, Wood began to develop his land, hiring laborers to cut timber, prepare fields, and plant an orchard. The Woods planned to settle into a congenial society surrounded by family and friends. Lola's uncle, Dr. Richard Mackubin, lived on the nearby plantation of Strawberry Hill, and Elk Ridge, also in the vicinity, was home to her sister Mary Cass and Mary's husband, Jim Hammond. Lola's widowed father dwelt in Baltimore, and Wood family members resided in Washington.

A final visit to Secretary of the Navy Isaac Toucey brought Wood's welcome posting to the naval academy as instructor of naval tactics and nautical gunnery. He reported for duty on 14 February 1860. The Woods rented a home in Annapolis but continued to manage Woodland, which was worked with hired laborers. The only slaves the Woods owned were a cook and a house servant. Wood's ever-increasing commitment to the many activities of the farm caused him to comment about his teaching, "I do not take a great deal of interest in it. I have not the same relish for my duties I once had."[14] His strenuous effort to avoid a cruise with the academy cadets was an indication of his split loyalty between the navy and his home and hearth. Since his separation from Lola and his absence on the death of their first child, Wood had been disenchanted with his naval career; and if the country had remained at peace, he probably would have ended his days as a Maryland farmer and businessman.

The stirring political events of the presidential election of 1860 intruded into Wood's comfortable world that summer when the Democratic convention at Charleston splintered into factions over the issue of extending slavery in the territories. Three separate conventions were subsequently held in Baltimore. Although aware of the convention for Constitutional Union candidate John Bell, Wood attended the Democratic convention (at which his uncle Richard Taylor was a Louisiana delegate) that nominated Stephen A. Douglas of Illinois. Since Douglas was an unacceptable candidate for the South, the Southern delegates withdrew and reconvened to nominate the sitting vice president, John C. Breckinridge of Kentucky. In August Wood escorted President Buchanan and Secretary Toucey on a visit to Annapolis. A week later he embarked on a trip to Minnesota to visit scenes of his childhood. From St. Paul he returned by way of Chicago, Niagara Falls, and another former home in Buffalo, New York. Lola, who was pregnant, remained at home.[15]

The excitement generated by the four-way race for the presidency and the deepening crisis in the Union caused growing concern in the Wood family. Undecided between Bell and Breckinridge, Wood sought guidance in late September from his brother and father as well as Senator Davis. By mid-October he was of a mind to "cling to the Union, let what will come," but he also stated, "The country is getting fairly awkward in regard to the Division between North and South. I hope and pray they may be stifled." Wood predicted that the election of Republican Abraham Lincoln would mean that "three or four states at least will go out of the Union." His own future depended on Maryland's stance, but Wood began to lean toward the Southern viewpoint.[16] On 11 November, when a son, Zachary Taylor Wood, was born in the middle of the national crisis, Wood wrote, "I pray this may long continue a bright and joyful day in the family."[17]

Providing the catalyst for further secession, South Carolina left the Union in December 1860. Six more Southern states followed by February 1861. Although his father and father-in-law stood for the Union and Maryland was deeply divided, Wood's affinity for the South was reinforced by discussions with Stephen R. Mallory of Florida and Davis, both of whom had resigned their seats in the U.S. Senate when their states seceded and both of whom urged him to join the Southern cause.

In early February the seven seceded states organized the Confederate States of America in Montgomery, Alabama, electing Jefferson Davis as provisional president. Baltimore was so heavily secessionist that president-elect Lincoln, en route to Washington for his inauguration, had to pass through the city in disguise. Wood was not immune to the rapid acceleration of events in March and April that culminated in the firing on Fort Sumter in Charleston harbor and the secession of four more states. His divided loyalties left him unsure as to his future course of action. In late March he wrote, "I trust that we shall avoid a conflict. I never could engage in one"; but after Fort Sumter fell, he reflected, "I feel perfectly miserable; belong neither to North or South."[18] He spent the following evening discussing "the present disrupting situation" with his father, who was "for the Union unconditionally," a fact that caused Wood to declare, "I wish sometimes I could feel so."[19] Since Maryland, surrounding the national capital, could not be allowed to secede, Federal troops were sent in force to occupy Baltimore, precipitating a riot and inflicting civilian casualties.

After the secession of Virginia, Wood wrote: "We are fearing an attack here and every preparation has been made for one. From the North and the South all are struggling to reach Washington. Near it a great battle must be fought. My sympathies for the South are becoming more and more enlisted. I must soon quit."[20] On Sunday, 21 April, the day that young Zack was christened, a Massachusetts regiment landed in Annapolis and towed the *Constitution* to Newport, Rhode Island, where the naval academy was to be relocated. Wood was in-

censed, writing, "I have resigned. My blood is boiling over with indig-
nation, but I must keep quiet."[21] In Washington he reassured his father
of his determination to "maintain a neutral position between the members of my family," but the breach widened between father and son.
The family was already split, for Wood's brother Robert had resigned
from the U.S. Cavalry to join the staff of Confederate General Braxton
Bragg, and his uncle Richard Taylor from Louisiana, whom Wood
highly respected, became a Confederate brigadier general.

Through the summer Wood's unease intensified as Maryland's former governor and other officials were arrested on suspicion of dis-
loyalty; but the agricultural life at Woodland, gathering crops and
tending livestock, went on as if the stirring events of the war were in
some other land. By September, however, Wood reached his decision,
buried the family silver, and on the night of the fourteenth crossed
the Potomac River with Lola and Zack in an open boat that nearly
swamped during an unexpected squall. The family made it overland to
Fredericksburg and then by train to Richmond.[22] At the Confederate
capital Wood was warmly received by President Davis and sent over to
renew his acquaintance with Secretary Mallory. His commission as a
lieutenant in the C.S. Navy was dated from 4 October. Wood had
joined the Confederacy so late that little was available except an assignment to the Potomac River batteries at Evansport, Virginia, on Quan-
tico Creek and Aquia Creek. He had just enough time to find housing
for Lola and Zack in Petersburg before he reported for duty.[23]

While Wood was refining his considerable gunnery skills on the
Potomac, Secretary Mallory had embarked the Confederate navy on
an enterprise that would change world history—the construction of
the ironclad ram css *Virginia*. When Federal forces inexplicably abandoned the Gosport Navy Yard near Norfolk in May 1861, the facility
was only partially destroyed. The occupying rebels garnered intact
machinery, heavy equipment, supplies, about twelve hundred naval
guns, and the invaluable dry dock. Most of the damaged ships present
were aged wooden sailing vessels of little value; the sole exception was
the modern steam frigate uss *Merrimack*, which had been in the yard
for refitting. She was found sunk and burned to the waterline but still
salvageable. The *Merrimack* hulk was raised and placed in the dry
dock. To the plans of Lieutenant John M. Brooke and under the
supervision of naval constructor John L. Porter, she was reconstructed
as an ironclad steam-powered ram, mounting a battery of ten heavy
guns. The powerful vessel was armored with four inches of iron plate,

The Chesapeake

but the defective engines, although rebuilt by chief engineer William P. Williamson, remained her weakness.[24]

The largest Southern ironclad to see service, the *Virginia* was just over 262 feet long. At 178 feet, her armored casemate alone was longer than the later css *Albemarle*. The *Virginia* was the flagship of the energetic Captain Franklin Buchanan, commodore of the James River defenses. His first officer was the gunnery expert Lieutenant Catesby ap R. Jones, who had outfitted and armed the vessel. Secretary Mallory, Commodore Buchanan, and Lieutenant Jones assembled an outstanding group of officers eager to serve on a vessel that, although untried, appeared to have the potential to alter the course of the war. Wood was detached from the Potomac batteries on 20 November, took a holiday leave with Lola, who was again pregnant, and reported for duty at Gosport in January. He was assigned the important post commanding the *Virginia*'s aft pivot gun, a newly cast seven-inch Brooke rifle.[25]

Nearing completion, the giant ironclad was launched on 17 February 1862. About a week later, at the Brooklyn Navy Yard, a smaller armored craft of John Ericsson's extremely radical design, incorporating a revolving gun turret, was commissioned the USS *Monitor*. These ships carried the hopes of their respective countries, and the race was on to see which would first be ready for combat. In the final stages of arming and outfitting, the *Virginia* was still woefully short of seamen, but over the next few weeks she would be manned by a patched-together crew from the army, which had swept up many experienced sailors. Also available was the remnant of crews from the recently vanquished North Carolina "mosquito fleet." Wood was sent to the front lines at Yorktown, where he recruited eighty sailors and gunners for the ship. With workmen cluttering the *Virginia* right up until she sailed on her trial run, there was scant room or time to train the crew, test the engines, or even fire the guns. Wood and his friend Lieutenant Charles C. Simms, who was in charge of the bow rifle, trained their gun crews on the nineteen-gun battery of the receiving ship, the former *United States*, the venerable frigate now called the *Confederate States*.[26]

On 8 March 1862 the *Virginia* cast off for Hampton Roads on her maiden voyage, which most of the onlookers thought was a test run. Leaving the harbor, the great ironclad was "saluted by the waving of caps and handkerchiefs; but no voice broke the silence of the scene; all hearts were too full for utterance." As the *Virginia* steamed down the Elizabeth River, accompanied by the gunboats *Beaufort* and *Raleigh* and a fleet of spectator craft, the soldiers in the batteries stood on the ramparts cheering her on. The officers were distressed that the anemic engines could drive the heavy ironclad no more than five knots, and the great weight and deep draft of the ship made the helm so sluggish that it took half an hour to turn. Nevertheless, the commodore, "Old Buck," believed the strengths of the weapon he commanded far outweighed its weaknesses, and he was ready to do battle.[27]

Steering directly across the great bay, the *Virginia* headed straight for Newport News and the unsuspecting USS *Congress* (fifty guns) and the USS *Cumberland* (thirty guns), which were festooned with drying clothes. Down the bay near Fortress Monroe were the USS *Minnesota*, the USS *Roanoke*, the USS *St. Lawrence*, and several gunboats. Sallying out of the James River, the Confederate gunboats—the CSS *Patrick Henry*, the CSS *Jamestown*, and the CSS *Teaser*—engaged the shore batteries and then rendezvoused with the *Virginia*. At less than a mile the Union ships and shore batteries opened fire on the peculiar vessel, which to a Union officer on the *Congress* looked like "the roof of a very big barn belching forth smoke as from a chimney on fire."[28] The buttoned-up *Virginia* steamed inexorably on without returning fire until at close range the bow rifle opened on the *Cumberland*, dismounting a cannon, and a broadside was directed into the *Congress* in passing. The Union return fire was ineffective, glancing or bouncing off the slanted casemate of the ironclad. Boring in on the *Cumberland*, the *Virginia* rammed her, opening a hole in her side "wide enough to drive in a horse and cart." As the *Virginia* backed away and turned, leaving her broken ram in the stricken enemy, Wood fired his stern rifle at the *Congress* for the first time. The *Cumberland* sank rapidly, with the crew manning the guns until the decks were submerged. Wood wrote that "no ship was ever fought more gallantly."[29]

Pounded for over an hour by the *Virginia* and her consorts, the *Congress* finally surrendered after her commander was killed. As the *Beaufort* and the *Raleigh* came alongside to receive the surrender of the *Congress*, Union troops and shore batteries opened fire, killing and wounding friend and foe alike. Buchanan was so angered by this violation of a truce that he ordered the *Congress* to be bombarded by heated shot until she was on fire. She burned all afternoon, and during the night disintegrated in a spectacular explosion. When Buchanan was wounded by rifle fire, Lieutenant Jones took command. All of the large Union ships coming to aid the *Congress* had grounded, but the *Roanoke* and the *St. Lawrence* had been towed to safety, leaving the *Minnesota* alone in harm's way. Although the *Minnesota* had been damaged by the *Virginia*'s fire, it was decided that it was too late in the day to risk venturing into shallow water to destroy her. The victorious *Virginia* anchored for the evening near Confederate batteries at Sewell's Point.[30] The Confederates listed thirty-four casualties, and the *Virginia*, the target of a hundred cannon, had suffered only superficial damage. When the wounded were landed, Wood telegraphed Lola, "Thank Heaven all well. Great victory." Union killed and wounded, mostly on the *Congress* and the *Cumberland*, totaled over three hundred, about two-thirds of them dead or missing.[31] That night the *Monitor* fortuitously arrived with orders to save the *Minnesota*.

The next morning as the *Virginia* steamed toward the *Minnesota* to finish her, the bizarre-looking *Monitor* appeared. To Wood she seemed a "pigmy" beside the adjacent frigate. Upon seeing the newcomer, a Confederate sailor blurted out, "A tin can on a shingle!"[32] The two ships, the first armored vessels in history to engage in combat, approached each other warily and then began firing as rapidly as they could. After four hours of continuous shelling at distances ranging from half a mile to point-blank, no more than minor damage was done to either vessel. The *Virginia* attempted to ram and board her pesky opponent, but the nimble *Monitor* maneuvered away from her ponderous foe. Wood finally scored a direct hit on the pilot house of the *Monitor*, damaging it and seriously wounding the ship's commander, Lieutenant John L. Worden. The *Monitor* withdrew into shoal water, drawing ten feet less than the *Virginia*. After waiting an hour for the *Monitor* to return, the *Virginia* steamed back to Portsmouth.[33] Thus ended the battle that made the world's navies obsolete. Both sides claimed victory. The Confederates carried the first day, killing and wounding scores of men and sinking two formidable warships and damaging another. Although the two ironclads fought to a draw, the *Monitor* had prevented further destruction of the Union fleet. For the next two months, since the North would not risk the *Monitor* in battle, the *Virginia* dominated Hampton Roads, denying Union forces entrance to the James River.

Wood took Buchanan's report of the battle and the colors from the surrendered *Congress* to Richmond. He was hailed by crowds at railroad stations along the route and was persuaded to recount over and over the story of the epic clash. At Richmond he was accompanied by Secretary Mallory to the president's house and a meeting with cabinet secretaries Judah P. Benjamin and James A. Seddon, among others. Wood gave his account of the two days and was questioned until midnight. In his final report, Buchanan commended Wood, saying, "Lieutenant Wood handled his pivot gun admirably, and the executive officer testifies to his valuable suggestions during the action. His zeal and industry in drilling the crew contributed materially to our success."[34] In the euphoria following the great achievement of the *Virginia*, the South paid scant attention to the fact that Ericsson's odd little vessel had countered their great hope. Buchanan was meritoriously promoted to the rank of admiral, and Lieutenant Jones became a commander. Wood's reward was a visit to his home at Petersburg a few hours after the birth of a daughter, Elizabeth Simms Wood, on 13 March, only four days after the momentous battle.[35]

With Buchanan wounded, command of the South's great ironclad went to the combative Commodore Josiah Tattnall. Several times in

April the repaired *Virginia* sallied out into Hampton Roads, tempting the *Monitor* to another round; but the Union vessel, restrained by orders, would not take up the challenge. Since General George B. McClellan's amphibious campaign to take Richmond was under way on the peninsula, the ironclads checkmated each other. The *Virginia* blocked the James River, while the *Monitor* protected the York River for the North. The abandonment of Confederate defenses on the lower peninsula panicked the defenders of Portsmouth, who with little provocation destroyed and evacuated the invaluable Gosport Navy Yard on 9 May. With her support base eliminated, the crew of the *Virginia*, which had too deep a draft to ascend the James, made a herculean effort to lighten her, but she was still too heavy. Realizing that a battle under such circumstances would be suicidal for both ship and men, Commodore Tattnall chose to preserve the experienced crew intact. At his order, the crew ran the ship aground on Craney Island, burned her, and marched away to man the vital James River batteries. Last to disembark, Wood and Lieutenant Jones set fire to the vessel, watching grimly as she was shattered to bits when her magazine exploded.[36]

With the *Virginia* out of the way, a Union squadron of two wooden gunboats and three ironclads—the *Monitor* and the lightly armored USS *Galena* and USS *Naugatuck*—made an assault up the nearly defenseless James River to take Richmond, hoping to end the war. From Richmond the *Virginia* crew was ordered to join other sailors from the James River Squadron, some seven miles downstream at fortified Drewry's Bluff, a ninety-foot-high ridge that dominated the river. For two agonizing days the naval contingent labored noon and night in heavy rain and "bottomless mud" to erect a battery, place obstructions in the river, and sink vessels to block the channel. By 15 May five heavy guns were mounted just in time to confront the Union flotilla, which smartly steamed up in the morning with the flagship *Galena* in the van and anchored six hundred yards downriver from the bluff.

On the previous day Wood had been detailed to command a scouting party of sharpshooters. He crossed the river and hid his scouts in the woods near Chaffin's Bluff, where he was reinforced by Confederate infantry. When the Union ships opened fire on the battery, Wood's marksmen concentrated their harassing musketry on the wooden gunboats, several times clearing their decks of the gun crews. After a three-hour bombardment, the fort suffered some damage, but the rapid and accurate plunging fire from the bluff severely punished the *Galena*, causing so many casualties that the flotilla withdrew.[37]

Although the battery at Drewry's Bluff was responsible for winning the battle, Wood and his sharpshooters were commended by Lieutenant Jones, who reported, "The enemy was excessively annoyed by their fire. His position was well chosen and gallantly maintained in spite of the shell, shrapnel, grape, and cannister fired at them."[38] Wood readily grasped the concept of combined army-navy operations, noting that if the Yankee fleet had been supported by a landing force, Richmond might have fallen as easily as New Orleans had earlier. The Southern victory at Drewry's Bluff saved Richmond, and the series of great battles on the peninsula, which began at Fair Oaks on 31 May and ended with General Lee's savage assaults of the Seven Days in late June, drove McClellan's invasion force back to northern Virginia.

Following the Confederate success, Wood had time to secure Secretary Mallory's approval for initiating small-boat raids on enemy shipping in the Chesapeake. Constructing boats and recruiting and training crews took time, but Wood's careful preparations paid off on 7 October when he seized and burned the Union supply schooner *Frances Elmore*. Augmented by acting Lieutenant Sidney S. Lee Jr. and his crew from the *Patrick Henry*, Wood moved his operation south to Mathews County and began nightly forays out on the bay searching for prey. Twenty miles off the mouth of the Rappahannock River, around midnight on 28 October, as the raiders stealthily approached the merchant ship *Alleghanian*, a lookout shouted a warning, but it was too late. Wood led his men on board and secured the vessel without firing a shot. The cargo of guano (fertilizer) was of no value to Wood and his men, but they did loot the vessel's provisions and equipment. Prior to burning his prize, Wood set some of the prisoners free, but he detained the officers. Soon after the boarding party left the *Alleghanian*, nearby Union gunboats saw the blaze and were able to extinguish it, although by then the vessel was little more than a smoldering hulk.[39]

With the Federal fleet alerted, Wood was temporarily assigned to duty on the unfinished ironclad css *Richmond*, but President Davis had more important duty in mind for his talented nephew. In February Wood was appointed colonel in the cavalry and aide-de-camp to the president, the rank dating from 23 January 1863.[40] On the same day the president ordered Wood on an inspection tour of the batteries, the navy yards, and the warships at Wilmington, Charleston, Savannah, Mobile, Port Hudson, and Vicksburg. The president needed an accurate assessment of the defense needs of these important installations from someone in whom he had complete confidence. Wood's particular relationship with the president and his dual rank enabled him to serve effectively as a liaison in joint army-navy operations. He left the next day for Wilmington and was able to suggest improvements to the batteries and the river obstructions. His main recommendation concerned the lack of heavy guns for the forts. He observed that there was "perfect accord between the military and naval commanders; both are working with spirit"; however, other reports indicated that interservice rivalry was customarily strong at Wilmington. He made similar recommendations at all of his stops, and many of them were carried out. Wood's inspection tour, although not so dramatic as his small-boat and high seas raids, generated key improvements to the defenses of vital ports and stands as one of his most important services to the Confederacy.[41]

Back in Richmond by late March, the restless Wood soon became discontented with staff duty and developed a plan to cut out a warship on the Chesapeake. He left Richmond on 12 August with eighty-two men and officers and four boats on wagons. Four days later they launched the boats on the Piankatank River and rowed twenty-five miles down to the Chesapeake. Wood established camp about two miles from the river's mouth, where the boats and crew could be concealed during the day until a prize was located. Unfortunately, a Union patrol boat discovered the Confederates, who drove it away in a brief skirmish. Now flushed from cover, Wood shifted his operation to the Rappahannock River and established liaison with Colonel Thomas L. Rosser of the Fifth Virginia Cavalry. In stormy weather about one o'clock in the morning of 23 August, at the river's mouth the Confederates located the side-wheel steamer USS *Satellite* and the USS *Reliance*, each armed with two guns. Deciding to attack both gunboats, Wood split his force. His contingent boarded the *Satellite* almost without warning and quickly secured control of the gunboat, wounding several and killing one of the Union crewmen. Lieutenant Frank L. Hoge led the boarding party to the *Reliance*. After hailing him three times, the deck watch opened fire, but the Confederates were on board by the time a general alarm had been given. The rest of the crew, caught by surprise, rushed on deck into a general melee; the commander, Henry Walters, was seriously wounded; but resistance did not crumble until Wood sent over another boat with reinforcements. Of the raiders, Lieutenant Hoge, Midshipman Henry S. Cooke, and two crewmen were wounded.[42]

At daylight Wood took command of the larger *Satellite*, commissioned the prizes as Confederate gunboats, and steamed up the Rappahannock to Urbanna, where the wounded and nearly seventy prisoners were turned over to Colonel Rosser, who detailed thirty sharpshooters to the vessels. After the limited supply of coal was divided between the ships, the Confederate gunboats sallied forth into the bay the following night. Under the command of Lieutenant Albert G. Hudgins, the *Reliance* had to turn back en route because of a faulty engine. In the face of strong wind and swells, the *Satellite* steamed into the Chesapeake looking for prizes. After several hours of fruitless searching, Wood returned to the Rappahannock. The next evening the *Satellite* had a busy night, running down three prizes—the schooner *Golden Rod*, with a cargo of coal, the *Coquette*, and the *Two Brothers*. Refueling from the *Golden Rod*, Wood left the prizes at Urbanna in the care of Lieutenant Hudgins and ran back down to the Chesapeake. Anchored near the mouth of the river, Wood noted the rough water and sighted three gunboats heading in his direction. The *Satellite* retreated to Urbanna. In preparation for moving far upstream to Port Royal, Wood had the *Golden Rod* burned. Towing the other two prizes, the *Satellite* and the repaired *Reliance* steamed to Port Royal, where they received a cordial welcome. Approaching Union troops forced Wood to strip the vessels, salvage their engines, and scuttle them. For weeks after the raid, Union forces scoured the countryside and the waterways for Wood, although he and his men had long been safely back in Richmond.[43] For the destruction of two enemy gunboats and five merchant vessels and the seizure of valuable equipment and prisoners, Wood received a meritorious promotion to commander with date of rank from 23 August 1863.[44]

The recovery of the occupied rich agricultural region of northeastern North Carolina once again became a Confederate objective in the winter of 1864. Under prodding by General Lee, plans had been developed for another attack on New Bern. Since the last assault on New Bern in the spring of 1863 had failed largely because of fire from Union gunboats, Southern naval support was considered essential. Since neither of the ironclads under construction on the Neuse and Roanoke Rivers was ready for an attempt in January, Wood was assigned to cooperate with the army commanded by General George E. Pickett by capturing one of the enemy gunboats during the planned attack. Some thirteen thousand Confederate troops were concentrated at Kinston when the campaign began on 31 January.[45]

Wood gathered his naval contingent at Richmond. Orders went out to squadrons at Charleston, Wilmington, and Richmond for boat crews to be selected for a special operation under his command. Lieutenant George W. Gift was sent to Wilmington to gather the southern units and bring them by rail to the rendezvous at Kinston. Each man was to be warmly clothed, to have three days' rations, to be armed with a rifle, a cutlass, and a revolver, and to have forty rounds of ammunition. From the James River Squadron Lieutenant Hoge gathered sailors, marines, and boats. They were ordered to meet Wood on the morning of 28 January. Commanded by Lieutenant Benjamin P. Loyall, this unit rowed down to Petersburg, where the boats were placed on railroad flat cars. The men traveled in the boats, presenting quite a spectacle to onlookers at railroad depots in Virginia and North Carolina. Lieutenant Loyall wrote, "It was a novel sight to see a train like that—Jack sitting upon the seats of the boats and waving his hat to the astonished natives, who never saw such a circus before."[46] They arrived in Kinston at two o'clock in the morning of 31 January.[47]

Wood wasted no time having the boats promptly unloaded, dragged to the Neuse River, and launched. Lieutenant Gift's Wilmington contingent followed in two large launches that carried a total of ninety men and were armed with boat howitzers. Since the journey to New Bern, which was only thirty miles overland, was twice as far by the winding river, the boats hurriedly set out, rowing silently with muffled oars. Only an occasional startled flock of ducks broke the deep silence of the night. All the next day the crews rowed steadily through dense, deserted woodland. About eleven o'clock that evening the river suddenly broadened into the wide estuary at its mouth. When they sighted New Bern, Wood had the boats hidden in a creek. While the exhausted men rested and ate, Wood explained for the first time the mission to capture a gunboat during the land attack on the town's fortifications. About 3:30 A.M. on 1 February, distant firing signaled the beginning of General Pickett's demonstration, and the three gunboats present—the USS *Lockwood*, the USS *Underwriter*, and the USS *Hull*—responded by moving into position to protect the Federal earthworks. The *Lockwood* steamed up the Trent River, leaving the *Hull* and the side-wheel steamer *Underwriter* in the Neuse. The *Hull* ran aground, leaving only the four-gun *Underwriter* in position, moored close to shore with guns trained inland to contest any rebel assault.[48]

During the day Lieutenant Gift and Lieutenant Philip Porcher from Charleston arrived with the launches, but the entire contingent of

The USS *Underwriter* was cut out and burned at New Bern, North Carolina, on 2 February 1864. (North Carolina Division of Archives and History, Raleigh)

some 250 sailors and marines remained hidden. Wood established contact with General Pickett and made final preparations for the attack. On a reconnaissance at dusk he and Loyall located a gunboat on the waterfront.[49] When they returned, the unit was organized in two divisions, led by Wood and Lieutenant Loyall. About midnight the raiders shoved off. A short distance downstream, the deeply religious Wood gathered the boats in close and offered a prayer for success. Midshipman Thomas J. Scharf wrote of this moment, "It was a strange and ghostly sight, the men resting on their oars with heads uncovered, the commander also bareheaded, standing erect in the stern of his boat; the black water rippling underneath, the dense overhanging clouds pouring down sheets of rain, and in the blackness beyond an unseen bell tolling as if from some phantom cathedral."[50]

The ship's bell tolled five times for 2:30 A.M., guiding the silent raiders stealthily to their prey. From the darkness the hull was suddenly discernible, and twice a hail, "Boat ahoy!," went unanswered. An alarm rattle was sounded, and the crew rushed on deck. Wood now shouted, "Give way!," and the order was echoed by his officers. The rebel raiders rowed with all their strength and the boats fairly flew over the last yards to the enemy's side. Midshipman Scharf fired his howitzer just before his boat struck the hull. The Confederate marines rose and fired a volley as the raiders came alongside. Grapnels were thrown over the sides, and as the rebels boarded, they were met with bursts of musketry from the crew. The raiders, armed with cutlasses and pistols, gave a yell and rushed madly into the Union sailors. Scharf wrote that "the onslaught was furious," and the Southerners forced the Yankees "pell-mell" off the deck and down below. The cost was high. The *Underwriter*'s captain, Jacob Westervelt, lay dead, along with two of his men; in addition, a number of crewmen were wounded, two mortally. Six of the raiders were dead or dying, and twenty-two were wounded.[51]

The bloody ten-minute struggle ended with a Confederate triumph. Unsurprisingly, however, the hellish din of the fight had alerted the Union garrison. As retrained guns in the adjacent batteries opened fire at point-blank range, a shocked Wood learned from his engineer that the boiler fires were so low that it would take too long to raise enough steam pressure to move the prize. With shells exploding around them, there was not even time to cut the anchor cables and tow her. After such human sacrifice it was an appalling choice, but Wood gave the order to secure the prisoners and abandon and burn the prize. All of the wounded who could be found were gathered, the guns were loaded and pointed toward the town, and the raiding party pulled away from the *Underwriter*; minutes later she was a "mass of flames." As the Southerners rowed away in a hail of musketry, the score of prisoners riding in the last boat in line discovered that by mistake their boat held only two rebel guards. The prisoners quickly overpowered the guards and returned safely to New Bern, but the raiders retained about two dozen other captives. Taking one last look at their handiwork from the safety of the darkness, the Confederates saw "the lurid light flaming in the sky" and heard "the dull, heavy booming sound" of the guns and shells exploding.[52]

Although the raid had been a spectacular success, Wood had failed to capture a gunboat, and General Pickett, who had been lukewarm about the campaign from the beginning, used this excuse to withdraw. The more aggressive General Robert F. Hoke, who had planned the operation and was convinced that a vigorous assault would carry the Union lines, reluctantly retreated. The Southern public blamed the failure to take New Bern on the army and Pickett's lack of nerve, while Wood and the navy won new laurels. Within two weeks the Confederate Congress passed a joint resolution commending Wood on all of his raids, for his "daring and brilliantly executed plans" that resulted in the capture and destruction of the two gunboats and five transports on the Chesapeake and his successful raid on the *Underwriter*.[53] Union Admiral David D. Porter wrote that "this was rather a mortifying affair for the navy."[54] Federal assistant secretary of the navy Gustavus V. Fox, who had been reading up on the British naval tradition of cutting-out, put matters even more bluntly, describing Wood's exploits as "disgraceful" to the Northern service and expressing his hope that a commander of Wood's ability and inclination would emerge in the U.S. Navy.[55]

Keenly disappointed over the failure when victory had seemed so close, Wood remained committed to reconquest of strategically important eastern North Carolina. Sharing Wood's opinion, Hoke convinced General Lee to allow him to keep his brigade in the state. Since a warship was necessary for coastal operations, it was fortunate that the two river ironclads were near completion. The CSS *Albemarle* was so nearly ready for service that Hoke's objective became Plymouth on the Roanoke River. Wood, who respected both General Hoke and Commander James W. Cooke of the *Albemarle*, served as liaison in the successful army-navy campaign that took Plymouth on 19 April.[56]

Back in Richmond that summer, Wood became involved in a desperate scheme to capture Washington. Twenty thousand Confederate prisoners from Point Lookout, Maryland, would be released, armed, and linked with cavalry to reinforce an infantry raid from the Shenandoah Valley under General Jubal Early. Wood's role was to ferry troops and arms from Wilmington to free the prisoners from Point Lookout. In four days' time he had the guns and some eight hundred troops ready to embark from Wilmington on 9 July. Early's forces were in place on time outside Washington, but General Grant reacted swiftly and moved reinforcements to the panic-stricken capital. Davis called off the mission on 10 July when he realized that the plans were public knowledge. Unbeknown to the Southerners, the prisoners had already been hastily transported to New York.[57]

In mid-July the swift British-built steamer *Atalanta*[58] ran the blockade into Wilmington for the fourth time. The iron-hulled ship was 220 feet in length and powered by two one-hundred horsepower engines driving twin screw propellers that could push the vessel to more than fourteen knots, making her one of the fastest ships at sea. The speed and maneuverability of the vessel attracted the attention of the Confederate navy, which purchased her at a premium. Wood was assigned command of the ship on 23 July and was charged with converting her to an armed cruiser. Rechristened the css *Tallahassee*, she was armed with three pivot-mounted rifles, a one-hundred-pounder, a thirty-pounder, and a twelve-pounder. Wood used cotton bales to shield the boilers and carried extra coal in bags on deck to extend her cruising range. His 120-man crew consisted of experienced river sailors from the James River Squadron; however, few of them had sailed on the ocean.[59]

With the *Tallahassee* ready to go to sea, the intrepid Wood took her down to Fort Fisher on 4 August. Two successive nights he grounded in New Inlet, so on the third try he went downriver, passing over the bar by Fort Caswell. While the *Tallahassee* was silently threading her way between two blockaders, they opened fire, but she quickly disappeared into the darkness. By daybreak the cruiser had cleared Frying Pan Shoals and turned toward the northeast. Soon two blockaders appeared, steaming at full speed toward the ship, but the raider rapidly outpaced them. Initially she encountered only neutral vessels, but on 11 August about eighty miles off New York harbor the *Tallahassee* took her first prize, the schooner *Sarah A. Boyce*, which was in ballast. After removal of the crew, provisions, medicine, and charts, the *Boyce* was scuttled. The next prize was a pilot boat, the schooner *James Funk*, which was taken about twenty miles from the harbor entrance. Wood manned the pilot boat, using it as a tender to lure ships to the *Tallahassee*. By the end of the day, five more ships had been taken, four of them destroyed and one bonded to receive the paroled prisoners. Wood had plans to raid New York, but he could neither persuade nor coerce the captured pilots to guide him into the harbor. The next day six more prizes were captured, including the large ship *Adriatic*, which was crowded with German immigrants going to New York. Again a vessel was bonded to take the passengers, and the *Adriatic* was burned.

Knowing that U.S. cruisers would be converging on New York to trap the raider, Wood ended his productive mini-blockade and sailed up the New England coast, destroying two more vessels on 13 August and burning his tender. Running low on fuel off the Maine coast, the *Tallahassee* seized the *James Littlefield*, fortuitously loaded with a cargo of coal. When rough seas prevented recoaling at sea, Wood reluctantly scuttled the prize. Over the next three days, 15–17 August, the *Tallahassee* decimated the Maine fishing fleet and coasters, taking sixteen prizes. Although the vessels were small, they were an important component of the regional economy. Nearly out of coal, the

The swift css *Tallahassee*, under Wood's command, went on a raid that terrorized the east coast of the United States in the summer of 1864. (Maritime Museum of the Atlantic, Halifax, N.S.)

cruiser entered Halifax, Nova Scotia, on 18 August, hoping to replenish fuel and supplies. Over twelve days, the rebel raider had seized thirty-two prizes off the coast of the United States and spread consternation in major ports, especially New York, as well as in small fishing villages. Not since the raid of the css *Tacony* a year earlier had New England been in such a furor about a "rebel pirate."[60]

At Halifax Wood was surprised to find the behavior of the port admiral and the lieutenant governor cold, uncooperative, and bordering on the offensive. Since it was obvious by 1864 that the South was losing the war, cordial treatment in neutral ports could no longer be assumed, except in Bermuda and Nassau, where blockade running was still an economic boon. The *Tallahassee* was entitled to a forty-eight-hour stay and refueling. Wood's request for several days to replenish his coal bunkers initially was granted; however, by the next morning he was told that he must leave in twenty-four hours and could have only enough coal to return to Wilmington. The cruiser was briefly surrounded by armed guard boats, but they were withdrawn when Wood protested. After the Confederate agent in Halifax managed to slip a little extra coal on board in record time, Wood sailed on the night of 19 August after forty hours in port.[61]

Hampered by low fuel, the *Tallahassee* could no longer seek prizes, but she ran across her last victim, the brig *Roan*, on the twentieth and burned her. Wood headed his ship directly toward Wilmington, approaching the outer ring of blockaders on 26 August and outrunning two pursuers. That night he headed toward New Inlet just outside the surf line. Nearly colliding with the USS *Monticello*, the bold Wood veered out for sea room, narrowly missing two other blockaders. They opened fire on what they thought was a blockade runner, but the mystery ship, to their surprise, returned fire. Four blockaders on that exciting night exchanged shots in the brief running battle, but the elusive raider was gone almost before they knew she was there. Wood gave them a parting broadside and vanished at fourteen knots into New Inlet. After the cruiser dropped anchor under the guns of Fort Fisher, Wood mustered the crew on deck and said a prayer of thanksgiving. At dawn, while raising her ensign, the *Tallahassee* and the fort exchanged twenty-one-gun salutes, and she then steamed upriver to Wilmington.[62]

The remarkable voyage of the *Tallahassee* under Wood's command boosted the morale of the Confederacy, which had been absorbing bad news from military defeats all summer. In twenty days the cruiser had taken thirty-three prizes off the coast of the United States, frightened the eastern seaboard with her foray, and made the U.S. Navy look incompetent. Commander Wood's raid gave a new direction for Confederate commerce raiding. Heretofore, most of the raiders had been purchased and outfitted abroad, manned largely by foreign crews, operated entirely on distant oceans, resupplied from their victims, and destined never to see the nation they represented. In contrast, the *Tallahassee* was purchased and outfitted in Wilmington, manned by experienced officers and crewmen of the Confederate States Navy, raided the almost sacrosanct sea lanes on the shoreline of the United States, and returned safely to her home port. The Confederacy had briefly attempted privateering, with mixed results, in the early months of the war, but the CSS *Tallahassee* was the first navy cruiser directed to operate from a Confederate home base.[63] Disguised as the CSS *Olustee*, the *Tallahassee* made one more voyage, destroying six more vessels, while her sister ship, the CSS *Chickamauga*, took seven prizes. Commerce raiding from Wilmington was ended when the local military authorities complained that since the blockade had been strengthened to stop the cruisers, more blockade runners had been taken. Everyone realized that blockade running was far more important to the Confederacy's existence than preying on Northern commerce could ever be.

Returning to a hero's welcome, Wood learned that his cruise had been a tonic to the Southern people, who were demoralized by escalating defeat. He was detached from the *Tallahassee* on 2 September and ordered to report to Richmond to resume his duties as an aide to the president. The preceding several months had been dangerous and hectic for him, and he was glad to be home but saddened that his daughter, Elizabeth, had died while he was at sea. Wood settled into the routine of serving on the president's staff and cherished the months at home in Richmond with Lola and Zack, whom he had moved there from Petersburg. On 10 February 1865 Wood was meritoriously promoted to the rank of captain in the provisional navy for his destruction of the *Underwriter* and his command of the *Tallahassee*.[64]

After Fort Fisher surrendered in January 1865 and the port of Wilmington was closed, the Confederacy's ability to keep armies in the field diminished rapidly. The starving and ragged troops in the trenches around Petersburg began to drift home that winter, and the army dwindled away in bits and pieces. From his personal observation of the army, Wood had sensed that the end was near, and on 28 March he took Lola, Zack, and newborn daughter Lola, only thirteen days old, to Greensboro, North Carolina, by rail. Back in Richmond, on 2 April Wood was attending services with the president at St. Paul's Episcopal Church when a courier interrupted with an urgent dispatch from General Lee notifying Davis that the thinly manned lines had been overwhelmed by a Union attack and the city must be evacuated immediately. Since Davis's wife, Varina, and their children had already left Richmond two days earlier for Charlotte, North Carolina, there was little to do at the president's office except pack government documents. Along with most of the cabinet, the presidential party boarded a train for Danville that night. As they pulled out of the city, the sky was aglow from burning supplies, and dull explosions were heard as the ironclads of the James River Squadron were destroyed. The presidential train arrived at Danville the next afternoon. Security was provided by midshipmen of the Confederate naval academy and sailors from the fleet commanded by Admiral Raphael Semmes.[65]

On 8 April Wood went to Greensboro on a two-day leave to visit his family. There he received word to remain in town since the government was being transferred to Greensboro. Arriving on 11 April, the cabinet members, army officers, and President Davis were housed in railroad cars. Since no one came forward to house the fugitive Davis, Wood persuaded him to share rented rooms with his family. On the twelfth, Davis received the crushing news that Lee had surrendered at Appomattox. Although he wished to continue the war, at a council held in the Wood home his cabinet and generals advised him that it

A Confederate escape party including John Taylor Wood and Secretary of War John C. Breckinridge hijacks a sloop from Union deserters off south Florida. This 1893 illustration from *Century Magazine* was based on a sketch by Wood. (North Carolina Collection, Wilson Library, University of North Carolina, Chapel Hill)

was time to capitulate. General Joseph E. Johnston, whose men were still fighting in North Carolina, left the council and returned to his army to negotiate a surrender to General William T. Sherman.[66]

On 15 April Wood sent his family back to Richmond and went south with the presidential party, traveling by horseback and wagon. Upon arriving in Charlotte, Davis learned that his wife had preceded him into South Carolina. The last full cabinet meeting of Davis's administration was held there, and on 26 April the president's caravan, including cabinet officers and a large cavalry escort, set out, attempting to reach the Trans-Mississippi Army, which had not yet surrendered. Over the next several weeks cabinet secretaries Mallory, Judah Benjamin, and John C. Breckinridge left the president's party, and the escort began to melt away. On 7 May, Davis joined his wife's caravan; but three days later near Irwinville, Georgia, diligent Union cavalry units, spurred on by the offer of a $100,000 reward for the president's capture and rumors of treasure in the convoy, surrounded the Davis camp, ending the flight. In the confusion, Wood bribed a trooper and hid in the undergrowth of a nearby swamp until everyone had left the area.[67]

When Wood reemerged from hiding, he joined a cavalry lieutenant with two worn-out horses and departed for Florida. Six days later near Madison, Florida, Wood met Kentuckians General John C. Breckinridge, the Confederacy's last secretary of war, and Colonel James Wilson. Because they were from states that had remained in the Union, all three believed they were subject to charges of treason and felt it necessary to leave the country. By 26 May, accompanied by two enlisted men and Breckinridge's servant, Tom, they exchanged their horses for a rowboat and started up the St. Johns River on an extraordinary escape odyssey that ended in Cuba on 11 June. For two and a half weeks they existed on the edge of starvation, traded for food with Seminole Indians, seized a sloop from Yankee deserters, fought a running battle with renegades and pirates, and weathered a severe storm at sea. Dressed in rags, with long, stringy hair and beards, they had no trouble convincing a Union patrol boat that they were Confederate deserters.[68]

When they landed in Cárdenas, Cuba, they registered their sloop as *No Name* and sold it, splitting the proceeds. Wood moved on to Havana and shipped out on a former blockade runner for Halifax, Nova Scotia. From there he traveled to Quebec, then to Montreal and a joyous reunion with Lola and the children on 15 July. In September Wood moved his family to Halifax, where he formed a partnership, Wilkinson, Wood and Company, with former blockade runner and naval lieutenant John Wilkinson. An unreconstructed rebel, Wood flew the Confederate flag over Wilkinson, Wood and Company for the remainder of his life.

Wood found peace in Halifax and became a prominent citizen of Nova Scotia. He succeeded in commerce and marine insurance and was an agent for steamship companies. As a member of the Halifax Chamber of Commerce, he spoke publicly and wrote for newspapers, promoting the development of the port city. He acquired a racing yacht and became vice commodore of the Royal Nova Scotia Yacht Squadron. Of their eleven children, the Woods raised nine, and Wood and his family were staunch members of Saint Luke's Anglican Church. John Taylor Wood died on 19 July 1904. His descendants have been noted for their many years of distinguished service to the Royal Canadian Mounted Police.[69]

*The "Shenandoah,"
originally called the "Sea
King," was the last and
most dangerous of all the
Confederate cruisers.*
—*Admiral David Dixon
Porter, 1886*

James T. Waddell

The *Shenandoah* Masters the North Pacific

In 1864 the Civil War was in its third year, and the Confederate States were beleaguered on all fronts. In the Virginia and Georgia theaters the two most important Confederate field armies gave ground in face of superior Union force. Grant's unrelenting juggernaut pressed Lee back toward Richmond and into the trenches of Petersburg by late June, while Sherman adroitly maneuvered Johnston to the gates of Atlanta a month later. Weakening Southern morale had been bolstered periodically throughout the war by the exploits of Confederate high seas raiders, but on 19 June 1864 off Cherbourg, France, the famed css *Alabama* was sunk in action with the uss *Kearsarge*, leaving the css *Florida* as the sole Confederate cruiser at sea. To Secretary of the Navy Stephen R. Mallory, it was essential to reinforce the *Florida*, for at this late date in the war the cruisers were the only offensive power remaining to the Confederacy. In August Mallory launched a new campaign from Wilmington, North Carolina, by arming former blockade runners and sending them out as the css *Tallahassee* and the css *Chickamauga* to harass the eastern seaboard of the United States. Although the prizes taken were mostly inconsequential coastal traders and fishing boats, the flames of burning vessels off New York harbor, Long Island, and the Maine coast sent tremors of near panic through Northern merchants, financial markets, and insurance companies, as well as the populace of Northern seaports and coastal towns. Mounted by the waning Confederacy, such a sea threat had no effect on the outcome of the war; yet it challenged the vaunted dominance of the U.S. Navy and gave Southerners some satisfaction that the North too was paying a price for the wanton devastation wrought by the blue-clad hordes crushing the life out of the Confederacy.

Mallory's response to the loss of the *Alabama* was to send orders to the canny Confederate naval agent in Europe, Commander James D. Bulloch in Liverpool, to acquire a new cruiser immediately and dispatch it to the previously untouched vast Pacific Ocean to destroy the valuable U.S. whaling fleet. The Pacific strategy grew out of consultations in the Navy Department among Mallory, Commander John M. Brooke, and Lieutenant Robert R. Carter, Bulloch's able assistant. Both Brooke and Carter had served in the Pacific in a prewar navy scientific expedition that charted the routes of whales and the whaling fleet.[1] When his orders arrived, Bulloch was elated to find in port the *Sea King*, a sleek merchant vessel that had "charmed" both him and Carter a year earlier in Glasgow, Scotland, before her maiden voyage to Bombay, India. He described the *Sea King* as a "fine" full-rigged ship with powerful auxiliary engines and a retractable screw propeller. She was 222 feet long and rated at 1,160 tons with a draft of sixteen feet. The hull was soundly constructed of teak on an iron frame. She was a fast sailer, her log recording a run of 330 miles in twenty-four hours. Always under the surveillance of Thomas H. Dudley, the dogged U.S. consul in Liverpool, Bulloch shrewdly stayed away from the vessel and worked quietly through English contact Richard Wright in purchasing the *Sea King*. Purportedly bound for India for her new owner, the ship was ballasted with coal and sailed to London. English Captain Peter Corbett, a former blockade runner, was granted a power-of-attorney to sell her at any time after she left London.[2]

As the *Sea King* prepared for a voyage to the Far East, Union spies at Liverpool were keeping close watch on Bulloch, who had also recently purchased the *Laurel*, a fast steam packet that Bulloch was sure the Union agents knew would make an ideal blockade runner. Advertising a forthcoming voyage to Havana, the packet received heavy crates, labeled as machinery, that hid cannon, arms, and ammunition. In the weeks before the *Laurel* was scheduled to leave, young men drifted singly into Liverpool, registered at different hotels and inns, and then booked passage on the steamer.

By early October both vessels were ready to sail. Using the telegraph, Bulloch ordered the *Sea King* to leave on the morning of the eighth, and during the day word was received by the men of the *Laurel* that she would sail that evening. At the mouth of the Thames the *Sea King* slipped past U.S. warships, which had been distracted by a suspicious-looking Spanish vessel. Under cover of darkness, the *Laurel*, commanded by English-born Confederate officer Lieutenant John F. Ramsay, sailed unmolested from Liverpool. Both vessels left under secret orders to sail to Funchal in the Portuguese Madeira Islands off the Moroccan coast. One of the passengers on board the *Laurel* was Lieutenant James I. Waddell, with orders to take command of the *Sea King*, outfit her as a Confederate States cruiser, and proceed to the Pacific to destroy the New England whaling fleet.[3]

Descended from some of North Carolina's most distinguished families—Waddell, Moore, and Nash—James Iredell Waddell was born 13 July 1824 in Pittsboro, the county seat of Chatham County, in the heart of the Piedmont. Waddell was the son of Francis Nash Waddell, an attorney, and Elizabeth Davis Moore Waddell. When his parents relocated to Louisiana for his father to manage a family estate, young James was left in the care of his grandmother, Sarah Waddell, and was educated in a private school. He said of his childhood in Pittsboro, "I must have been an incorrigible youngster. All the deviltry committed in and out of that hamlet the mothers of my playmates laid at my door."[4] It is likely that he was overindulged by a doting grandmother, and he retained fond memories of his early life. Because of his grandmother's poor health, the boy went to live with his grandfather, Alfred Moore of Moorefields in Hillsborough. At age thirteen he attended Bingham's School, the noted classical academy in Orange County. Upon their return to North Carolina, his parents settled at Moorefields.[5]

Through his grandfather's acquaintance with U.S. secretary of the navy George E. Badger of Raleigh, Waddell received an appointment as acting midshipman on 10 September 1841. He was ordered to report to Norfolk in December for duty on the 120-gun ship-of-the-line USS *Pennsylvania*, commanded by Commodore William B. Shubrick. Built over a span of fifteen years and launched in 1837, the *Pennsylvania* was the largest sailing man-of-war ever in the United States Navy.

In her day she was considered the most powerful ship in the world, but she proved too expensive to keep at sea in peacetime.[6] When the seventeen-year-old Waddell arrived on the docks at Norfolk, a fledgling midshipman who had never been away from the rolling hills and villages of Piedmont North Carolina, he "was astonished" at the wonders of the exciting world he had entered in the nearby navy yard. He stared up at the gigantic *Pennsylvania*, realizing that it was now his home; of the moment, he would later recall, "I had never seen a boat, I had no conception of a ship-of-war, or other floating armament."[7] He vowed to himself to look and listen carefully, learn quickly, and maintain "a silence" that he remembered "was wonderful for one so young." The veteran Commodore Shubrick instilled in his young charge the philosophy of military service in a democracy, advising him to "remember that you are now a servant of the people. . . . They are taxed for your support, and you shall at all times be respectful to the people."[8]

To the neophyte Waddell, service on the *Pennsylvania* seemed "an endless undertaking," and the ship was filled with more people than he had ever before seen at one time. Once presented to the officer of the deck, he was assigned quarters and stood the midnight to 4:00 A.M. watch on his first night on board. Ignorant of what he was to be watching for, he kept a "sharp lookout." Naive and immature for his age, Waddell was shocked by the "gruff manner and stern tone" of the officers.[9] His four years in boarding school had not prepared him for life in the midshipman's berth of boys and adolescent youths trying to act like men and sometimes practicing most of the imaginable vices of the day—cursing, smoking, drinking, gambling, and whoring. Fortunately, he also found kindred spirits among the midshipmen, talented and serious-minded young men of high moral character. After being insulted by Archibald H. Waring, an older midshipman, in May 1842 he engaged in a duel, receiving a serious hip injury from a pistol shot. He was on medical leave recuperating for eleven months, and he walked with a limp the rest of his life. When he returned to active duty in April 1843, he reported to the sloop uss *Vandalia* in the Gulf of Mexico. During his three years on the *Vandalia*, the ship was ravaged three times by yellow fever, losing a number of men and officers. In 1846 Waddell was transferred to the ten-gun brig uss *Somers* at Pensacola.[10]

In 1844 Democrat James K. Polk was elected president on an expansionist platform, calling for complete acquisition of Oregon and the annexation of Texas. Polk's victory emboldened Congress to pass a joint resolution on annexation before he took office. When Mexico broke diplomatic relations, General Zachary Taylor marched his army into Texas in the summer of 1845 and by the following March had reached the Rio Grande. Hostilities began in April 1846.

Beginning in April 1845 the Gulf Squadron, including the *Somers*, operated between Pensacola and Veracruz, Mexico, under Commodore David Connor. A year later, in support of Taylor's expedition, the squadron appeared at Veracruz in force. Since Mexico had no navy, there was little to do beyond blockade duty. In May the *Somers* was detached with other ships to protect Taylor's base at Point Isabel, just above the Rio Grande. Waddell was not destined for lengthy inactivity, however, and in October was posted to the naval school at Annapolis. He returned to Pensacola on the store ship USS *Relief* and arrived in Annapolis on January 1847. He was at the naval school for over two years and was rated a passed midshipman 29 September 1849, with a date of rank of 10 August 1847. Waddell was first assigned to the national observatory in Washington and then to an instructor's position at the naval school. While at Annapolis, he met, courted, and on 16 November 1848 married Anne Sellman Iglehart, the daughter of James Iglehart, a merchant of Annapolis, and established a permanent home near the future naval academy. The Waddells had a daughter, Anne, and settled into the life of the naval academy community.[11]

Waddell was ordered to a year's sea duty on the frigate USS *Independence*, the flagship of the Mediterranean Squadron. While he was on a return voyage to the United States on the *Relief*, he became ill and was placed on medical leave for several months. In 1851 he was assigned to a tour of duty with the coast survey, and then he returned to the naval academy as an instructor. From there he went on a three-and-a-half-year assignment on the sloop USS *Germantown* on the coast of South America. While on this cruise Waddell was promoted to lieutenant on 15 September 1855 and served as the ship's navigator. After a seven-week leave at home, he was assigned to the store ship USS *Release* on a voyage to Panama to ferry supplies to the Pacific Squadron. On the return voyage yellow fever struck everyone in the crew of the *Release* except one seaman and a boy. Once Waddell, who was the first officer to become ill, had recovered enough to return to duty, as the sole able-bodied officer on board, he sailed the vessel; when the pilot refused to come on board the fever-ridden ship at Matanzas, Cuba, Waddell guided the *Release* into the harbor there. His commander, L. M. Brasher, wrote a special commendation for Waddell's "excellent con-

James I. Waddell became a lieutenant in the U.S. Navy in 1855 and was on the faculty of the naval academy in 1858–59 when this portrait was painted. (North Carolina Museum of History, Raleigh)

duct" doing "duties most trying." After returning to the United States, Waddell served briefly as the executive officer on the receiving ship for new recruits at Baltimore and then returned to teach navigation at Annapolis.[12]

The years at Annapolis, the most pleasant of Waddell's naval service, were spent at home with his wife, friends, and family. He was described in 1858 as being over six feet tall, "with a powerful frame, weighing more than two hundred pounds, well proportioned, with a fine person. His features were well cut, betokening resolution and decision. He had a noble bearing, intelligence kindled his eye, and withal gracious and courtly, he was radiant with kindliness." Anne Waddell was petite, in temperament "a lovely and affectionate woman." The couple had lost their only child, and "the life of each seemed centered in the other. Though long married, they still were lovers."[13]

No talented naval officer remained ashore very long, and in July 1859 Waddell was ordered to report to San Francisco to the USS *Saginaw*, which was under construction. Commissioned in January 1860, the *Saginaw* was a side-wheel steamer mounting four heavy guns. Not until Waddell arrived at San Francisco did he realize that it would be

Waddell's wife, Anne Sellman Iglehart of Annapolis, known in the family as Sell, shared her husband's wartime experiences in Europe. In 1865, during the CSS *Shenandoah*'s cruise, she was under Union military house arrest. (North Carolina Division of Archives and History, Raleigh)

six more months before the ship could go to sea, time that he could have passed at home with Anne. The vessel steamed out for Hong Kong on schedule in the spring of 1860. During a cruise in the Gulf of Chihli or Bohai, Waddell witnessed a joint British-French attack on Chinese fortifications, part of hostilities designed to subject China to further European economic exploitation. Back in Hong Kong Waddell was ordered on 15 December to return to New York on the sloop USS *John Adams*.[14]

Increasingly, news of the political turmoil at home confronted all Southern-born officers with an agonizing dilemma: what to do if indeed their states left the Union and a war between the states occurred. Waddell wrote that he "hoped there would be peace between the sections," although he had privately decided that if war came he would "go South" to be with his family.[15] On the long voyage home no news was received until November 1861 when the sloop reached the isolated island of St. Helena in the South Atlantic. By then the war had been under way seven months, and the latest news was of the Confederate victory in July at Bull Run, or Manassas. On 20 November a saddened Waddell wrote his resignation to the secretary of the navy, saying, "In thus separating myself from associations which I have cherished for twenty years, I wish it to be understood that no doctrine of the rights of secession, no wish for disunion of the States impel me, but simply because, my home is the home of my people in the South, and I cannot bear arms against it or them."[16]

Waddell remained on the *John Adams* and continued to fulfill his duties. When he reached New York, "war excitement was intense." He declined the offer to command a wing of the bombardment fleet being organized by Commander David D. Porter for the coming attack on New Orleans. To be allowed to return home to Annapolis he was forced to take an oath of loyalty, which he did under protest. Once home he wrote to President Abraham Lincoln about his ambiguous situation, explaining that since his family resided in the South and he had brothers serving in the Confederate army, it was "impossible that I could bear arms against the South in this war." The reply from Secretary of the Navy Gideon Welles, which Waddell received on 28 January, was a dismissal from the service.[17]

Waddell's attempt to collect back pay in New York had been refused, and upon his reapplication Secretary Welles wrote that if he would take an oath to "take no part in the war" his account would be settled. Waddell considered that this reply was tantamount to a bribe and was so dishonorable that it relieved him from his oath. In expectation of arrest, he began to make plans to escape to the Confederacy. Contacting the underground network of border state smugglers, Waddell approached a butcher, known simply as the "fat man," at the Marsh Market in Baltimore, gave the proper recognition phrase, and made arrangements to leave the next night from Carroll Island. Waddell left his wife, promising to send for her as soon as he could, and with a companion set out in a heavy downpour for the island. There he was given a tinfoil-wrapped package for Judah P. Benjamin, who had until a few days earlier been Confederate secretary of war and was now secretary of state. As head of the military department, Benjamin had been engaged in intelligence gathering, and Waddell was trusted to be a courier, which placed his life in jeopardy if he was caught. At Carroll Island Waddell paid a $100 passage and boarded a schooner commanded by a "Yankee skipper" more interested in money than in politics. The schooner sailed down the bay, avoiding Union gunboats, and landed the refugees on Great Wicomoco River in Northumberland County, Virginia. From there it was a short overland trek by wagon to the Rappahannock River and Confederate lines. In Richmond Waddell applied for a commission as a lieutenant in the Confederate States Navy, which he received on 27 March.[18]

No seagoing command was available, so Waddell, who had some knowledge of the forthcoming Union attack on New Orleans, was immediately sent to that city, as the crisis there was coming to a head. The most important port and the largest and wealthiest city in the South, New Orleans was a key objective in the Union goal to win control of the Mississippi River, dividing the South and depriving it of its richest region. From Illinois Commodore Andrew Foote's ironclad flotilla posed a distant threat, but imminent danger appeared at the mouth of the Mississippi, where a great fleet was gathering, commanded by Commodore David G. Farragut. At the age of sixty, the Tennessee-born Farragut, with fifty years in the U.S. Navy, was pulled from a desk job in New York to head up the most important Union naval assignment of the war. This surprising appointment was probably at the behest of Farragut's foster brother, David Dixon Porter, who had planned the operation and now commanded the mortar fleet. By late February 1862 Union ships began to gather off the Mississippi delta, and a month later a Union army of 18,000 men commanded by General Benjamin F. Butler arrived by sea. On 27 March, the very day that Waddell was commissioned in the Confederate navy, the Union fleet began its movement up the flooded Mississippi. Farragut had under his command forty-six vessels mounting 286 guns, plus Porter's twenty-one mortar schooners.

Facing the Union invasion force was an impossibly tangled Southern command morass divided among national, state, army, navy, and private authorities. Nevertheless, a hot reception of river obstructions, mines, fire rafts, and a fleet of gunboats and ironclads was being prepared to supplement the 126 heavy guns of Forts Jackson and St. Philip. Confederate hopes were pinned on the completion of two huge ironclads, the css *Louisiana* and the css *Mississippi*, whose keels had been laid in October 1861. Although the ships were scheduled to have been ready by February 1862, the usual delays, shortages, and lack of technology and equipment that would frustrate Confederate shipbuilding efforts throughout the war had stymied their construction. Both of the ironclads were over 260 feet long and broad beamed. The *Louisiana* mounted sixteen guns, and the *Mississippi* would have twenty guns. Completed except for her engines, the *Louisiana*, with workmen aboard her laboring frantically, was towed on 20 April to a mooring above Fort St. Philip to serve as a floating battery. The barn-like *Mississippi*, to which Waddell had been assigned as first lieutenant, was being constructed by Nelson and Asa Tift and was not launched until 17 April, the day before Porter's mortar fleet began a lengthy bombardment of the forts. In retrospect, the *Mississippi*, which was potentially powerful enough to maintain command of much of the river, was so far behind schedule that she should have been towed out of danger, but desperation ruled the day in New Orleans. The Tifts drove their workmen to finish what was commonly believed to be a ship so powerful that she could single-handedly stop the Union invasion.

Less than a week after the *Mississippi* had been launched, Farragut commenced his assault on the forts and his drive to take New Orleans with a flotilla of twenty-four ships and gunboats and nineteen mortar schooners mounting 302 guns. Opposing him were the Confederate forts and fourteen gunboats, including two ironclads, with a total of only 166 guns. To their detriment, most of the Confederate cannon were stationary, but the South's fatal flaw was its confused command structure, which resulted in an uncoordinated defense. Nevertheless, the night passage by the forts was one of the most dramatic and terrible scenes of the war, unmatched for horror in Farragut's long military career. As hundreds of guns roared in all directions and fire rafts floated helter-skelter through the maelstrom of warships, the Confederate fleet was utterly annihilated, and Union forces also suffered scores of killed and wounded. On the morning of 25 April the battered but triumphant Union fleet anchored near the New Orleans levee, facing a chaotic and burning city where mobs looted and ran amok in the streets. Just upstream at the Tift shipyard, an all-out struggle to move the *Mississippi* had been under way for twenty-four desperate hours. Despite all efforts, the two assigned steamers were unable to budge the massive vessel, so Commander Arthur Sinclair went down to New Orleans to find additional towboats, leaving Waddell in command with orders to burn the ship if the enemy approached. On the devastated waterfront Sinclair found that all remaining boats had fled, were burning, or were sinking. As he returned upriver to the Mississippi valley's last remaining hope, he was shattered to see a pall of black smoke above his burning ironclad, for he knew there was nothing left now on the river to prevent Farragut from linking up with Foote's squadron far to the north.[19]

Waddell went to Vicksburg with the remnant of the Confederate naval command and immediately received orders to return to Richmond. There he was reassigned as an ordnance officer to the shore battery on the James River at Drewry's Bluff. With the loss of the css *Virginia*, the James River and Richmond lay virtually defenseless as a Union squadron spearheaded by the ironclad uss *Galena* cautiously worked its way upstream through mines and obstructions. On Drewry's Bluff, just seven miles downstream from Richmond, Waddell joined the naval contingent that confronted the Union fleet on 15 May in a three-hour duel which stopped the Union gunboats and saved Richmond from immediate capture. That summer the fortifications were expanded and more guns mounted, until Drewry's Bluff seemed impregnable. While Waddell was on active duty, Anne remained in Annapolis, keeping in touch through mutual friends and correspondence. Waddell continued to serve in the naval battery through the fall and was promoted to the rank of first lieutenant from 2 October 1862.[20]

In January 1863 Confederate ironclads at Charleston sallied forth and mauled Federal blockaders, temporarily driving them out to sea. The Union response was to gather a fleet of monitors off Charleston, with the possibility of penetrating the network of Confederate batteries in the harbor and taking the city, despised in the North as the birthplace of secession. At Confederate naval headquarters in Richmond, Waddell joined other enterprising officers to consider the problem of how best to capture the monitors if they made it into Charleston harbor. He was then ordered to report to Charleston on 18 February to Lieutenant William A. Webb, who organized "the forlorn hope." The plan was to send boarding parties from small boats and steamers to jam the turrets with wedges, blind the pilot house with blankets, cast explosives down the smokestack, and drop incendiaries and smoke bombs through the turret openings. Spar torpedoes also were to be mounted on the steamers. Fortunately for both sides, there was never an opportunity to try these suicidal tactics, and Waddell soon received orders to proceed from Charleston to Europe.[21]

Meanwhile, Commander Bulloch, following his 1862 coup of sending the commerce raiders *Florida* and *Alabama* to sea from England, was pursuing the other goal of Confederate naval strategy—to provide seagoing ironclads to break the blockade of Southern ports. By the spring of 1863 Bulloch and Commander James H. North had under contract in Great Britain and France five powerful ironclads and four conventional cruisers in various stages of construction. The most advanced were the two ironclad rams being built at Liverpool by the Laird brothers, who had completed the *Alabama*. Despite the incessant spying of Union agents, it had been possible to mask the *Florida* and the *Alabama* as merchant vessels, but there was no way that the turreted ironclad rams could be portrayed as anything other than future warships. As Southern high seas raiders cut swaths of destruction across the Atlantic, Union diplomatic pressure on Britain became increasingly intense, and Union espionage was nearly frantic in an effort to prevent any more Confederate vessels from going to sea. Bulloch countered the hardening British attitude toward his ships by maneuvering a sale to a Paris trading house, Bravay and Company, which was ostensibly brokering the ironclads for Egypt. This deal fell through when Bulloch's personal secretary, Clarence Younge, betrayed him and sold information to United States officials. Britain ultimately seized the ironclads in October 1863 and bought them for the Royal Navy the next year.[22]

Early in 1863, when it appeared that a Confederate fleet was near completion in Europe, Secretary Mallory dispatched officers to man these ships, and Waddell was slated to be a first lieutenant on one of the Laird rams. Waddell left Charleston on 19 March on the blockade runner *General Beauregard*, headed to Bermuda. After a month he took passage on a British packet to Halifax, Nova Scotia. There he telegraphed home and received the devastating news that his only child, Anne, had died two months earlier. He sent for his wife to join him at Halifax, and they proceeded on to England with a contingent of Confederate naval officers. Although Waddell kept in touch with Confederate authorities, he and Anne spent the next two months touring Europe, visiting France, Switzerland, Germany, Belgium, Scotland, and Ireland. The Waddells returned to Liverpool at the end of July, and Anne left for Maryland in mid-August. When the Laird rams were impounded, Waddell sent for Anne again and settled into a long wait in England and France divided among Liverpool, Calais, and, chiefly, Paris. Anne remained with her husband until he assumed command of the *Shenandoah*.

With a vision of his mighty battle fleet shaping up in Europe, Secretary Mallory dispatched for its command the high-ranking Commodore Samuel Barron Sr., accompanied by more junior officers. Barron arrived in Liverpool in October 1863 after the Laird rams had been seized and then went on to Paris, where he established his naval headquarters. As the long months passed, Waddell became restless, and in July 1864 he considered an offer to captain a blockade runner at £1,000 per trip. Commodore Barron approved the command, but Anne Waddell convinced her husband to decline.[23]

Then, at last, the long wait was over for Waddell. When Bulloch's

Waddell in a photo-
graph probably taken in
the fall of 1864 before
he left England on the
CSS *Shenandoah*. He
held the rank of lieuten-
ant commanding in the
Confederate States
Navy and is wearing
commander's rank.
(Naval Historical Cen-
ter, Washington, D.C.)

orders to replace the *Alabama* arrived on 30 August 1864, he immediately sent his broker, Richard Wright, to Glasgow to find a suitable
vessel. The purchase of the *Sea King* in September touched off a rapid
chain of events flawlessly orchestrated by Bulloch. A tender, the *Laurel*, which easily passed for a blockade runner, was loaded in Liverpool
with the armament for the future raider, and the *Sea King*, commanded
by British Captain Peter Corbett, was sent to London to await orders.
On 5 September in Paris Waddell was appointed "lieutenant commanding" by Commodore Barron and ordered to Liverpool. Within a
week he and his wife had taken an apartment in Liverpool, and Waddell reported to Bulloch. On 28 September Lieutenant Carter returned
from Richmond with details of the projected cruise as well as the
whaling chart published by world-famous oceanographer and Confederate officer Commander Matthew F. Maury. By 6 October all of the
cruiser's officers had been sent by Commodore Barron to Liverpool,

where they were living singly in rooming houses and inns, having no knowledge of their assignment except to await orders from Bulloch. Bulloch set the escape of the cruiser in motion by notifying Lieutenant William C. Whittle Jr., the executive officer of the cruiser, to proceed to London. Although young, Whittle had seen considerable service on the cruiser css *Nashville*, the *Louisiana* at New Orleans, and the css *Chattahoochee*. At London Whittle checked in to Wood's Hotel under the name of W. C. Brown. At eleven o'clock on the morning of 7 October, he sat with a newspaper and a white napkin in a coat buttonhole in the hotel restaurant, where he was approached by an agent, Richard Wright, and told to join the *Sea King* that night. In the early morning darkness of 8 October Whittle boarded the *Sea King*, which then sailed down the Thames, apparently bound for Bombay, India.[24]

With the *Sea King* safely away, a telegraphed coded message was sent to Bulloch, who then got word to Lieutenant Ramsay that the *Laurel* was to leave that night. The "passengers" were notified by messenger to be aboard about eight o'clock that evening. Acting Master's Mate Cornelius E. Hunt remembered that as he strode silently toward the wharf through the dense, chilly mist he saw several of his comrades walking alone in the gloom but did not speak to them for fear of notice by Union spies. He was apprehensive about the long-anticipated sea adventure, which might lead to wealth and fame or, just as easily, to a "felon's doom." Yet, as the voyage began, he felt that he was "too young and hopeful to long contemplate the dark side of the case; the ship I was to join was afloat; the ocean was before us, and, sailor-like, I was content to put my trust in Providence, Neptune, and the Southern Confederacy."[25]

The *Laurel* steamed away, bound officially for Havana, Cuba, with a coaling stop at Funchal in the Madeira Islands. In his cabin Waddell opened and read his orders from Commodore Barron and lengthy sailing instructions from Commander Bulloch, who wrote, "You are about to proceed upon a cruise in the far-distant Pacific, into the seas and among islands frequented by the great American whaling fleet, a source of abundant wealth to our enemies and a nursery for their seamen. It is hoped that you may be able to greatly damage and disperse that fleet, even if you do not succeed in utterly destroying it."[26] Bulloch anticipated that Waddell could recruit from the *Sea King* and the *Laurel* the more than one hundred crewmen needed to handle the ship and work the guns. He would be on his own on the other side of the world in the stormy northern Pacific and the hostile Arctic Ocean.

Back in Liverpool, U.S. consul Dudley was again thwarted when the *Laurel* slipped through his grasp. His information on the steamer was partly correct in that she was carrying guns, equipment, and crew "for a piratical cruise against the United States," but he had exaggerated notions about the number of men aboard. Even more unfounded was his belief that the Northern merchant fleet's worst nightmare, the notorious Captain Raphael Semmes of the late *Alabama*, was to command the new raider. By the end of the month the U.S. agent in Funchal confirmed Dudley's suspicion that the Confederates had indeed managed to slip another high seas marauder through his network.[27]

The *Laurel* entered the harbor at Funchal on 16 October and waited for the *Sea King*. At night on the eighteenth the lookout spied a full-rigged ship standing off the mouth of the harbor. The next morning the stranger displayed the recognition flag, and both ships cleared the harbor. In the nearby cluster of islets known as Las Desertas off the island of Porto Santo, the two vessels anchored and were lashed alongside for the transfer of the cargo and coal from the *Laurel*. As first officer, Lieutenant Whittle took charge of the outfitting. Supplemented by hired local fishermen, officers and men labored in tandem around the clock, and by the next morning, 19 October, the deck of the *Sea King* was strewn with guns, equipment, and supplies. The crewmen were called aft, where Captain Corbett announced the sale of the vessel to the Confederacy as a commerce raider. Waddell, dressed in full C.S. Navy uniform, then read his commission and declared the *Sea King* to be the css *Shenandoah*. He offered an enlistment bounty of £15, but only four men joined. With five men from the *Laurel* and the Confederate naval personnel who had been quietly included among the passengers, Waddell had a disappointing total of only twenty-three officers and nineteen crewmen, far short of the minimum required for handling the ship.[28] The wary sailors remembered all too well the past summer's disastrous battle and heavy casualties sustained when the *Alabama* sank off Cherbourg.

Accustomed to the shipshape ways of the old navy, Waddell was "much discouraged" by the lack of response, and on Lieutenant Whittle's advice he called a council of officers to decide whether they should continue the cruise. When the officers unanimously agreed to work the ship alongside the crew, the Confederate ensign was hoisted and, with parting salutes, at six o'clock in the evening the *Laurel* and the *Shenandoah* slipped their bonds and sailed away in opposite directions. The first task was to clear the decks of the "hopeless confusion" of boxes, trunks, casks of beef and bread, and guns. With Waddell at the helm, the other officers joined the men "barefooted and with trousers rolled up," storing provisions and supplies, cutting gunports, and mounting the battery of four eight-inch smooth-bore shell guns, two Whitworth rifled thirty-two pounders, and two twelve-pound howitzers. Until the magazine was constructed, the powder was stored in a cabin next door to the captain's quarters. Once the decks were cleared, they were scrubbed and holystoned, the brass was polished, and the *Shenandoah* took on the appearance of a squared-away man-of-war.[29] The men of the cruiser did not know that on 7 October, the day before the vessel had sailed from London, the *Florida* had been taken by a night assault in the neutral port of Bahia, Brazil. This violation of Brazil's neutrality created an international diplomatic incident, and it left the *Shenandoah* the sole Confederate raider on the high seas.

On 28 October a sail was spotted and the rebel raider began her first chase. In about an hour the crew of the *Shenandoah* could make out the British ensign on the ship she was pursuing. The ship's design appeared to be so American that the raider closed in and fired a blank to halt the vessel. She turned out to be the *Mogul* of London, one of the many American vessels that had been sold to the British to avoid destruction. Two days later, after a two-hour chase, the crew of the raider boarded and took the ship's first prize, the bark *Alina* from Maine. She was loaded with railroad iron, and vessel and cargo were valued at $95,000. The officers were paroled and the crew temporarily confined in irons, except for six who joined the C.S. Navy. The order was given to scuttle the prize, and the *Shenandoah's* carpenter went over to drill holes in the hull.[30] As the *Alina*, the first of many prizes, went down, Master's Mate Hunt looked on with "a curious heart-heaviness that none but a sailor can understand, to see the gallant old barque sink into her orcas grave." With all sails set, the *Alina* went down "right bravely" about four o'clock, stern first, with her bow high in the air. Hunt found it appalling to watch for the first time as a ship sank, especially one intentionally scuttled. To him it was like standing at a deathbed witnessing "the sinking away of a soul into the ocean of eternity."[31]

The cruise settled into a pattern of searching for ships and determining whether they were foreign-owned or legitimate prizes. Once a vessel was taken, the crew was removed from the prize, which was then looted of any supplies or equipment needed for the *Shenandoah*.

Personal baggage of captured crewmen was not rifled, although prisoners were first kept in irons in the locked top-gallant forecastle. This was done to encourage recruitment as well as for the safety of the short-handed cruiser. Captured officers were granted parole and given the freedom of the ship. Neutral vessels were used to convey prisoners away.

On 5 November the schooner *Charter Oak* of San Francisco was stopped and, before being burned, looted of provisions, particularly preserved fruit and canned tomatoes, and furniture for the officers' cabins and the wardroom. Waddell wrote that his ship's compartments were poorly furnished. He started the cruise with nearly bare quarters in "as cheerless a spot as ever the sun shone on," so the boats returned laden with welcome sofas, chairs, and tables from the nicely appointed *Charter Oak*. For the first time the cruiser had women and children aboard, as the passengers on the prize included the captain's wife and his sister-in-law and her son, who were housed aboard the *Shenandoah* in one of the two cabins available to Waddell. The *Charter Oak* was the first of many prizes burned; two days later the same fate befell the *D. Godfrey* of Boston and her cargo of lumber and beef. On 10 November a Danish brig, the *Anna Jane*, was hailed, and her captain agreed to take the prisoners to Rio de Janeiro.[32]

Between 10 and 13 November the rebels destroyed two prizes, the New York brig *Susan* and the schooner *Lizzie M. Stacy* from Boston, and bonded the clipper ship *Kate Prince*, which was carrying a neutral-owned cargo. On the fifteenth, when the equator was reached, the *Shenandoah* was visited by "King Neptune" and his court to initiate all on board who had never before crossed into the Southern Hemisphere. The grotesque "king" appeared with a large trident and an outlandish wig. Men brought before him were mock shaved with tar and soap and a barrel hoop razor and blasted with a stream of water from the pump. The whole crew enjoyed the tomfoolery of the age-old naval ritual.

For nearly three weeks all sails encountered proved to be neutral, until on 4 December, in sight of the isolated island of Tristan da Cunha, a Yankee whaler, the *Edward*, was found hove to, engaged in cutting up a right whale. The *Shenandoah* lay alongside the whaler for two days restocking the larder. After burning the *Edward*, the cruiser took her crew to Tristan da Cunha, which towered nearly seven thousand feet above the Atlantic, and left the men in the tiny settlement there with adequate provisions. Much later Waddell learned that

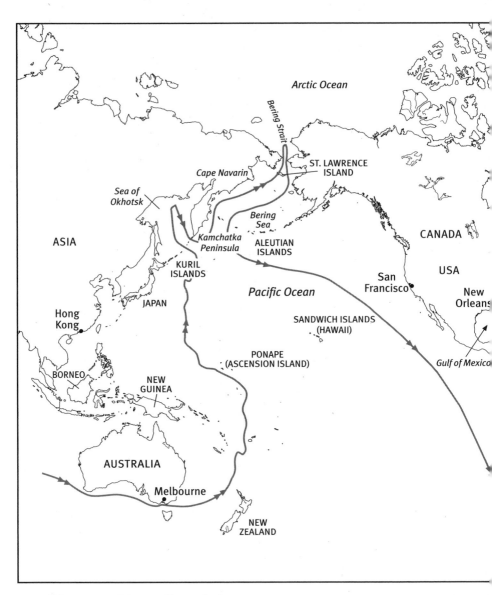

The voyage of the css *Shenandoah*

twelve hours after the cruiser's departure the uss *Iroquois*, close in pursuit, called at the island.[33]

The day after sailing from Tristan da Cunha, the cruiser's crew discovered damage in the propeller coupling, to which the engineers made a temporary repair. Waddell decided to avoid Cape Town and push on across the Indian Ocean to Australia. The *Shenandoah* rounded the Cape of Good Hope well below 40° south latitude and was now racing

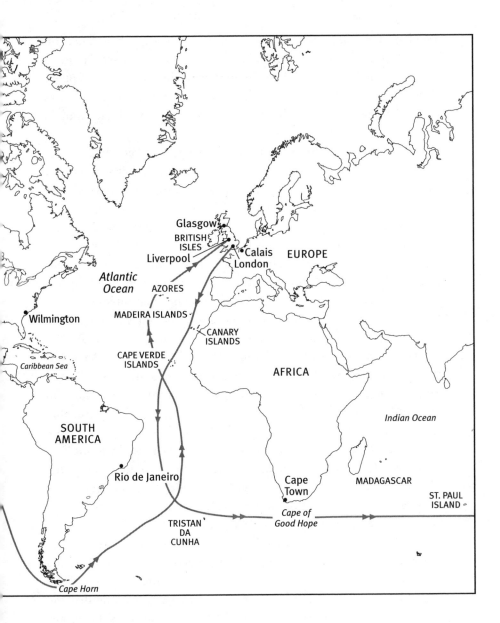

before the "roaring forties," the sustained winds blowing from the west. Seas were high, and the raider weathered several severe gales in which mountainous waves broke over the ship, forcing the gunports to be smashed open to drain the deck. Under a leaden sky, day after day, the ship drove east with reefed topsails, buffeted by snow, hail, squalls, high winds, and huge waves. On a rainy 29 December the *Shenandoah* was wallowing under short sail in a broken cross sea when a sail was spied approaching astern. Those aboard the unsuspecting American bark *Delphine* from Bangor, Maine, were dismayed to see the rebel ensign hoisted and a gun fired in answer to their hail. The captain, William G. Nichols, tried to save his ship by pleading that his wife was sickly and might die if she left the *Delphine*. Surgeon Charles Lining, sent over to attend to the invalid, reported that the lady in question was not only in "robust health" but fine-looking, cultured, and strong-willed. Lillian Nichols came on board with her maid, her son, a caged canary, and all of her possessions except her piano. Her initial surliness soon softened under the attention paid her by the young, gallant officers of the raider, and she provided an attractive and welcome diversion in the wardroom for the remainder of the voyage to Australia.[34]

The new year of 1865 brought a brief stop at the desolate French-owned island of St. Paul, where the ship's officers bargained for fish and chickens and brought back a pet penguin. The three-week run from St. Paul to Australia was uneventful, and on 25 January the *Shenandoah* was met at the Melbourne harbor entrance by a pilot who agreed to take her in when informed of the disabled propeller coupling. Proceeding into the bay, the cruiser was surrounded by a fleet of local steamboats and launches crowded with curious residents who were titillated by the visit of a notorious "rebel pirate." Confirmation that the Confederacy had "a great many friends" in the city came from the cheering crowds on the boats and on the wharves. Assistant Surgeon Fred I. McNulty wrote that as the *Shenandoah* moved into the harbor, "never was conquering flag at peak hailed with such honors as were given us upon that bright, tropical morning. . . . Flags dipped, cannon boomed, and men in long thousands cheered."[35]

The *Shenandoah* was cordially received as well by local officials and was granted permission by the governor to make the extensive repairs she needed. When the vessel was hauled out in the government slip and the damage was inspected, it proved to be so serious that the cruiser's stay lengthened into nearly a month. Waddell took the opportunity to write an extensive report to Secretary Mallory and Commodore Barron, unaware that his message would be sent into a void. Before the ship was laid up, she was virtually besieged by throngs of curious Australian visitors, who crowded on board after her first day in port. Local clubs hosted the officers, while balls and other entertainments were held for the exotic visitors. Amid the festivities, Union sympathizers encouraged desertion, anonymous threats were made, and Union diplomatic pressure began to have an effect.[36]

After a harrowing passage through the "roaring forties," the CSS *Shenandoah* entered the port of Melbourne, Australia, on 25 January 1865 for repairs and supplies. (North Carolina Division of Archives and History, Raleigh)

The Confederates also hoped clandestinely to replace the deserters and fill out their crew with adventure-seeking Australians; but to recruit actively was a violation of neutrality. Soon Waddell was embroiled in a controversy with the local police over "Charlie the cook," an alleged recruit whom he repeatedly denied harboring, although he exercised his rights and declined to allow officials to search the ship. The crisis reached a climax on 14 February when the ship was surrounded by police and a detachment of Royal Artillery. Waddell still refused to back down, but "Charlie" and three others were discovered, set ashore, and immediately arrested. The "Charlie" incident was not resolved until a trial after the *Shenandoah* had left, but the cruiser was released and allowed to take on coal and provisions for departure. Despite his public stance of innocence in the "Charlie" affair, Waddell looked the other way as some forty-two Australians were secretly brought on board the vessel on the evening before her departure.[37]

As the *Shenandoah* set off across the Pacific, the stowaways crawled out from every nook and cranny of the ship, including fourteen from the hollow iron bowsprit, where they had nearly suffocated. The "old sea-dogs" were brought before Waddell and with straight faces solemnly declared to a man that they were native-born Southerners who wished to defend their country. With the Australian contingent Waddell could muster about one hundred officers and men, fully manning the ship for the first time. News of the cruiser's presence had dispersed the whalers in the South Pacific, so Waddell skirted the New Zealand coast and headed north, running into severe storms. At Drummond Island natives reported that no whalers had been seen, but a few days later a trading schooner reported that there were ships at Ponape in the Caroline Archipelago.

On 26 March the *Shenandoah* crossed the equator into the North Pacific, her appointed cruising ground. April Fool's Day found the Confederates approaching Ponape harbor, which held four whalers— the *Edward Cary*, the *Hector*, the *Pearl*, and the *Harvest*. The local pilot, an escaped Australian convict, took them through the tricky channel in the reef, and the raider anchored so as to block the exit. Four boats with armed prize crews were sent to pay visits to the unsuspecting prey. As soon as the boats were under way, the Confederates hoisted their colors and fired a gun, startling the natives gathered on the beach and sending them scurrying into the undergrowth. Bowing to the inevitable, the whalers hauled down their colors. After the prizes were plundered for anything useful to the cruiser, the natives were allowed to take what was left. This was a rare opportunity for the islanders, whom the whaling fleet had exploited for years, and "they made the most of it," swarming over the doomed hulks all day. The ships were then burned over a period of several days.[38]

The next day the tribal chief, King Ish-y-paw, accepted Waddell's invitation to visit the *Shenandoah* and arrived with his court retainers, decked out in flower wreaths and grass skirts, in a fleet of seventy war canoes colorfully decorated with bright cloth. The heavily tattooed courtiers were escorted to the captain's cabin, where they were offered a smoke and plied with schnapps. The king was paid with old muskets and tobacco to keep watch over the cruiser's moorings. On another visit the royal party toured the ship and was most astonished by the engine room. The king was presented with a sword, and in return, on the day before the ship's departure, he offered two chickens and a dozen coconuts as a present to his brother ruler, the great warrior Jeff Davis. Leaving all the prisoners with adequate provisions, the cruiser weighed anchor on 13 April to continue her mission. During the pleasant interlude at Ponape, half a world away the momentous first week in April had seen the collapse of the Confederate army in Virginia, the evacuation of Richmond, and Lee's surrender at Appomattox. Ish-y-paw's brother sovereign was now a fugitive in his own country.[39]

Setting a northerly course, Waddell steered the *Shenandoah* across the Pacific through the snowy Kuril Islands. For five weeks the raider did not cross the wake of another ship, and there were only gales to break the monotony. On 21 May the raider entered the Sea of Okhotsk and headed toward the Siberian coast of Kamchatka. A week later, in heavy ice floes, the whaler *Abigail* of New Bedford was taken and burned, the first prize since the cruiser had left Ponape. During the plundering, the crew got into a store of trade whiskey, and many of them ended up drunk and in irons over the next three days. Hunt wrote that "it was the most general and stupendous 'spree' I ever witnessed." When the crew sobered up, these sailors from temperate climes spent a miserable three weeks dodging ice floes in the cold, dreary, and empty Sea of Okhotsk before turning south to reenter the North Pacific.[40]

Rounding the Kamchatka Peninsula, the *Shenandoah* entered the Bering Sea in a heavy fog on 16 June in search of the whaling fleet that had so far eluded her. Five days passed before lookouts spotted drifting whale meat off Cape Navarin. The cruiser followed the current and on the morning of 22 June came upon the *William Thompson* and the *Euphrates*, followed over the next two days by the *Milo*, the *Sophia Thornton*, the *Jireh Swift*, and the *Susan Abigail*. All six of the prizes were plundered for ship's stores and provisions and burned, except for the *Milo*, which was bonded and received all of the prisoners. One of the Yankee skippers told Waddell that the war was over, but he had no way to confirm this startling news. Although an April newspaper on the *Susan Abigail* was filled with the discouraging accounts of Richmond's fall and Lee's surrender, it also included a proclamation from President Davis from Danville, Virginia, pledging to continue the war with redoubled effort.[41]

The next day the *Shenandoah* enjoyed a brief interlude off the island of St. Lawrence, surrounded by several Eskimo kayaks, which approached the ship to trade furs and walrus tusks for tobacco and whiskey. Then, on 25 June, the seizure and destruction of the *General Williams* began a four-day bonanza that netted eighteen whalers, of which fifteen were burned. On the first day, as the cruiser closed on her clustered quarry, the scene was "indescribably beautiful," with the sun's rays reflecting from "glittering fields of ice." Off the starboard bow a whaleboat was being towed hell-for-leather on a "Nantucket sleigh ride" by a right whale that it had just harpooned. Other ships were flensing, or cutting up, whales lashed alongside, while still others were rendering oil from the blubber in cooking vats. Seals swam around the ships or rested on the drifting ice. Of the six whalers caught that day, four were burned and two were bonded to take home the 250 prisoners, who were so numerous that they had been towed behind the raider in whaleboats during the capture of the fleet.[42]

Although the whalers were in close proximity, the *Shenandoah* had to steam slowly through drifting ice to reach each one. On 28 June the raider made her greatest haul, taking eleven prizes. There was no escape for her victims, for the ice hemmed them in; moreover, most were anchored, processing their catches. Again the large number of prisoners, about four hundred, so threatened the safety of the ship that they were placed in towed boats. Nine of the oil-laden whalers burned quickly and brightly, illuminating the horizon "with a fiery glare presenting a picture of indescribable grandeur, while the water was covered with black smoke mingled with flashes of fire." To Master's Mate Hunt, "the last act in the bloody drama of the American civil war had been played." Hearing that there were a number of whalers in the polar sea, the *Shenandoah* passed through the Bering Strait into the Arctic Ocean on 29 June but could see only a vast, unbroken field of ice. The cruiser turned back at 66°40′ north latitude, none too soon, as the strait was closed by drifting ice shortly after she passed through. With no fresh prey in sight, Waddell decided to sail south out of the treacherous fog and ice of the Bering Sea. By 5 July the *Shenandoah* was through the Aleutian Islands into the Pacific, having successfully completed her mission of scouring the Arctic seas of the New England whaling fleet.[43]

Over the next month Waddell headed generally southeast toward California, with a vague plan of possibly raiding, and extracting ransom from, San Francisco. Hoping to contact a neutral ship offshore for intelligence about the port's defenses, on 2 August he stopped the English bark *Barracouta* and learned from the captain and a recent newspaper that the war was indeed over. Surgeon Lining wrote that it was "doomed to be one of the blackest of all the black days of my life, for from to-day I must look forward to begin life over again, starting where I cannot tell, how I cannot say—but I have learned for a certainty that I have no country." The battery was immediately struck and stowed in the hold, and the ship was completely disarmed. From that date the *Shenandoah* ceased hostile operations against the United States, but the problem remained that most of her prizes had been seized after the war had ended. It also was clear from the newspapers that Waddell and his men were being sought as pirates.[44]

With the possibility of piracy charges eliminating the United States as a destination, Waddell favored returning to Great Britain, where, he hoped, Bulloch could provide funds to pay the crew. Initially swayed by his men to sail to the nearest British port of Sydney, Australia, within twenty-four hours Waddell, probably thinking of the numerous problems he had had with Melbourne officials, changed course, heading south toward Cape Horn and Europe. He also was influenced by the belief that the United States Navy's pursuit would head toward the North Pacific. Some of the crew, upset by his apparent vacillation, petitioned him to reconsider Australia, to which he responded with a promise to enter the first English port.[45]

The *Shenandoah* was now headed for the long, lonely voyage around dangerous, tempestuous Cape Horn. As weeks passed, the monotony and low morale bred rumors and some cases of drunkenness, dereliction of duty, and insubordination, even among the officers. Waddell ran the ship with the lighter hand of a merchant captain instead of a naval officer, but overall the routines established by many months at sea as a man-of-war were maintained. By 15 September the cruiser rounded the cape in a gale and headed north through a field of icebergs into the Atlantic. The nearness of Cape Town, which at least qualified as a colonial British port, brought another flurry of petitions by officers and crew anxious to end the voyage, but the effort subsided after a majority of the watch officers voted for Liverpool. Seventy of the crew backed the captain by signing a petition expressing satisfaction with his decision. When Waddell realized that the *Shenandoah* would become the only Confederate ship to circumnavigate the globe, he sent champagne to the wardroom to celebrate.[46]

The *Shenandoah* forged steadily onward to the north, stealthily avoiding all passing ships, and crossing the equator for the last time on 11 October. Again the monotony, broken only by occasional squalls, led to some quarrels and a near duel. Toward the end of the voyage, two crewmen died of old illnesses—the first fatalities of the entire cruise—a remarkable record, considering the length and conditions of the voyage. The last anxious moment came about five hundred miles southeast of the Azores when a vessel that looked suspiciously like a U.S. man-of-war seemed to be closing on the *Shenandoah*. Waddell placed the ship on steam for the first time since leaving the Bering Sea and that night changed course to shake the stranger. He later determined that the vessel was probably the USS *Saranac*.[47]

At daylight on 5 November the *Shenandoah* made a perfect landfall at the entrance to St. George's Channel, even though the ship's chronometer had not been rated since Melbourne. On the approach to Liverpool, not knowing what their reception would be, Waddell divided the prize money taken prior to the end of the war among the officers and crew, declining his rightful share. Around midnight a pilot boarded to take the ship up the Mersey River. When told that he was on the Confederate raider, his surprised reply was that he thought the ship was still in the Arctic. At 9:00 A.M. on 6 November the graceful raider dropped anchor for the last time, ending a round-the-world odyssey of 58,000 miles and returning with a war record of thirty-eight captures valued at over a million dollars and more than a thousand prisoners. The *Shenandoah* had fired the last shot of the Civil War on 29 June to halt a neutral vessel. On 6 November Waddell mustered the crew for a ceremonial lowering of the last Confederate flag, six months after the war had ended.[48]

The *Shenandoah*, at anchor next to the HMS *Donegal*, was an embarrassment to the British government, which no longer wished to be reminded of the depredations visited on the United States by the Confederate cruisers acquired in Britain. Waddell's letter to Foreign Secretary Lord John Russell surrendering the *Shenandoah* to Great Britain brought a gunboat and guard to keep the crew from leaving. Within two days, Crown judges ruled that the ship could be turned over to the United States as the successor government to the Confederacy. All Southern crew members would be allowed to leave. When the muster was held on 10 November, the 133 officers and men on board stepped up and unabashedly declared, one and all, that they were from one of the Southern states. Waddell bid them farewell, thanking them for doing their duty in defending their lost country, and the crew responded with three cheers for the captain. The next day Waddell secured enough funds from Commander Bulloch to make partial payments toward what was owed the crew.[49]

The *Shenandoah* was turned over to the United States. Consul Dudley hired a merchant captain to sail her across the Atlantic in late November, but within two weeks she returned, badly damaged by a severe gale. The former cruiser lay at anchor at Liverpool until she was purchased for $108,000 by the Sultan of Zanzibar for use as his luxury yacht. After he apparently lost interest in the project, the *Shenandoah* was outfitted as the merchant vessel *Majidi* and plied the seas of Southeast Asia for over a decade. In 1879 the historic ship foundered on a reef in the Indian Ocean and was lost.[50]

Waddell took a home in Waterloo, a suburb of Liverpool, where he waited for his wife to join him. Anne had returned to her family in Annapolis after the *Laurel* left Liverpool. When news of the *Shenandoah*'s depredations reached Washington, Anne Waddell was placed under house arrest in January 1865 and then released under bond to remain in the United States, in effect as a hostage. She was subsequently granted parole on condition that she not communicate with her husband. In December 1865, bitter over his wife's restraint, Waddell wrote, "So ends my naval career, and I am called a pirate. I made New England suffer, and I do not regret it. I cannot be condemned by any honest-thinking man."[51] The family garnered political support for Anne's release, and soon she was able to join him. By the fall of 1867 the exiles had returned home to Annapolis and were living with Waddell's in-laws, the Igleharts. Waddell occupied his time by working on his memoir of the now-famous cruise.[52]

To support his family Waddell saw no choice but to return to the sea, and in New York in 1870 he secured a master's license for steam navigation. By 1875 he was in California, where he had been offered a position with the British-owned Pacific Mail Steamship Company. Initially, there was some opposition to him in San Francisco because of his war record, so he returned to Annapolis and built a home there. He was summoned back to California in the fall of 1876 and offered command of the new passenger ship, *City of San Francisco*, which was built to operate from Panama to Japan and Australia. On his first cruise to Melbourne since the war, he was welcomed by crowds drawn by his notoriety and by pleasant memories of his exciting stay in 1865. After several uneventful voyages, on 16 May 1877 the liner ran on an uncharted reef near Tartar Shoal, Mexico, and a gash was ripped in her hull. Some thirteen miles offshore, Waddell turned the stricken vessel toward the coast and grounded her about three miles from shore. Following the rescue of the 251 passengers and crew without loss of life, Waddell was the last to leave the vessel as she went under. He was exonerated in the hearing on the ship's loss and remained with the Pacific Mail Company as an agent to establish new ship lines.[53]

Waddell returned to Annapolis in 1882 and became the commander of the Maryland State Fishery Force, charged with enforcing state fishing laws on the Potomac River and Chesapeake Bay. Oyster poaching ended when Waddell's armed police boat, *Leila*, caught a fleet of Virginia boats illegally dredging in Maryland waters, drove three of the "oyster pirates" aground in a skirmish, sunk one by howitzer fire, and scattered the remainder.

From his Annapolis office Waddell wrote his brother Guion in April 1885: "I have been a wanderer on the face of the earth for so many years." Eleven months later the "wanderer" died suddenly at his home on 15 March 1886. In honor of Annapolis's famous adopted son, the Maryland state legislature adjourned and came as a group to the funeral. There, officers from the naval academy and Confederate veterans were bound together in paying homage to a great sea captain, "the last Rebel."[54]

Glossary of Nautical Terms

Aft, after: toward the stern of a vessel.

Bark, barque: a three-masted vessel with square-rigged foremast and mainmast and fore-and-aft rigged mizzenmast.

Beam: the breadth of a ship.

Beat to quarters: the drum call to battle stations.

Bowsprit: a large spar extending over the bow of a ship from which the jib sails are set.

Brig: a two-masted vessel with square-rigged foremast and mainmast.

Brigantine: a two-masted vessel with square-rigged foremast and mainmast, except for the mainsail, which is fore-and-aft rigged.

Bulkhead: partition between cabins in a vessel.

Bulwark: the raised sides of a vessel above the deck.

Bumboat: a boat in port selling provisions, supplies, and services to a vessel.

Cable: thick rope to which an anchor was attached.

Canister: a shot made up of small iron balls packed in a tin case.

Capstan: an upright winch situated near the fore part of a ship, used principally to weigh the anchors.

Careen: to heel a ship on her side for hull cleaning and repairs.

Carronade: a short cannon of large caliber used for close-range fighting.

Chains: the hardware used to secure the lower shrouds of a mast to the ship's side.

Chaser: a long gun used in a chase, mounted on the bow or stern.

Commodore: a senior captain holding temporary rank as a squadron or fleet commander.

Cutting-out: the capture of a prize in port by small boats at night.

Flag officer: rank equivalent to commodore or admiral.

Forecastle: the forwardmost part of the upper deck, or the portion beneath it, where the enlisted sailors sling their hammocks.

Frigate: a fast square-rigged, three-masted naval vessel carrying twenty-eight to fifty guns.

Galliot: a small boat rigged with a single mast and oars.

Grape shot: small iron balls in a canvas bag used against personnel.

Haul: to pull, as in "hauling a sheet."

Helm: the tiller or wheel used to control the rudder to steer the ship.

Hove to: a stationary ship turned into the wind.

Impressment: forcible drafting of seamen from shore or at sea, usually from merchant vessels.

Jib: a triangular sail set on the bowsprit to the foremast.

Kedge: a secondary anchor used in mooring or to move a ship that is in harbor or aground.

Keel: the main or bottom timber in a ship's frame to which the stem, most ribs, and stern are attached; a ship's backbone.

Line: any rope on a ship not used in setting the sails.

Lee, leeward: the side of the ship or shore sheltered from the wind.

Mainmast: the second mast of a vessel carrying two or more masts.

Master: the officer responsible for navigating and sailing the ship; also the captain of a merchant vessel.

Mate: on a merchant ship, a deck officer ranking below the captain; in the navy, a petty officer or noncommissioned officer.

Midshipman: a senior petty officer and candidate for a commission, ranking below lieutenant.

Mizzenmast: the mast nearest the stern of a vessel carrying three masts.

Packet: a regularly scheduled passenger and mail boat.

Periauger: an open workboat, the design probably derived from the log canoe, usually having two masts and oars; it was common on North Carolina sounds and rivers.

Pink: a small Dutch square-rigged coastal vessel with a narrow stern, often used for fishing.

Pinnace: a ship's longboat or tender equipped to be rowed or sailed.

Polacre: a Mediterranean ship-type of two or more masts, usually square-rigged.

Port: the left side of a vessel as one faces forward.

Quarter: plea for mercy or surrender; the denial of quarter meant a fight to the death.

Quarterdeck: the aft portion of the deck, usually raised on larger vessels, which is the command center of the ship, where the captain, master, and officer of the deck were stationed.

Quartermaster: a petty officer who assisted with steering, signaling, and navigation.

Reefers: slang for midshipmen.

Reefing: reducing the exposed sail area by rolling the sail up and tying it with reef points or line; masts could be reefed by shortening or taking down a section.

Schooner: a vessel with two or more masts that are fore-and-aft rigged.

Shallop: a ship's boat propelled by oars or a sail.

Sheets: rope attached to the sails and used to set them.

Ship-of-the-line: the multidecked battleship of the eighteenth and nineteenth centuries, mounting from seventy-four to more than a hundred guns.

Shrouds: the cables or ropes running from the mastheads to the sides of a vessel, which support the masts.

Sloop: A single-masted fore-and-aft rigged boat; ship sloops had three masts, and brig sloops had two.

Snow: the largest two-masted square-rigged vessel, usually a merchant ship.

Spars: all poles in a vessel's rigging, including the bowsprit, masts, and yards.

Starboard: the right side of a vessel as one faces forward.

Stays: part of the standing rigging that supports the masts; named for the mast, as in forestay or mainstay.

Sweeps: long, heavy oars used to row small sailing vessels; also a steering oar.

Swivel gun: a small cannon mounted on a swivel, usually on the top or rail of the bulwark.

Tender: an auxiliary to a man-of-war, usually a supply ship.

Topgallant: the mast above the topmast; also refers to the sail it carries.

Topsail: a sail set above the mainsail.

Windward: the side of the ship or shore against which the wind is blowing; also called the weather side.

Yard: a long, narrow spar attached to the mast to support the sails.

Notes

ABBREVIATIONS

BNL	*Boston News-Letter*
CFR	*Carolina Federal Republican* (New Bern, N.C.)
CSPCS	William N. Sainsbury, Cecil Headlam, et al., eds. *The Calendar of State Papers, Colonial Series, America and the West Indies.* 42 vols. London: 1860–.
DNCB	William S. Powell, ed. *Dictionary of North Carolina Biography.* 6 vols. Chapel Hill: University of North Carolina Press, 1979–96.
LC	Library of Congress, Washington, D.C.
NA	National Archives, Washington, D.C.
NCDAH	North Carolina Division of Archives and History, Raleigh
NHC	Naval Historical Center, Washington, D.C.
NWR	*Niles' Weekly Register* (Baltimore, Md.)
ORN	*Official Records of the Union and Confederate Navies in the War of the Rebellion.* 31 vols. Washington: Government Printing Office, 1894–1927. All references are to Series 1.
PRO ADM	Public Record office, Admiralty Papers
PRO CO	Public Record Office, Colonial Office Papers
SHC	Southern Historical Collection, Wilson Library, University of North Carolina, Chapel Hill

CHAPTER ONE

1. Stick, *Graveyard*, 244–57. The Underwater Archaeology Unit at Fort Fisher has documented nearly five thousand wrecks on the North Carolina coast.
2. Saunders, *Colonial Records*, 4:1306.
3. Homer, *The Odyssey*, trans. Robert Fagles, intro. and notes by Bernard Knox (New York: Viking Penguin, 1996), 219.

4. Johnson, *Pyrates*, 4. Originally published as *A General History of the Robberies & Murders of the Most Notorious Pyrates* (London, 1724), this popular narrative has been the single most influential source on the history of piracy in the Western Hemisphere. The most complete version available at present is the 1972 edition of Manuel Schonhorn. The theory first made public in 1931 that Johnson may have been Daniel Defoe was held widely until it was refuted in 1988. See Cordingly, *Under the Black Flag*, xix–xx, and Cordingly's introduction in Johnson, *Pirates*, xi–xiii, for a brief discussion of the matter.

5. Hughson, *Carolina Pirates*, 15. For a discussion of the effects of the Navigation Acts on the colonies, see Harper, *Navigation Laws*, and Andrews, *Colonial Period*, 4:36–37, 64–65, 86, 102–3.

6. Johnson, *Pyrates*, 3.

7. Rankin, *Golden Age*, 20–21.

8. Rediker, "Under the Banner," 205–8. This article was expanded into chap. 6 of Rediker, *Between the Devil and the Deep Blue Sea*. The estimate of 2,500 pirates in the era of Blackbeard and Bonnet (1717–18) is closer to contemporary observations. Rediker doubles this figure for the whole decade of 1716–26.

9. Johnson, *Pyrates*, 342.

10. Rediker, "Under the Banner," 209.

11. Johnson, *Pyrates*, 342–43.

12. Ibid., 211–12.

13. Ibid., 323–24.

14. Maclay, *American Privateers*, viii.

15. Clark, "Oration," 25.

16. An Act Concerning Letters of Marque, Prizes and Prize Goods, 26 June 1812, Customs Letters, 5:774, RG 45, NA.

17. Mahan, *Sea Power*, 1:300; 2:22.

18. Maclay, *American Privateers*, viii; Mahan, *Sea Power*, 1:297; Coles, *War of 1812*, 71–73; Chidsey, *American Privateers*, 137–38.

19. Mahan, *Sea Power*, 1:404, 406–7; 2:220–22; Maclay, *American Privateers*, viii; Coles, *War of 1812*, 98; Macintyre, *Privateers*, 168, 184.

20. Clark, "Address."

21. Dudley, *Going South*, 13, 34–55.

22. The navy yard is located in Portsmouth, across the river from Norfolk, but even in the nineteenth century it was commonly referred to as the Norfolk Navy Yard.

23. Quoted in Robinson, *Confederate Privateers*, 13, 16.

24. Tolbert, *Papers of John Willis Ellis*, 2:689–90.

25. *ORN*, 6:72.

26. Ibid., 1:60.

27. Porter, *Naval History*, 47.

28. Owsley, *Florida*, 159.

29. Ibid., 12, 160–61; Dalzell, *Flight from the Flag*, 232, 235–37, 239, 247; Silverstone, *Warships*, 209–18.

30. Owsley, *Florida*, 10.
31. Naval History Division, *Civil War Naval Chronology*, 5:118.

CHAPTER TWO

1. Internet web sites of the North Carolina Department of Cultural Resources, Division of Archives and History, Office of State Archaeology, and North Carolina Maritime Museum. Additional documents include Intersal Inc.; Assessment Plan for Shipwreck Site 003BUI: *Queen Anne's Revenge?*; Archaeological Investigation on the Possible Wreck of the "Queen Anne's Revenge": Blackbeard's Flagship, Week of 20–24 October 1997 and 27–31 October 1997; also news articles in *Beaufort Gam*, 23 October, 30 October 1997; *Daily News*, 23 October 1997; *News and Observer*, 3 November 1997.
2. Johnson, *Pyrates*, 96.
3. Ibid., 71; Lee, *Blackbeard*, 3–4, 175–76n; Moore, "Blackbeard," 31–32. There is no primary documentation for the claim that Blackbeard was a Drummond from Virginia. Lee, *Blackbeard*, 177n.
4. Charles Leslie, "Thirteen Letters from a Gentleman to His Friend" (1740), quoted in Gosse, *History of Piracy*, 193; *BNL*, 11–18 November 1717; Governor Walter Hamilton to Board of Trade, 6 January 1718, PRO CO 152/12; *CSPCS, 1717–1718*, 149.
5. *BNL*, 11–18 November 1717; Moore, "Blackbeard," 32.
6. Johnson, *Pyrates*, 84, 96.
7. Henry Bostock Deposition, 19 December 1717, PRO CO 152/12, quoted in Moore, "Blackbeard," 32; *CSPCS, 1717–1718*, 150–56.
8. Johnson, *Pyrates*, 84–85. The Ramillies wig is named for a 1706 victory of the Duke of Marlborough in the War of the Spanish Succession. The popular style, which had military origins, featured at the back a long tapered and plaited queue tied with black ribbons.
9. Ibid.
10. Ibid., 86.
11. Ibid., 71, 84.
12. Rediker, *Between the Devil and the Deep Blue Sea*, 267–68.
13. Woodes Rogers to Council of Trade, New Providence, 31 October 1718, *CSPCS, 1717–1718*, 372, 376–77; Johnson, *Pyrates*, 36–37, 41–42, 146, 615–17, 639, 643; Rankin, *Golden Age*, 88, 107.
14. Johnson, *Pyrates*, 71.
15. *BNL*, 11–18 November 1717; Tyler, "Howard the Pirate," 36–37.
16. Ernaud Deposition, Nantes, 27 April 1718, Folio 56, Archives Départementales de Loire-Atlantique; Dosset Deposition, Nantes, 13 October 1718, Folio 90, ibid. (copies from NCDAH, Underwater Archaeology Unit, Fort Fisher, N.C.; translations by Odile McGowan of Wilmington). Lieutenant Ernaud recorded that the *Concorde* was armed with fourteen guns, and Captain Dosset said sixteen. The encounter took place thirty to forty leagues (a league is three miles) from Martinique on latitude 14°30′ north.

While the rest of western Europe had been using the modern Gregorian calendar since the sixteenth century, England retained the Julian calendar until 1752. The French date for the capture of the *Concorde*, 28 November, has been adjusted by eleven days to 17 November to conform to the English calendar at the time.

17. The queen's name may have been a sentimental reminder of Blackbeard's days as a privateer before he became an outcast, but his use of "revenge" suggests a pirate's contempt for authority, which in 1717 was represented by George of Hanover, the German successor to the childless Queen Anne. By invoking the name of an earlier popular monarch, the stateless pirate thumbed his nose at government officials.

18. Governor Walter Hamilton to Board of Trade and Plantations, 6 January 1718, PRO CO 152/12; Henry Bostock Deposition, quoted in Moore, "Blackbeard," 32; *CSPCS, 1717–1718,* 149–51.

19. Captain Francis Hume to the Admiralty, Barbados, 16 February 1718, PRO ADM 1/1879; Johnson, *Pyrates,* 72. The Bay of Honduras is now called the Gulf of Honduras.

20. *Tryals of Major Stede Bonnet,* 44–45.

21. *BNL,* 16–23 June 1718.

22. Johnson, *Pyrates,* 74.

23. *Tryals of Major Stede Bonnet,* iii–iv, 45; Governor Robert Johnson to Lords Proprietors, Charles Town, 13 June 1718, PRO CO 5/1265; Johnson, *Pyrates,* 74–75, 87–91.

24. *Tryals of Major Stede Bonnet,* iv, 19, 45–46; Johnson, *Pyrates,* 75. Founded as Beaufort in 1713, the village was incorporated in 1723 and became the county seat of Carteret County. Despite local traditions, it is not likely that there are any extant structures in Beaufort that can be associated with Blackbeard. Paul, "Colonial Beaufort," 144–45.

25. Paschal, *Colonial Bath,* 1, 7, 9, 10, 15, 17–19, 23–25, 32, 40–42.

26. The key figures in the political controversy surrounding Blackbeard are profiled in Jacquelin Drane Nash, "Charles Eden," *DNCB,* 2:134; James D. Gillespie, "Tobias Knight," ibid., 3:380; Lawrence F. London, "Maurice Moore," ibid., 4:303–4; William S. Price Jr., "Edward Moseley," ibid., 332–33; and W. Conrad Gass, "Thomas Pollock," ibid., 5:116–17.

27. Johnson, *Pyrates,* 75.

28. Captain Ellis Brand to Secretary of Admiralty, Virginia, 6 February 1719, PRO ADM 1/1472.

29. Johnson, *Pyrates,* 76.

30. Cain, *Records of the Executive Council,* 84; Johnson, *Pyrates,* 76–77.

31. Cain, *Records of the Executive Council,* 85.

32. Ibid., 90.

33. Captain George Gordon to Admiralty, Virginia, 10 March 1718, PRO ADM 1/1826; Alexander Spotswood to Lord Carteret, Virginia, 14 February 1719, in Brock, *Letters of Alexander Spotswood,* 2:273–74; Johnson, *Pyrates,* 78–79. For background on Spotswood, see Dodson, *Alexander Spotswood.*

34. Brock, *Letters of Alexander Spotswood*, 2:273–74; Brand to Admiralty, 6 February 1719, PRO ADM 1/1472; Alexander Spotswood to Council of Trade, Virginia, 22 December 1718, *CSPCS, 1717–1718*, 430; Alexander and Lazell, *Ribbon of Sand*, 80–82.

35. Lieutenant Robert Maynard to Lieutenant Symonds, North Carolina, 17 December 1718, in Cooke, "British Newspaper Accounts," 306; *CSPCS, 1717–1718*, 431; Johnson, *Pyrates*, 80.

36. Captain George Gordon to Admiralty, London, 14 September 1721, PRO ADM 1/1826; Lee, *Blackbeard*, 113–21; Alexander and Lazell, *Ribbon of Sand*, 83–90.

37. Spotswood to Carteret, 14 February 1719, Brock, *Letters of Alexander Spotswood*, 2:275; Brand to Admiralty, 6 February 1719, PRO ADM 1/1472; Gordon to Admiralty, 14 September 1721, PRO ADM 1/1826; Lee, *Blackbeard*, 123; Johnson, *Pyrates*, 82–83, 87. A standard bulk container of the era, the hogshead held up to 140 gallons of liquid or 500 pounds of dry cargo, and the tierce had a capacity of 42 gallons. According to a Virginia legend, the top of Blackbeard's skull was fashioned into a silver-lined drinking bowl.

38. Alexander Spotswood to Secretary James Craggs Jr., Virginia, 26 May 1719, Brock, *Letters of Alexander Spotswood*, 2:316–17; Log of HMS *Pearl*, Capain George Gordon, 1–3 January 1719, National Maritime Museum, ADM L/P/32; Shomette, *Pirates in the Chesapeake*, 216; Johnson, *Pyrates*, 83, 87.

39. Cain, *Records of the Executive Council*, 79–80, 98–99; Price, *Higher-Court Minutes*, 198–201, 208–9.

40. Spotswood to Craggs, 26 May 1719; Alexander Spotswood to Lords of Trade, Virginia, 26 May 1719, Brock, *Letters of Alexander Spotswood*, 2:320–25.

41. Cain, *Records of the Executive Council*, 84, 87–91.

42. Johnson, *Pyrates*, 92.

43. Ibid., 82.

44. Labree, *Papers of Benjamin Franklin*, 7.

CHAPTER THREE

1. Johnson, *Pyrates*, 95.

2. Whistler, "Account of Barbados."

3. J. A. Doyle, quoted in Hughson, *Carolina Pirates*, 10.

4. *CSPCS, 1663–1668*, 382–83.

5. Sanders, *Barbados Records: Wills*, 1:37; Sanders, *Barbados Records: Baptisms*, 277.

6. Sanders, *Barbados Records: Marriages*, 1:114; Sanders, *Barbados Records: Baptisms*, 43, 56, 57, 286; Alleyne, "A Barbadian Pirate," 73.

7. Kent, *Barbados and America*, 197; Alleyne and Fraser, *Barbados-Carolina Connection*, 26, 31.

8. *BNL*, 28 October–4 November 1717; Johnson, *Pyrates*, 95–96.

9. *BNL*, 11–18 November 1717; also quoted in Moore, "Blackbeard," 32–33. Codd's account in the fall of 1717 records an alliance between Bonnet and Blackbeard five months earlier than was previously believed.

10. Captain Francis Hume to the Admiralty, Barbados, 16 February 1718, PRO ADM 1/1879. Governor Walter Hamilton to Board of Trade and Plantations, 6 January 1718, PRO CO 152/12; *CSPCS, 1717–1718*, 149.

11. Johnson, *Pyrates*, 5–6.

12. Ibid., 96.

13. *BNL*, 16–23 June 1718.

14. *Tryals of Major Stede Bonnet*, 37; Johnson, *Pyrates*, 96–97.

15. *Tryals of Major Stede Bonnet*, iii, 44–45; Johnson, *Pyrates*, 74–75.

16. *Tryals of Major Stede Bonnet*, 45–46; Johnson, *Pyrates*, 75. The archaeological evidence of the Beaufort Inlet shipwreck, which is probably the *Queen Anne's Revenge*, reveals that a kedge anchor was set in an effort to warp, or pull, the grounded vessel off the bar. This could be an indication that the wreck was not intentional.

17. *Tryals of Major Stede Bonnet*, iv, 11, 40, 45, 46; Johnson, *Pyrates*, 75, 97.

18. *Tryals of Major Stede Bonnet*, 46; Johnson, *Pyrates*, 97. A bumboat supplied the needs of ships in port by selling merchandise, providing everything from provisions to prostitutes.

19. *Tryals of Major Stede Bonnet*, 37, 39, 47–48; Johnson, *Pyrates*, 98–99. The name of the *Royal James* was a jab at the Hanoverian king George I, who had received the crown in 1714 at the death of his cousin Anne, the last of the Protestant Stuart monarchs. Her half-brother James, known as the Old Pretender, was excluded from the succession because he was Catholic. It was customary among the lawless element to express contempt for the government by drinking toasts to James or invoking his name.

20. *BNL*, 11–18 August, 18–25 August 1718.

21. *Tryals of Major Stede Bonnet*, 23.

22. Ibid., 13.

23. Ibid., 7, 13, 49.

24. Ibid., 50.

25. Ibid., 14, 48.

26. Ibid., 21–22, 30–31.

27. Governor Robert Johnson and Council to Council of Trade, Charles Town, 21 October 1718, *CSPCS, 1717–1718*, 366–67; McCrady, *South Carolina under the Proprietary Government*, 369, 397, 400; Alexander, *Henrietta Johnson*, 52–53.

28. *Tryals of Major Stede Bonnet*, iv.

29. Ibid., v, 50; Robert Johnson to Lords Proprietors, 21 October 1718, Charles Town, PRO CO 5/1265.

30. *Tryals of Major Stede Bonnet*, v. The "wiff" was a recognized distress signal indicating the need for assistance. The use here is sarcastic.

31. Ibid., 19–20, 26.

32. Ibid., v–vi. It is not known whether the black and the Amerindian were traveling with Bonnet or were already hiding on the island.

33. Ibid., 1; Johnson and Malone, *Dictionary of American Biography*, 18:649–50.

34. *Tryals of Major Stede Bonnet*, 3, 5.

35. Ibid., 12, 14, 23; Johnson, *Pyrates*, 105–6.

36. *Tryals of Major Stede Bonnet*, 8.

37. Ibid., 28–30.

38. Ibid., 37–38, 40.

39. Ibid., 42–43.

40. Johnson, *Pyrates*, 111–13; Bonnet's letter to Governor Johnson is quoted in Leland, *Stede Bonnet*.

41. Sherman, *Robert Johnson*, 34–36.

CHAPTER FOUR

1. "Otway Burns and the Snap Dragon," 407–8. Authorship of this essay is attributed to John H. Bryan Jr. in Battle, "Burns," 10.

2. Maclay, "Exploits of Otway Burns," 874.

3. Otway Burns Paper, 6 July 1809, Onslow Deeds, 4:29, Onslow County Clerk of Court and Register of Deeds Office (copy in SHC); Onslow Deeds, 3:120, ibid.; Tucker R. Littleton and Sarah McCulloh Lemmon, "Otway Burns Jr.," *DNCB*, 1:283.

4. Holdcamper, *Vessels*, 2:748; Theophilus Parker Share in the *Snap Dragon*, 7 October 1812, in Barbour, *Cruise*, 203; Nicholson, "American Privateer," 206.

5. Edward Pasteur to Francis Hawks, New Bern, 14 October 1812, Customs Letters, 1:229, RG 45, NA; Barbour, *Cruise*, 203; "Otway Burns and the Snap Dragon," 408. For background on Pasteur, see Watson, *New Bern*, 113, 122–23, 250, 323.

6. Commissions for the *Snap Dragon*, District of New York, Edward Pasteur, 27 August 1812; District of New Bern, Edward Pasteur, 14 October 1812; District of Beaufort, Otway Burns, 1 June 1813, 17 January 1814; District of New Bern, Edward Pasteur 21 May 1814; Customs Letters, 1:53, 229–31; 2:266; 6:n.p., RG 45, NA.

7. Joshua Whithead, Garrett Farrell, and others, on board the *Snap Dragon*, 19 December 1812; David —— and others, *Snap Dragon*, 16 January 1813, British Prisoners, RB, Boxes 575, 577, RG 45, NA.

8. "Otway Burns and the Snap Dragon," 408–10.

9. The Virgin Islands were discovered and named by Columbus in 1493. In 1666 the British took Tortola from the Dutch. St. Thomas, St. John, and St. Croix (Santa Cruz) were a Danish colony from 1754 to 1917, when they were sold to the United States. During the Napoleonic Wars the British seized and occupied the Danish islands in 1801 and again in 1807–15.

10. "Otway Burns and the Snap Dragon," 411–12; *NWR*, 4 September 1813.

11. "Otway Burns and the Snap Dragon," 412.

12. Ibid., 461–62.

13. Ibid., 462.

14. Ibid., 463.

15. *CFR*, 27 February, 20 March, 17 April 1813; *NWR*, 13 March 1813; "Otway Burns and the Snap Dragon," 463.

16. "Otway Burns and the Snap Dragon," 464.

17. Ibid., 464–66.

18. Ibid., 466.

19. Ibid., 466–67. The *Providence* had been an American privateer schooner from Rhode Island when it was captured by the HMS *Dominica*. *NWR*, 4 September 1813.

20. *CFR*, 27 February, 20 March, 17 April, 1 May 1813.

21. Commission, 1 June 1813, Customs Letters, 6:n.p., RG 45, NA; "Otway Burns and the Snap Dragon," 126–27.

22. *CFR*, 18 September 1813; "Otway Burns and the Snap Dragon," 127.

23. *CFR*, 18 September 1813; *NWR*, 4 September 1813; "Otway Burns and the Snap Dragon," 128–29. The *Ringdove* is identified as the armed sloop *Rifleman* in this narrative.

24. "Otway Burns and the Snap Dragon," 129.

25. *CFR*, 18 September 1813; "Otway Burns and the Snap Dragon," 129–30.

26. *CFR*, 18 September 1813; *NWR*, 4 September 1813; 18 September 1813; "Otway Burns and the Snap Dragon," 130–31.

27. *Raleigh Register and North Carolina Gazette*, 17 September 1813; *Wilmington Gazette*, 2 October 1813; *CFR*, 11 September 1813; "Otway Burns and the Snap Dragon," 205; Garitee, *The Republic's Private Navy*, 179; Chidsey, *American Privateers*, 46. In addition to the crews' and owners' shares, customs duties and contributions to seamen's welfare were paid from the sale. In a sale of seized cargo in Camden, Maine, the duties reported were 15 percent of the value, which was half the normal import duty, an incentive offered to privateers. *NWR*, 30 April 1814.

28. Otway Burns to James Monroe, Beaufort, 17 January 1814, Customs Letters, 1:53, RG 45, NA; *New Berne Weekly Journal*, 27 February 1896.

29. *New Berne Weekly Journal*, 27 February 1896.

30. Ibid.; *NWR*, 30 April 1814; Report of Prisoners by the Snap Dragon, Otway Burns, New Bern, 9 April 1814, British Prisoners, RB, Box 577, RG 45, NA.

31. Commission, 21 May 1814, Customs Letters, 1:230, RG 45, NA; *Raleigh Register and North Carolina Gazette*, 5 August 1814; *NWR*, 30 July 1814; Log of the sloop H.M.S. Martin, 30 June 1814, PRO, ADM 51/2557; Kert, *Prize and Prejudice*, 191, 213, 222; Barbour, "What Happened to the Snap Dragon?," 13; RA, U.S. Prisoners, Halifax, Nova Scotia, Box 567, Dartmoor, England, Box 566, RG 45, NA.

32. Sanders, *Carteret County Court Minutes*, 1456; Elliot, *Marriage Bonds*, 14;

Carteret Deeds, R:368, S:143, Carteret County Clerk of Court and Register of Deeds Office; *DNCB*, 1:283.

33. Carteret Deeds, S:143, U:156–57, 181–84, 390–91, V:234–35, Carteret County Clerk of Court and Register of Deeds Office; Sanders, *Carteret County Court Minutes*, 1413; Clark, "Oration," 57; *Raleigh Register and North Carolina Gazette*, 19 June 1818; Littleton, "First Steamboat," 9. Burns sold his shipyard in Swansboro in 1819. Onslow Deeds, 10:83, Onslow County Clerk of Court and Register of Deeds Office; Still, "Shipbuilding," 9.

34. Battle, "Burns," 23, 28.

35. Ibid., 23–24, 26–28; Max R. Williams, "Otway Burns, Jr.," in Garraty and Carnes, *American National Biography*, 4:26.

36. Carteret Deeds, U:156–57, 181–84, 390; V:18, Carteret County Clerk of Court and Register of Deeds Office; Otway Burns to John H. Bryan, Portsmouth, 26 February 1843, John H. Bryan Collection, NCDAH.

37. Bureau of Lighthouse Letters, 10:386; 14:82, 87; 15:24; 19:356–57, 392; 20:342, RG 26, NA. Romulus M. Saunders to Walter Forward, Washington, 25 February 1843, Series P, Box 2; Sylvester Brown to John C. Spencer, Ocracoke, 4 December 1843, Series P, Box 2; Elijah W. Pigott to Sylvester Brown, Portsmouth, 28 December 1843, Series P, Box 4; Otway Burns to John C. Spencer, Beaufort, 17 April 1844, Series P, Box 4, Lighthouse Service Correspondence, ibid.

38. Elliot, *Marriage Bonds*, 14; Old Burying Ground, Beaufort; Simpson and Taylor, *1850 Federal Census of Carteret County*, 3.

39. Maclay, "Exploits of Otway Burns," 874. The government was paying a bounty of $25 for each prisoner captured in 1813. *NWR*, 11 September 1813.

40. "Otway Burns and the Snap Dragon," 129, 205.

CHAPTER FIVE

1. Watson, *Wilmington*, 29–30, 33.

2. Lawrence F. London, "Edward Jones," *DNCB*, 3:317; Johnson, "Biographical Sketch," 1–2; Sarah McCulloh Lemmon, "Johnston Blakeley," *DNCB*, 1:173; Charles E. Brodine Jr., "Johnston Blakeley," in Garraty and Carnes, *American National Biography*, 2:929.

3. Johnson, "Biographical Sketch," 2.

4. Johnston Blakeley to Mary Jones, New York, 14 November 1808, in Johnson, "Biographical Sketch," 5–6.

5. Patton, "Glimpses," 317.

6. Henderson, *Southern Tour*, 104–8, 114–16.

7. Henderson, *Campus*, 38–40, 42; Snider, *Light on the Hill*, 26, 29–30.

8. Henderson, *Campus*, 73.

9. Connor, Wilson, and Lefler, *Documentary History*, 2:177.

10. Ibid., 2:496.

11. Ibid., 1:251, 254, 256, 257, 259, 269, 271, 280, 282, 283, 478; Snider, *Light on the Hill*, 31.

12. Connor, Wilson, and Lefler, *Documentary History*, 2:177; Snider, *Light on the Hill*, 36; Battle, *History*, 155.

13. Connor, Wilson, and Lefler, *Documentary History*, 2:498.

14. Johnson, "Biographical Sketch," 5.

15. Connor, Wilson, and Lefler, *Documentary History*, 1:308, 343, 346.

16. Battle, "Naval Hero," 6; Blakeley Service Record, Johnston Blakeley File, Box 20, ZB Series, NHC.

17. Knox, *Naval Documents*, 1:438–39; 2:121.

18. Paullin, *Rodgers*, 21.

19. Pratt, *Preble's Boys*, 255–75.

20. Paullin, *Rodgers*, 109–10; Kitzen, *Tripoli*, 79.

21. Paullin, *Rodgers*, 122; Kitzen, *Tripoli*, 81–82.

22. Allen, *Barbary Corsairs*, 324.

23. Blakeley Service Record, NHC.

24. Johnson, "Biographical Sketch," 5–6.

25. Blakeley Service Record, NHC.

26. Dudley, *Naval War*, 1:628; Chapelle, *Sailing Navy*, 145–46.

27. Dudley, *Naval War*, 1:385, 389–90.

28. Ibid., 1:21, 54n, 390, 394, 400, 425n.

29. Ibid., 2:54n, 88–89, 90n, 147, 159–60, 232, 233n; Blakeley Service Record, NHC; *NWR*, 4 September 1813.

30. Blakeley Service Record, NHC; Chapelle, *Sailing Navy*, 256, 263, 278; Perry, *"Wasp,"* 84–85; Dudley, *Naval War*, 2:43, 291.

31. Andrew Ritchie to Artemus Ward, Boston, 11 February 1817, GLB 22:238, NCDAH; Brodine, "Johnston Blakeley," 929.

32. Quoted in Pratt, *Preble's Boys*, 267–68.

33. David Geisinger, *Wasp* Journal, 2 May 1814, David Geisinger Collection, LC. Midshipman Geisinger was keeping his journal in sea time with the day beginning at noon. Other sources give the departure date as 1 May.

34. Geisinger, *Wasp* Journal, LC.

35. Ibid.; *NWR*, 29 October 1814.

36. *American State Papers*, 1:315–18; *NWR*, 29 October 1814; Geisinger, *Wasp* Journal, LC; Pratt, *Preble's Boys*, 268–71; Roosevelt, *Naval War*, 294–96; Mahan, *Sea Power*, 2:253–55.

37. Geisinger, *Wasp* Journal, LC; *NWR*, 19, 26 November, 3, 10 December 1814; Pratt, *Preble's Boys*, 271–72; Mahan, *Sea Power*, 2:255–57; Roosevelt, *Naval War*, 298–302.

38. Johnston Blakeley to William Jones, U.S.S. Wasp, 22 September 1814, Box 20, ZB Series, NHC; Johnson, "Biographical Sketch," 11; *NWR*, 19, 26 November 1814.

39. *NWR*, 19 November 1814.

40. Brodine, "Johnston Blakeley," 930.

41. Blakeley Service Record, NHC; *Letter from the Secretary of the Navy*, 3–4;

Extracts from the Annals of Congress, 14th Congress, 1st Session, 1815–16, Appendix, 1964; Johnston Blakeley Papers, NCDAH.

42. Johnson, "Biographical Sketch," 12–13, 16.

43. Ibid., 10; Ritchie to Ward, GLB 22:239, NCDAH; Blakeley Pension File, Records of the Veterans Administration, RG 15, NA.

44. William Miller to Mrs. Johnston Blakeley, Raleigh, 3 January 1817, GLB 22:202–3, NCDAH.

45. Jane A. Blakeley to William Miller, Boston, 14 April 1817, GLB 22:287, NCDAH.

46. Jane A. Blakeley to Edward Jones, Boston, 5 March 1817, Mary B. Hardin Collection, NCDAH; John Branch to Jane Blakeley, Raleigh, 13 October 1818, GLB 23:89, NCDAH; Newsome, "Blakeley," 164–66, 169. The Blakeley silver tea service was eventually repurchased by the state and may be seen at the North Carolina Museum of Art in Raleigh.

47. Parish Register, St. John's Episcopal Church, Christiansted, St. Croix, Blakeley Papers, NCDAH; Newsome, "Blakeley," 170–71.

CHAPTER SIX

1. John D. Davis, "Sketch of James Wallace Cooke," Beaufort, 1898, James Wallace Cooke Papers, SHC, 1–2; Cooke, "Henry Marchant Cooke," 38; Old Burying Ground, Beaufort; Carteret County Wills, D:117, Carteret County Clerk of Court and Register of Deeds Office; Sanders, *Carteret County Court Minutes*, 7:1379.

2. Newsome, "A Miscellany," 398–400.

3. John N. Maffitt to George Davis, New Hanover County, 17 August 1874, George Davis Papers, Duke University.

4. Crabtree and Patton, *"Journal,"* 420, 424.

5. Carteret County Deeds, W:257–59, Carteret County Clerk of Court and Register of Deeds Office.

6. Davis, "Sketch of James Wallace Cooke," 2–3, SHC; Chapelle, *Sailing Navy*, 340, 344, 355, 358, 400, 420.

7. Hinds, *Invasion*, 46; Davis, "Sketch of James Wallace Cooke," 2–3, SHC; *Register of Officers of the Navy of the United States*, 32–33; Chapelle, *Sailing Navy*, 385, 388.

8. Davis, "Sketch of James Wallace Cooke," 3, SHC; Crabtree and Patton, *"Journal,"* 421; Hinds, *Invasion*, 46–49.

9. Davis, "Sketch of James Wallace Cooke," 3–4, SHC; Crabtree and Patton, *"Journal,"* 421.

10. Scharf, *History*, 96–97, 140, 408n; *Register of Officers of the Confederate States Navy*, 40; Stephen R. Mallory to James W. Cooke, 15 June 1861, James W. Cooke File, Box 49, ZB Series, NHC.

11. Samuel Barron to James W. Cooke, 18 July 1861, Cooke File, NHC.

12. *ORN*, 1:50–52, 59–60, 67; 6:795; Tredwell, "North Carolina Navy," 299–300; Stick, *Outer Banks*, 117–18.

13. *ORN*, 6:784; Silverstone, *Warships*, 122, 239.

14. *ORN*, 6:784–89.

15. Daly, "Amphibious Division," 31; Reed, *Combined Operations*, 39.

16. *ORN*, 6:789. Parker, *Recollections*, 242–46.

17. *ORN*, 6:594; Parker, *Recollections*, 248–50; Stick, *Outer Banks*, 136–48.

18. *ORN*, 6:595, 597.

19. Ibid., 595; Parker, *Recollections*, 254–55.

20. *ORN*, 6:606–7.

21. Ibid., 596, 607–8; Parker, *Recollections*, 258–59; Scharf, *History*, 391. The *Appomattox* was burned when she was discovered to be too wide for the canal locks.

22. *ORN*, 6:597; Maffitt, "Reminiscences," 500.

23. Maffitt, "Reminiscences," 500–501.

24. Scharf, *History*, 391–92n; Maffitt, "Reminiscences," 500; Tredwell, "North Carolina Navy," 312. During the Civil War, officers usually, and sometimes enlisted men, could be sent home on parole. Parole was granted when an individual pledged his sacred honor that he would not take up arms or serve the war effort in any way until exchanged for an enemy prisoner.

25. *ORN*, 6:597.

26. French Forrest to James W. Cooke, 19 August 1862, Cooke File, NHC; *Register of Officers of the Navy of the United States*, 40.

27. Still, *Iron Afloat*, 150–51.

28. Elliott, "Albemarle," 318.

29. Elliott, "Albemarle," 316–17; Elliott, *Ironclad*, 88, 273–74. The dimensions given by Gilbert Elliott, the builder, in 1880 differ from those listed by the United States Navy surveyors in 1865; but the surveyors' figures, taken from measurements made by professional naval officers, should be more accurate than Elliott's memory fifteen years later. Also see John L. Porter's plans in Elliott, *Ironclad*, 160–61.

30. Elliott, "Albemarle," 315; Maffitt, "Reminiscences," 502; *ORN*, 8:844.

31. *ORN*, 9:799–800.

32. Crabtree and Patton, "*Journal*," 474; Elliott, *Ironclad*, 115–17.

33. Elliott, "Albemarle," 317–18; Elliott, *Ironclad*, 99, 118–21, 129; Crabtree and Patton, "*Journal*," 482. Smith's modified drill reduced the time for drilling a hole in the armor plate from twenty minutes to four minutes.

34. Elliott, "Albemarle," 318; Elliott, *Ironclad*, 166–67; Barefoot, *Hoke*, 127–28, 136–37.

35. *ORN*, 9:639–40, 644, 656–58, 772; Elliott, "Albemarle," 319–21; Nichols, "Fighting," 79–82; Elliott, *Ironclad*, 168–83.

36. Barrett, *Civil War*, 215–21; *ORN*, 9:658; Barefoot, *Hoke*, 148–50, 155–57, 159.

37. Elliott, *Ironclad*, 189–90; Barefoot, *Hoke*, 157–58, 160–65.

38. *ORN*, 9:769. Elliott, "Albemarle," 322; Roe, "Sassacus and Albemarle," Francis A. Roe Papers, LC.

39. *ORN*, 9:764–71, 773; Roe, "Sassacus and Albemarle," LC; Elliott, "Albemarle," 321–22; Elliott, *Ironclad*, 194–210; Holden, " 'Albemarle,' and 'Sassacus,' " 628–32; Nichols, "Fighting," 83–84.

40. *ORN*, 9:735, 742, 752; Elliott, *Ironclad*, 212.
41. Crabtree and Patton, *"Journal,"* 578–79; *ORN*, 10:627, 659, 687, 704.
42. *Register of Officers of the Navy of the United States*, 40; Elliott, *Ironclad*, 228, 242–43; *ORN*, 10:741. Cooke's promotion was in the provisional navy, which had been established by Congress in May 1863 to allow meritorious promotion of younger officers over older senior officers. The provisional navy gradually replaced the regular navy. Coski, *Capital Navy*, 20.
43. Cushing, "Destruction," 634–41; Warley, "Note," 641–42.
44. Crabtree and Patton, *"Journal,"* 669–70, 690.
45. Davis, "Sketch of James Wallace Cooke," 13, SHC.

CHAPTER SEVEN

1. Maffitt, *Nautilus*, 90–92; Speech of Commodore Jesse Elliot, 14 November 1843, John Newland Maffitt Papers, SHC.
2. Maffitt, *Life*, 19, 21–23, 30; Shingleton, *High Seas Confederate*, 2–4, 6.
3. Maffitt, *Life*, 30–31; John N. Maffitt to Eliza Maffitt, Pensacola, 26 April 1833, Maffitt Papers, SHC; Shingleton, *High Seas Confederate*, 8–9.
4. John N. Maffitt to William H. Maffitt, Pensacola, 7 January 1833, Maffitt Papers, SHC; Maffitt Service Record, John N. Maffitt File, Box 144, ZB Series, NHC; Silverstone, *Warships*, 128.
5. Maffitt Service Record, NHC.
6. Maffitt, *Nautilus*, 315.
7. Maffitt, *Life*, 47, 52–53, 137; Maffitt Service Record, NHC.
8. John N. Maffitt to Eliza Maffitt, Pensacola, 3 May 1839, Maffitt Papers, SHC.
9. John N. Maffitt to Eliza Maffitt, Veracruz, 1 June 1840, Maffitt Papers, SHC; Maffitt, *Life*, 54–55, 137.
10. John N. Maffitt to Eliza Maffitt, Pensacola, 3 May 1839, Maffitt Papers, SHC.
11. Maffitt, *Life*, 56–57.
12. Maffitt Service Record, NHC.
13. Maffitt, *Life*, 162.
14. Ibid., 66, 68, 70–72, 75.
15. Ibid., 64; Boykin, *Sea Devil*, 65.
16. Maffitt, *Life*, 85–86, 97, 99–100, 204–5.
17. Ibid., 136, 198; Shingleton, *High Seas Confederate*, 24–25; Maffitt Service Record, NHC.
18. Shingleton, *High Seas Confederate*, 118n.
19. Florie Maffitt to Maggie Maffitt, Washington, D.C., 31 March 1859, Maffitt Papers, SHC.
20. Maffitt, *Life*, 205–6.
21. Ibid., 206–7.
22. Ibid., 208, 211–14; John N. Maffitt to Eliza M. Hybart, 21 August 1860, Maffitt Papers, SHC.
23. Maffitt, *Life*, 215–16, 218.
24. Private Journal of Capt. John N. Maffitt, 1–3, Maffitt Papers, SHC.

25. Ibid., 4; *ORN*, 6:322.
26. Maffitt, "Reminiscences," 499; Private Journal, 6, Maffitt Papers, SHC; Jones, *Civil War at Sea*, 1:261–66; Scharf, *History*, 663–67; *ORN*, 12:297–98.
27. Private Journal, 6, Maffitt Papers, SHC; John N. Maffitt to Florie Maffitt, Coosawhatchie, 5 December 1861, ibid.; *ORN*, 12:319, 487; Jones, *Civil War at Sea*, 1:273–78.
28. Private Journal, 7, Maffitt Papers, SHC; John N. Maffitt to his children, Coosawhatchie, 20 December 1861, ibid.
29. Maffitt, "Blockade-Running," 626–27. Trenholm would become the Confederate secretary of the treasury.
30. Private Journal, 7, Maffitt Papers, SHC; Wise, *Lifeline*, 58–59.
31. *ORN*, 1:755–58. The *Oreto* was also known as the *Manassas*.
32. Bulloch, *Secret Service*, 1:51–52, 57–58, 152–53, 156–59; Hearn, *Gray Raiders*, 52–55; Silverstone, *Warships*, 211.
33. Semmes, *Memoirs*, 354.
34. Private Journal, 8–11, Maffitt Papers, SHC; *ORN*, 1:759; Stephen R. Mallory to John N. Maffitt, Richmond, 14 July 1862, Maffitt Papers, SHC.
35. Private Journal, 12–13, Maffitt Papers, SHC.
36. Ibid., 16–18; *ORN*, 1:760; John N. Maffitt to Florie Maffitt, 19 September 1862, Maffitt Papers, SHC.
37. Maffitt, *Life*, 253; John N. Maffitt to Florie Maffitt, Mobile Bay, 8 September and 19 September 1862, Maffitt Papers, SHC.
38. Maffitt, *Life*, 254.
39. Private Journal, 19–20, Maffitt Papers, SHC; *ORN*, 1:432; Sinclair, "Eventful Cruise." 418–19.
40. Private Journal, 20, Maffitt Papers, SHC; *ORN*, 1:464; Maffitt, *Life*, 261; Franklin Buchanan to John N. Maffitt, Mobile, 7 September 1862, Maffitt Papers, SHC.
41. *ORN*, 1:761; Stephen R. Mallory to John N. Maffitt, Richmond, 8 October 1862, Maffitt Papers, SHC.
42. *ORN*, 1:432–40, 459.
43. John N. Maffitt to Florie Maffitt, Mobile Bay, 11 January 1863, Maffitt Papers, SHC.
44. *ORN*, 2:639; Maffitt, *Life*, 265–67; Private Journal, 27–29, Maffitt Papers, SHC; Sinclair, "Eventful Cruise," 419–21; Silverstone, *Warships*, 211.
45. Private Journal, 29–30, Maffitt Papers, SHC; *ORN*, 2:674; Sinclair, "Eventful Cruise," 421; A. L. Drayton Diary, 19 January 1863, LC.
46. *ORN*, 2:642–43, 675–76; Private Journal, 30–32, 34–35, Maffitt Papers, SHC; Maffitt, *Life*, 275; Shingleton, *High Seas Confederate*, 67.
47. John N. Maffitt to Florie, Mary, John, and Colie Maffitt, 13 March 1863, Maffitt Papers, SHC; *ORN*, 2:676.
48. Private Journal, 35–38, Maffitt Papers, SHC; *ORN*, 2:676.
49. John N. Maffitt to Florie, Mary, John, and Colie Maffitt, 13 March 1863, Maffitt Papers, SHC.
50. Private Journal, 38–43, Maffitt Papers, SHC; Maffitt, *Life*, 280–87; *ORN*, 2:643, 677–79.

51. *ORN*, 2:330–31, 654–57; Crabtree and Patton, *"Journal,"* 417; Drayton Diary, 6 May–26 June 1863, LC; Hearn, *Gray Raiders*, 83–93, 312–13; Campbell, *Southern Fire*, 38–54.

52. *ORN*, 2:383–85, 653–54; Maffitt, *Life*, 291–95, 300–301; Shingleton, *High Seas Confederate*, 76–78.

53. Maffitt, *Life*, 304.

54. *ORN*, 2:654, 658–60; Shingleton, *High Seas Confederate*, 79–80.

55. Maffitt, *Life*, 305; Stephen R. Mallory to John N. Maffitt, Richmond, 7 August 1863, Maffitt Papers, SHC.

56. *ORN*, 2:657–60; Maffitt, *Life*, 321–22. The *Florida*'s last cruise, under the command of Lieutenant Charles M. Morris, began from Brest in February 1864 and ended in October in Bahia, Brazil. There the ship was seized by the USS *Wachusett* in violation of Brazil's neutrality. She was secretly scuttled by the U.S. Navy in Hampton Roads in November to end the diplomatic controversy. Owsley, *Florida*, 110–55.

57. Maffitt, *Life*, 327–28; Vandiver, *Bermuda*, 58, 132; Wise, *Lifeline*, 108, 239; Shingleton, *High Seas Confederate*, 87–89; *ORN*, 2:613; 9:806; Boykin, *Dare Devil*, 238, 241–42.

58. Maffitt, *Life*, 335–39; *ORN*, 10:457–58.

59. Crabtree and Patton, *"Journal,"* 578–79.

60. Sprunt, "Blockade Running," 396, 410, 441; Maffitt, "Blockade-Running," 30–32; Maffitt, *Life*, 340–43; Vandiver, *Bermuda*, 144, 146.

61. Maffitt, "Blockade-Running," 32–33.

62. Maffitt, *Life*, 350–54; Campbell, *Fire and Thunder*, 155–64; Shingleton, *High Seas Confederate*, 97–98; Stephen R. Mallory to John N. Maffitt, Richmond, 24 February 1865, Maffitt Papers, SHC.

63. Maffitt, *Life*, 354, 356–59. The war between Paraguay and the alliance of Brazil, Argentina, and Uruguay took place between 1865 and 1870.

64. George H. Preble to John N. Maffitt, Boston, 27 June 1867, Maffitt Papers, SHC; Maffitt, *Life*, 359.

65. Maffitt, *Life*, 360–62, 382.

66. Ibid., 399.

67. Ibid., 397–98.

68. Ibid., 363–68, 375; John N. Maffitt to Emma Martin, New York, 23 July 1870, Maffitt Papers, SHC; Shingleton, *High Seas Confederate*, 101.

69. Maffitt, *Life*, 383; Shingleton, *High Seas Confederate*, 102.

70. Maffitt, *Life*, 423–25. Lambert was the chaplain on the *Constitution* and other frigates on which Maffitt served. Emma Maffitt to John N. Maffitt, Wilmington, 6 January 1886, Maffitt Papers, SHC.

CHAPTER EIGHT

1. Luraghi, *Confederate Navy*, 300.

2. Shingleton, *Wood*, 62, 64–65; *ORN*, 5:118–19.

3. Shingleton, *Wood*, 2, 4; Thurston, *Skipper*, 45n.

4. Shingleton, *Wood*, 7.

5. Wood Service Record, John Taylor Wood File, Box 239, ZB Series, NHC.

6. Wood, "Slaver," 451–52, 455, 457–62. Liberia had been acquired by the American Colonization Society in 1821 and a year later was first settled by former slaves. Under the auspices of the society, it was proclaimed an independent republic, and the last governor, Joseph J. Roberts, became the first president. As the governor of Grand Bassa explained to Wood, the American freedmen existed on the coast with "sufferance only from the natives."

7. Wood Service Record, NHC.

8. Shingleton, *Wood*, 5; Thurston, *Skipper*, 41.

9. John Taylor Wood to Lola Wood, Genoa, 14 September 1858, John Taylor Wood Papers, SHC. In the lengthy correspondence to his wife written on this cruise, he signed his name J. Taylor Wood and may have used Taylor as his given name. This signature continued throughout his life.

10. John Taylor Wood to Lola Wood, Muzia, 19 September 1858, Wood Papers, SHC. The marble bust was later purchased by the U.S. government from a Wood descendant.

11. John Taylor Wood to Lola Wood, Leghorn, 9 and 10 August 1859, Wood Papers, SHC.

12. John Taylor Wood to Lola Wood, Leghorn, 14 August 1859; John Taylor Wood to Lola Wood, Muzia, 21 August 1859; John Taylor Wood to Lola Wood, New York, 16 December 1859, Wood Papers, SHC.

13. John Taylor Wood Diary, Washington, 2–3 January, 12 January, 6 February 1860, Wood Papers, SHC.

14. Ibid., Annapolis, 17 February 1860.

15. Ibid., 8 May, 19 June, 23 June, 15–31 August 1860; Wood Service Record, NHC.

16. Wood Diary, 24 September, 10 October, 7 November, 23 November 1860, Wood Papers, SHC.

17. Ibid., 11 November 1860.

18. Ibid., 21 March, 15 April 1861.

19. Ibid., 16 April 1861.

20. Ibid., 20 April 1861.

21. Ibid., 21 April, 1861; Wood Service Record, NHC; Shingleton, *Wood*, 15–16.

22. Shingleton, *Wood*, 18–19.

23. Wood Service Record, NHC; Shingleton, *Wood*, 25.

24. Wood, "First Fight," 692–94; Davis, *Duel*, 8–12.

25. Stephen R. Mallory to John Taylor Wood, Richmond, 20 November 1861, Wood File, NHC; Wood, "First Fight," 694; Davis, *Duel*, 36, 39–40.

26. Wood, "First Fight," 695; Davis, *Duel*, 35–36.

27. Wood, "First Fight," 696; Parker, *Recollections*, 271–72.

28. Reaney, "Gun-Boat 'Zouave,'" 715; Wood, "First Fight," 696–700.

29. Wood, "First Fight," 698; *ORN*, 7:44; Davis, *Duel*, 86–95.

30. Wood, "First Fight," 698–700; Parker, *Recollections*, 274–78; Davis, *Duel*, 98–104.

31. *ORN*, 7:42, 44–45; Parker, *Recollections*, 278–79; Davis, *Duel*, 105, 109–10; Thurston, *Skipper*, 133.
32. Colston, "Watching the 'Merrimac,' " 714.
33. *ORN*, 7:46; Wood, "First Fight," 701–3; Davis, *Duel*, 112–35.
34. *ORN*, 7:47.
35. Wood, "First Fight," 705; *ORN*, 7:62–63; Thurston, *Skipper*, 125.
36. Wood, "First Fight," 705–10.
37. *ORN*, 7:357–58, 369–70; Scharf, *History*, 713–16; Wood, "First Fight," 711; Shingleton, *Wood*, 48–53.
38. Wood, "First Fight," 711.
39. *ORN*, 7:137–41; 8:167–69; Shingleton, *Wood*, 65–67.
40. Thurston, *Skipper*, 156.
41. Jefferson Davis to John Taylor Wood, Richmond, 9 February 1863, Wood File, NHC; *ORN*, 8:859–60, 862–63; Shingleton, *Wood*, 69–73.
42. *ORN*, 5:335–41, 344–45; Shingleton, *Wood*, 75–83.
43. *ORN*, 5:344–45; Shingleton, *Wood*, 85–89.
44. *Register of Officers of the Confederate States Navy*, 216. Wood was paid $6,683.25 prize money for the destruction of the *Satellite* and the *Reliance*. He likely received prize money for the *Underwriter* as well. Receipt, James A. Semple to John Taylor Wood, 10 January 1864, Wood File, NHC.
45. Barefoot, *Hoke*, 105–8, 111; Barrett, *Civil War*, 202–6.
46. Loyall, "Capture," 326.
47. *ORN*, 9:449–51; Scharf, *History*, 395.
48. *ORN*, 9:441–42, 452–54; Scharf, *History*, 395–96. George W. Gift to Ellen Shackelford, Newbern, N.C., 2 February 1864; Kinston, N.C., 7 February 1864, Wood Papers, SHC; Castlen, *Hope*, 163–64.
49. Loyall, "Capture," 328.
50. Scharf, *History*, 397; Conrad, "Capture," 94–95.
51. *ORN*, 9:440–41, 452–54; Scharf, *History*, 398–99; Loyall, "Capture," 329–30; George W. Gift to Ellen Shackelford, Kinston, N.C., 5 February, 7 February 1864, Wood Papers, SHC; Conrad, "Capture," 95–96; Castlen, *Hope*, 165–66.
52. *ORN*, 9:441, 452, 458; Scharf, *History*, 400–401; Conrad, "Capture," 97–98.
53. *ORN*, 5:346.
54. Porter, *Naval History*, 472.
55. *ORN*, 9:589.
56. Ibid., 658.
57. Ibid., 10:281, 721–22; Shingleton, *Wood*, 116–18.
58. Although this vessel was also called the *Atlanta*, it is clear that her British builders originally named her for the swift-running huntress of Greek mythology. Shingleton, "Atlanta," 11–12.
59. Wood, "Dash," 409; *ORN*, 3:706; Hearn, *Gray Raiders*, 129; Shingleton, *Wood*, 118–24.
60. Wood, "Dash," 409–14; *ORN*, 3:701–4; Hearn, *Gray Raiders*, 130–35; Shingleton, *Wood*, 124–37.

61. Wood, "Dash," 414–16; *ORN*, 3:702, 704–10; Hearn, *Gray Raiders*, 135–37; Shingleton, *Wood*, 136–39.

62. Wood, "Dash," 416; *ORN*, 3:170–74, 703–4; Hearn, *Gray Raiders*, 137–38; Shingleton, *Wood*, 140–41.

63. The lightly armed CSS *Nashville* did make a voyage in 1861–62 from Charleston, returning to Beaufort, North Carolina, and taking two prizes; however, the primary purpose of the voyage was diplomatic, and the prizes were almost incidental. The CSS *Sumter*, the first Confederate cruiser, was manned and outfitted in New Orleans, and the CSS *Florida* came to Mobile for equipment and reinforcements for a shorthanded crew ravaged by yellow fever. Neither of these famous cruisers ever returned to the Confederacy.

64. Stephen R. Mallory to John Taylor Wood, Richmond, 2 September 1864, Wood File, NHC; *Register of Officers of the Confederate States Navy*, 216.

65. Wood Diary, Richmond, 2–3 April 1864, Wood Papers, SHC; Davis, *Long Surrender*, 14–15, 21, 29–31, 52–54; Shingleton, *Wood*, 146–49.

66. Wood Diary, Greensboro, 8–12 April 1865, Wood Papers, SHC; Davis, *Long Surrender*, 62–63, 68–72; Shingleton, *Wood*, 149–53.

67. Wood Diary, Greensboro, 15 April 1864, Charlotte, 20–26 April, 10 May 1864, Wood Papers, SHC; Wood, "Escape," 110; Davis, *Long Surrender*, 79, 87–94, 125, 138, 147–48.

68. Wood Diary, 10 May–11 June 1865, Wood Papers, SHC; Wood, "Escape," 111–23; Shingleton, *Wood*, chaps. 10 and 11; Davis, *Long Surrender*, 163–67.

69. Wood Diary, 12 June–16 July 1865, Wood Papers, SHC; Thurston, *Skipper*, 356, 369–71, 391; Wood Obituary, *Herald*, 20 July 1904; Shingleton, *Wood*, 198–206, 224n. Wood records the boat name as "No Value" in his diary.

CHAPTER NINE

1. Bulloch, *Secret Service*, 2:130.

2. Ibid., 125–28; Merli, *Great Britain*, 227–30.

3. Bulloch, *Secret Service*, 2:129–32.

4. Waddell, *Memoirs*, 53.

5. Will of Alfred Moore, Orange County, North Carolina, 6 January 1837, James Iredell Waddell Papers, NCDAH. When Moorefields was willed to the Waddells, it became their family homeplace.

6. Chapelle, *Sailing Navy*, 338–39, 370–74.

7. Waddell, *Memoirs*, 54.

8. Ibid.

9. Ibid., 55.

10. Ibid., 56; Stephen R. Wise, "James Iredell Waddell," in Garraty and Carnes, *American National Biography*, 22:426.

11. Waddell, *Memoirs*, 57, 59–60; Charles Waddell to Francis N. Waddell, Petersburg, Virginia, 11 September 1867, Waddell Papers, NCDAH. In the family his wife was known as Sell.

12. Waddell, *Memoirs*, 60–62; L. M. Brasher to Francis N. Waddell, Matanzas, 27 July 1857; James I. Waddell to Thomas Corwin, Hillsborough, September 1851, Waddell Papers, NCDAH.

13. Ashe, "Waddell," 128.

14. Waddell, *Memoirs*, 63–64, 66; Silverstone, *Warships*, 24.

15. Waddell, *Memoirs*, 65.

16. Ibid., 66.

17. Ibid., 66–69.

18. Ibid., 69–74. Waddell's editor confused Great Wicomoco River, Virginia, with Wicomico River, Maryland. Ibid., 72.

19. Jones, *Civil War at Sea*, 2:chaps. 4 and 5; Luraghi, *Confederate Navy*, 108, 131, 157–63; "Opposing Forces," 73–75.

20. John Taylor Wood to Lola Wood, Drewry's Bluff, 24 May 1862, 5 July 1862, John Taylor Wood Papers, SHC; *ORN* 8:850; William C. Whittle Sr. to James Iredell Waddell, Vicksburg, 27 April 1862, James Iredell Waddell File, Box 226, ZB Series, NHC.

21. Waddell, *Memoirs*, 75–76; Scharf, *History*, 687–89.

22. Bulloch, *Secret Service*, 1:382–85, 389, 391, 401–5; Roberts, "Bulloch and the Confederate Navy," 320–26, 330–35, 341–47; Spencer, *Confederate Navy in Europe*, 70–71, 78–79, 81–84, 110–11; Merli, *Great Britain*, 182–83, 195–210.

23. James Iredell Waddell Diary, United States Naval Academy; Waddell, *Memoirs*, 76–77; Forrest, *Odyssey in Gray*, 43, 90, 178, 211; Spencer, *Confederate Navy in Europe*, 107–10; Luraghi, *Confederate Navy*, 269, 271; Hill, *Sea Dogs*, 229.

24. Bulloch, *Secret Service*, 2:126, 130–34; Whittle, "Cruise," 241; Hearn, *Gray Raiders*, 253.

25. Hunt, *Shenandoah*, 13.

26. *ORN*, 3:749, 758; Waddell, *Memoirs*, 82–83.

27. *ORN*, 8:344–45.

28. Waddell, *Memoirs*, 91–95, 100–101, 103; Whittle, "Cruise," 242–43; Riley, "Shenandoah," 166; *ORN*, 8:757, 759, 785; Hunt, *Shenandoah*, 21–22; Hearn, *Gray Raiders*, 257–60. There is a one-day discrepancy in dates written in early log entries, caused by the twelve-hour difference between sea time and civil time. Since the sea day began at noon, the date of commissioning was recorded as 20 October, which was 19 October civil time. On 8 November the log entries were shifted to civil time. The different accounts also vary slightly in the combination of officers and crewmen aboard the *Shenandoah* at the beginning of the cruise. When the berth deck was cleared, Waddell set the ship's capacity at 120.

29. Waddell, *Memoirs*, 96, 99–101; Whittle, "Cruise," 244–45; Mason, "Last of the Confederate Cruisers," 602–3; Riley, "Shenandoah," 167.

30. *ORN*, 8:785; Waddell, *Memoirs*, 104–5; Lining, "Journal," 128; Grimball, "Career," 119–20.

31. Hunt, *Shenandoah*, 32–33.

32. Waddell, *Memoirs*, 107–9; *ORN*, 8:786; Hunt, *Shenandoah*, 35–40, 42; Riley, "Shenandoah," 168; Whittle, "Cruise," 245–46; Mason, "Last of the Confederate Cruisers," 603.

33. Waddell, *Memoirs*, 110–13; Lining, "Journal," 129; Whittle, "Cruise," 246; Hunt, *Shenandoah*, 43–45, 49–52, 55–59.

34. Waddell, *Memoirs*, 116–20; Hunt, *Shenandoah*, 64–69, 72–76; Hearn, *Gray Raiders*, 272–73; Mason, "Last of the Confederate Cruisers," 605–6; Riley, "Shenandoah," 170; Grimball, "Career," 121–22.

35. Riley, "Shenandoah," 170.

36. *ORN*, 8:759–63; Waddell, *Memoirs*, 124–30; Mason, "Last of the Confederate Cruisers," 606; Grimball, "Career," 122; Hunt, *Shenandoah*, 101–5.

37. *ORN*, 8:769–74; Lining, "Journal," 138–39; Waddell, *Memoirs*, 131–35; Mason, "Last of the Confederate Cruisers," 606–7.

38. Waddell, *Memoirs*, 139–40, 142–46; Lining, "Journal," 139, 141–42; Hunt, *Shenandoah*, 113–17, 122–29; Whittle, "Cruise," 250–51; Mason, "Last of the Confederate Cruisers," 607–8. In the nineteenth century Ponape was also known as Ascension Island.

39. Waddell, *Memoirs*, 151–55; *ORN*, 8:788–89; Whittle, "Cruise," 251; Lining, "Journal," 142–43; Hunt, *Shenandoah*, 129–37.

40. Waddell, *Memoirs*, 157–58; Lining, "Journal," 146–48; Hunt, *Shenandoah*, 155.

41. Waddell, *Memoirs*, 162–67; Lining, "Journal," 148–49; *ORN*, 8:790–91. Since the *Shenandoah* passed the International Date Line going east, 22 June was recorded twice, lasting forty-eight hours. *ORN*, 8:790.

42. Waddell, *Memoirs*, 167–70; Hunt, *Shenandoah*, 172–73, 188–92; *ORN*, 8:792.

43. Waddell, *Memoirs*, 171–72; Hunt, *Shenandoah*, 196–205, 208–9; *ORN*, 8:791.

44. Lining, "Journal," 152; Waddell, *Memoirs*, 175–76; *ORN*, 8:791; Grimball, "Career," 124–25.

45. Lining, "Journal," 152–53; Hunt, *Shenandoah*, 222–23; Waddell, *Memoirs*, 176–78.

46. Lining, "Journal," 158–59; Waddell, *Memoirs*, 179; Hunt, *Shenandoah*, 228–32.

47. Lining, "Journal," 161–63; Waddell, *Memoirs*, 179–81; Hunt, *Shenandoah*, 232–33, 237.

48. Waddell, *Memoirs*, 181–84; Lining, "Journal," 162.

49. James I. Waddell to Earl Russell, Liverpool, 5 November 1865, Waddell Papers, NCDAH; Waddell, *Memoirs*, 182–84; Lining, "Journal," 163; Hunt, *Shenandoah*, 247–48, 260–61. There is no evidence to support Hunt's charge that Waddell withheld some of the funds due the crew. Hunt's credibility was compromised when he became the only member of the *Shenandoah*'s crew to desert. Hunt, *Shenandoah*, 252–57, 262–63.

50. Waddell, *Memoirs*, 50–51; Bulloch, *Secret Service*, 2:186–87; Hearn, *Gray Raiders*, 301.

51. James I. Waddell, Waterloo, 27 December 1865, quoted in Hunt, *Shenandoah*, 266–70.

52. Charles E. Waddell to Francis N. Waddell, Petersburg, Va., 11 September 1867, Waddell Papers, NCDAH. The lieutenant governor of Maryland interceded for Mrs. Waddell, who appealed to the president for release. Christopher Cox to President Andrew Johnson, Annapolis, 6 February 1866, Waddell File, NHC.

53. James Iredell Waddell Scrapbooks, United States Naval Academy; Waddell, *Memoirs*, 47–48; Morgan, *Dixie Raider*, 330–31.

54. Waddell Scrapbooks, United States Naval Academy; James I. Waddell to Guion Waddell, Annapolis, 14 April 1885, and Lizie H. Welsh to Mrs. Guion Waddell, Annapolis, 4 April 1886, Waddell Papers, NCDAH; untitled newspaper clipping, Charleston, S.C., 1872. ibid.; Obituary, *The American*, 15 March 1886, ibid.

Bibliography

PRIMARY SOURCES

Manuscripts

Archives Départementales de Loire-Atlantique, Nantes, France
    Deposition of Captain Pierre Dosset
    Deposition of Lieutenant François Ernaud
Carteret County Clerk of Court and Register of Deeds Office, Beaufort, N.C.
    Carteret County Deeds
    Carteret County Wills
Duke University, Perkins Library, Durham, N.C.
    George Davis Papers
Library of Congress, Manuscript Division, Washington, D.C.
    A. L. Drayton Diary
    David Geisinger Collection
    Francis A. Roe Papers
National Archives, Washington, D.C.
    Naval Records Collection of the Office of Naval Records and Library, Record
        Group 45
      British Prisoner Rolls and Lists
      Letters from Collectors of Customs to the Secretary of State Relating to
            Commission of Privateers, 1812–13, 6 vols.
      U.S. Navy Subject Files, 1812–15
      U.S. Prisoners Rolls and Lists
    Records of the U.S. Coast Guard, Record Group 26
      Bureau of Lighthouses, Fifth Auditor's Office, Lighthouse Letters, 31 vols.
      Lighthouse Service, Correspondence Relating to Early Lighthouses
    Records of the Veterans Administration, Record Group 15
      Navy and Privateer Applicants for Pensions
National Maritime Museum, Greenwich, U.K.
    Admiralty Logs

Naval Historical Center, Washington, D.C.
  Operational Archives, Early Records Collection, ZB Series
North Carolina Archives, Division of Archives and History, Raleigh
  British Records Collection
  North Carolina State Records
    Governors' Letterbooks
      John Branch, 1817–20, GLB 23
      William Miller, 1816–17, GLB 22
    Private Collections
      Johnston Blakeley Papers
      John H. Bryan Collection
      Mary B. Hardin Collection
      Edward Teach (Blackbeard the Pirate) Papers
      James Iredell Waddell Papers
Onslow County Clerk of Court and Register of Deeds Office, Jacksonville, N.C.
  Onslow County Deeds
Public Record Office, London
  Admiralty Papers
  Colonial Office Papers
United States Naval Academy, Special Collections, Nimitz Library, Annapolis,
    Md.
  Photo Album, Class of 1861
  James Iredell Waddell Diary and Scrapbooks
University of North Carolina, Wilson Library, Chapel Hill
  Southern Historical Collection
    James Wallace Cooke Papers
    George Washington Gift Letters
    John Newland Maffitt Papers
    John Taylor Wood Papers

Published Documents

American State Papers: Naval Affairs. 4 vols. Reprint. New York: Arno Press,
  1979.
Brock, R. A., ed. *The Official Letters of Alexander Spotswood, Lieutenant
  Governor of the Colony of Virginia, 1710–1722.* 2 vols. Richmond: Virginia
  Historical Society, 1882.
Cain, Robert J., ed. *Records of the Executive Council, 1664–1734.* Vol. 7 of *The
  Colonial Records of North Carolina* [2nd ser.]. Raleigh: Division of Archives
  and History, 1984.
Callahan, Edward W., ed. *List of Officers of the Navy of the United States and of
  the Marine Corps from 1775 to 1900.* Reprint. New York: Haskell House, 1969.
Connor, Robert D. W., Louis R. Wilson, and Hugh T. Lefler, eds. *A
  Documentary History of the University of North Carolina, 1776–1799.* 2 vols.
  Chapel Hill: University of North Carolina Press, 1953.
Dudley, William S., ed. *The Naval War of 1812: A Documentary History.* 2 vols.
  to date. Washington: Naval Historical Center, 1985–92.

Elliot, Ethel T., comp. *Marriage Bonds of Carteret County, North Carolina.*
Beaufort: n.p., n.d.

Knox, Dudley W., ed. *Naval Documents Related to the United States Wars with the Barbary Powers: Naval Operations including Diplomatic Background from 1785 through 1807.* 6 vols. Washington: Government Printing Office, 1939–44.

Labree, Leonard W., ed., *The Papers of Benjamin Franklin.* Volume 1, *1 January 1706 through 31 December 1734.* New Haven: Yale University Press, 1959.

Letter from the Secretary of the Navy, Transmitting the Official Account of the Capture of the British Sloop of War Reindeer, By the United States' Sloop Wasp, Commanded By Captain Johnston Blakeley on the Twenty-Eighth June Last. Washington: Roger C. Weightman, 1814.

Nichols, Roy F., ed. "Fighting in North Carolina Waters." *North Carolina Historical Review* 40 (January 1963): 75–84.

Official Records of the Union and Confederate Navies in the War of the Rebellion. 31 vols. Washington: Government Printing Office. 1894–1927.

Price, William S., Jr., ed. *North Carolina Higher-Court Minutes, 1709–1723.* Vol. 5 of *The Colonial Records of North Carolina* [2nd ser.]. Raleigh: Division of Archives and History, 1974.

Register of Officers of the Confederate States Navy, 1861–1865. Washington: Government Printing Office, 1931.

Register of the Commissioned and Warrant Officers of the Navy of the United States; Including Officers of the Marine Corps and Others for the Year 1860. Washington: n.p., 1860.

Sainsbury, William N., Cecil Headlam, et al., eds. *The Calendar of State Papers, Colonial Series, America and the West Indies.* 42 vols. London, 1860– .

Sanders, Joanne McRee, ed. *Barbados Records: Baptisms, 1637–1800.* Baltimore: Genealogical Publications, 1984.

———. *Barbados Records: Marriages, 1693–1800.* 2 vols. Houston: Sanders Historical Publications, 1982.

———. *Barbados Records: Wills and Administrations.* 3 vols. Baltimore: Genealogical Publications, 1979.

Sanders, Rebecca W., comp. *Early Carteret County Court Minutes, 1810–1820.* Morehead City: n.p., n.d.

Saunders, William L., ed. *The Colonial Records of North Carolina.* 10 vols. Raleigh: State of North Carolina, 1886–90.

Simpson, Thelma D., and David R. Taylor, comps. *1850 Federal Census of Carteret County, North Carolina.* Baltimore: Genealogical Publishing Co., 1972.

Tolbert, Noble J., ed. *The Papers of John Willis Ellis.* 2 vols. Raleigh: Department of Archives and History, 1964.

The Tryals of Major Stede Bonnet and Other Pirates, viz . . . Who were all condemn'd for Piracy . . . At the Admiralty Sessions held at Charles-Town in the Province of South Carolina, on Tuesday the 28th of October, 1718. and by several Adjournments continued to Wednesday the 12th of November, following. To which is Prefix'd An Account of the Taking of the said Major Bonnet, and the rest of the Pirates. London: Benjamin Cowse, 1719.

Vandiver, Frank E., ed. *Confederate Blockade Running through Bermuda, 1861–1865: Letters and Cargo Manifests.* Austin: University of Texas Press, 1947.

Whistler, Henry. "An Account of Barbados in 1654." Transcribed by Neville Connell. *Journal of the Barbados Museum and Historical Society* 5 (1937–38): 184–85.

Memoirs and Diaries

Bulloch, James D. *The Secret Service of the Confederate States in Europe.* 2 vols. 1884. Reprint. New York: Thomas Yoseloff, 1959.

Castlen, Harriet G. *Hope Bids Me Onward.* Savannah: n.p., 1945.

Clark, Walter, ed. *Histories of the Several Regiments and Battalions from North Carolina in the Great War, 1861–65.* 5 vols. Raleigh: State of North Carolina, 1901.

Colston, R. E. "Watching the 'Merrimac.'" In *Battles and Leaders of the Civil War*, edited by Robert V. Johnson and Clarence C. Buel, 1:712–14. 4 vols. 1887. Reprint. New York: Thomas Yoseloff, 1956.

Conrad, Daniel B. "Capture and Burning of the Federal Gunboat 'Underwriter,' in the Neuse, off Newbern, N.C., in February, 1864." *Southern Historical Society Papers* 19 (January 1891): 93–100.

Crabtree, Beth G., and James W. Patton, eds. *"Journal of a Sesech Lady": The Diary of Catherine Ann Devereux Edmondston, 1860–1866.* Raleigh: Division of Archives and History, 1979.

Cushing, William B. "The Destruction of the 'Albemarle.'" In *Battles and Leaders of the Civil War*, edited by Robert V. Johnson and Clarence C. Buel, 4:634–40. 4 vols. 1887. Reprint. New York: Thomas Yoseloff, 1956.

Davis, Jefferson. *The Rise and Fall of the Confederate Government.* 2 vols. New York: D. Appleton, 1881.

Elliott, Gilbert. "The Ram Albemarle: Her Construction and Service." In *Histories of the Several Regiments and Battalions from North Carolina in the Great War, 1861–65*, edited by Walter Clark, 5:315–23. 5 vols. Raleigh: State of North Carolina, 1901.

Forrest, Douglas French. *Odyssey in Gray: A Diary of Confederate Service, 1863–1865.* Edited by William N. Still Jr. Richmond: Virginia State Library, 1979.

Grimball, John. "Career of the Shenandoah." *Southern Historical Society Papers* 25 (January 1897): 116–26.

Holden, Edgar. "The 'Albemarle' and the 'Sassacus.'" In *Battles and Leaders of the Civil War*, edited by Robert V. Johnson and Clarence C. Buel, 4:628–33. 4 vols. 1887. Reprint. New York: Thomas Yoseloff, 1956.

Hunt, Cornelius E. *The Shenandoah; or the Last Confederate Cruiser.* New York: G. W. Carlton and Company, 1867.

Johnson, Robert V. and Clarence C. Buel, eds. *Battles and Leaders of the Civil War.* 4 vols. 1887. Reprint. New York: Thomas Yoseloff, 1956.

Lining, Charles E. "Journal of Chas. E. Lining, C.S.S. Shenandoah." In *A Calendar of Confederate Papers*, edited by Douglas S. Freeman. Richmond: Confederate Museum, 1908.

Loyall, Benjamin P. "Capture of the 'Underwriter.'" In *Histories of the Several Regiments and Battalions from North Carolina in the Great War, 1861–65*, edited by Walter Clark, 5:325–33. 5 vols. Raleigh: State of North Carolina, 1901.

Maffitt, Emma Martin. *The Life and Services of John Newland Maffitt.* New York and Washington: Neale Publishing Co., 1906.

Maffitt, John N. "Blockade-Running." *The United Service: A Monthly Review of Military and Naval Affairs* 6 (June 1882): 626–33; 7 (July 1882): 14–32.

——. *Nautilus, or Cruising Under Canvas.* New York: United States Publishing Co., 1871.

——. "Reminiscences of the Confederate Navy." *The United Service: A Monthly Review of Military and Naval Affairs* 3 (October 1890): 495–514.

Mason, John T. "The Last of the Confederate Cruisers." *Century Magazine* 56 (August 1898): 600–610.

Parker, William H. *Recollections of a Naval Officer, 1841–1865.* 1883. Reprint. Annapolis: Naval Institute Press, 1985.

Reaney, Henry. "How the Gun-Boat 'Zouave' Aided the 'Congress.'" In *Battles and Leaders of the Civil War*, edited by Robert V. Johnson and Clarence C. Buel, 1:714–15. 4 vols. 1887. Reprint. New York: Thomas Yoseloff, 1956.

Riley, James. "The Shenandoah." *Southern Historical Society Papers* 21 (1893): 165–76.

Semmes, Raphael. *Memoirs of Service Afloat: During the War Between the States.* 1868. Reprint. Baton Rouge: Louisiana State University Press, 1996.

Sinclair, G. Terry. "Confederate Commerce-Destroyers: II. The Eventful Cruise of the 'Florida.'" *Century Magazine* 56 (July 1898): 417–27.

Sprunt, James. "Blockade Running." In *Histories of the Several Regiments and Battalions from North Carolina in the Great War, 1861–65*, edited by Walter Clark, 5:353–451. 5 vols. Raleigh: State of North Carolina, 1901.

Tredwell, Adam. "North Carolina Navy." In *Histories of the Several Regiments and Battalions from North Carolina in the Great War, 1861–65*, edited by Walter Clark, 5:299–313. 5 vols. Raleigh: State of North Carolina, 1901.

Waddell, James I. *CSS Shenandoah: The Memoirs of Lieutenant Commanding James I. Waddell.* Edited by James D. Horan. New York: Crown, 1960.

Warley, Alexander F. "Note on the Destruction of the 'Albemarle.'" In *Battles and Leaders of the Civil War*, edited by Robert V. Johnson and Clarence C. Buel, 4:641–42. 4 vols. 1887. Reprint. New York: Thomas Yoseloff, 1956.

Whittle, William C., Jr. "The Cruise of the Shenandoah." *Southern Historical Society Papers* 35 (1907): 235–58.

Wood, John Taylor. "The Capture of a Slaver." *Atlantic Monthly* 86 (September 1900): 451–63.

——. "Confederate Commerce-Destroyers: I. The 'Tallahassee''s Dash into New York Waters." *Century Magazine* 56 (July 1898): 408–17.

——. "Escape of the Confederate Secretary of War." *Century Magazine* 47 (November 1893): 110–23.

——. "The First Fight of Iron Clads." In *Battles and Leaders of the Civil War*, edited by Robert V. Johnson and Clarence C. Buel, 1:692–711. 4 vols. 1887. Reprint. New York: Thomas Yoseloff, 1956.

Newspapers

American (Annapolis, Md.)
Beaufort Gam
Boston News-Letter
Carolina Federal Republican (New Bern, N.C.)
Daily News (Jacksonville, N.C.)
Herald (Halifax, N.S.)
New Berne Weekly Journal
News and Observer (Raleigh, N.C.)
Niles' Weekly Register (Baltimore, Md.)
Raleigh Register and North Carolina Gazette
Wilmington Gazette

SECONDARY SOURCES

Alexander, Forsyth, ed. *Henrietta Johnson*. Winston-Salem: Old Salem, 1991.
Alexander, John, and James Lazell. *Ribbon of Sand: The Amazing Convergence of the Ocean and the Outer Banks*. Chapel Hill: Algonquin Books, 1992.
Alford, Michael. *Traditional Work Boats of North Carolina*. Beaufort: North Carolina Maritime Museum, 1990.
Allen, Gardner W. *Our Navy and the Barbary Corsairs*. 1905. Reprint. Hamden, Conn.: Archon Books, 1965.
Alleyne, Warren. "A Barbadian Pirate." *The Bajan* 6:73.
Alleyne, Warren, and Henry Fraser. *The Barbados-Carolina Connection*. London: Macmillan Caribbean, 1988
Andrews, Charles M. *The Colonial Period of American History*. 4 vols. New Haven: Yale University Press, 1936.
Ashe, Samuel A. "Captain James Iredell Waddell." *North Carolina Booklet* 13 (October 1913): 126–44.
Barbour, Ruth P. *Cruise of the Snap Dragon*. Winston-Salem: John F. Blair, 1976.
———. "What Happened to the Snap Dragon?" *The State* 48 (November 1980): 12–14.
Barefoot, Daniel W. *General Robert F. Hoke: Lee's Modest Warrior*. Winston-Salem: John F. Blair, 1996.
Barrett, John G. *The Civil War in North Carolina*. Chapel Hill: University of North Carolina Press, 1963.
Battle, Kemp P. *History of the University of North Carolina from Its Beginning to the Death of President Swain, 1789–1868*. Raleigh: Edwards and Broughton, 1907.
———. "A North Carolina Naval Hero and His Daughter: Captain Johnston Blakeley." *North Carolina Booklet* 1 (January 1901): 3–15.
———. "Otway Burns, Privateer and Legislator." *North Carolina University Magazine*, n.s., 19 (November 1901): 1–30.

Boykin, Edward. *Sea Devil of the Confederacy: The Story of the Florida and Her Captain, John Newland Maffitt*. New York: Funk & Wagnalls Co., 1959.

Browning, Robert M., Jr. *From Cape Charles to Cape Fear: The North Atlantic Blockading Squadron during the Civil War*. Tuscaloosa: University of Alabama Press, 1993.

Burns, Walter F., comp. *Captain Otway Burns: Patriot, Privateer, and Legislator*. New York: n.p., 1905.

Campbell, R. Thomas. *Fire and Thunder: Exploits of the Confederate States Navy*. Shippensburg, Pa.: Burd Street Press, 1997.

———. *Southern Fire: Exploits of the Confederate States Navy*. Shippensburg, Pa.: Burd Street Press, 1997.

Carr, Albert Z. *The Coming of War: An Account of the Remarkable Events Leading to the War of 1812*. Garden City, N.Y.: Doubleday & Co., 1960.

Carr, Dawson. *Gray Phantoms of the Cape Fear: Running the Civil War Blockade*. Winston-Salem: John F. Blair, 1998.

Carse, Robert. *Blockade: The Civil War at Sea*. New York: Rinehart & Co., 1958.

Chapelle, Howard I. *The History of the American Sailing Navy: The Ships and Their Development*. New York: W. W. Norton, 1949.

Chidsey, Donald Barr. *The American Privateers*. New York: Dodd, Mead & Co., 1962.

———. *The Wars in Barbary: Arab Piracy and the Birth of the United States Navy*. New York: Crown Publishers, 1971.

Clark, Walter. "Address at the Dedication of the Otway Burns Monument, Burnsville." Supplement, *The Eagle* (Black Mountain, N.C.), 2 August 1909.

———. "Oration at the Dedication of the Otway Burns Memorial, Beaufort, 1901." In *Captain Otway Burns: Patriot, Privateer, and Legislator*, compiled by Walter F. Burns, 15–65. New York: n.p., 1905.

Coles, Harry L. *The War of 1812*. Chicago: University of Chicago Press, 1965.

Cooke, Arthur L. "British Newspaper Accounts of Blackbeard's Death." *Virginia Magazine of History and Biography* 61 (July 1953): 304–7.

Cooke, James L. "Henry Marchant Cooke." *The Heritage of Carteret County*, edited by Charles O. Pitts Jr., 2:38. 2 vols. Beaufort: Carteret Historical Research Association, 1984.

Cooney, David M. *A Chronology of the U.S. Navy: 1775–1965*. New York: Franklin Watts, 1965.

Cordingly, David. *Under the Black Flag: The Romance and Reality of Life among the Pirates*. New York: Random House, 1995.

Coski, John M. *Capital Navy: The Men, Ships and Operation of the James River Squadron*. Campbell, Calif.: Savas Publishing Co., 1996

Daly, Robert W. "Burnside's Amphibious Division." *Marine Corps Gazette* 35 (December 1951): 30–37.

Dalzell, George W. *The Flight from the Flag: The Continuing Effect of the Civil War upon the American Carrying Trade*. Chapel Hill: University of North Carolina Press, 1940.

Davis, Burke. *The Long Surrender*. New York: Random House, 1985.

Davis, William C. *Duel between the First Ironclads.* New York: Doubleday & Co., 1975.

Dodson, Leonidas. *Alexander Spotswood: Governor of Colonial Virginia, 1710–1722.* Philadelphia: University of Pennsylvania Press, 1932.

Dudley, William S. *Going South: U.S. Navy Officer Resignations and Dismissals on the Eve of the Civil War.* Washington: Naval Historical Foundation, 1981.

Durkin, Joseph T. *Stephen R. Mallory: Confederate Navy Chief.* Chapel Hill: University of North Carolina Press, 1954.

Elliott, Robert G. *Ironclad of the Roanoke: Gilbert Elliott's Albemarle.* Shippensburg, Pa.: White Mane Publishing Co., 1994.

Ferguson, Eugene S. *Truxtun of the Constellation: The Life of Commodore Thomas Truxtun, U.S. Navy, 1755–1822.* Baltimore: Johns Hopkins University Press, 1956.

Forester, Cecil S. *The Age of Fighting Sail: The Story of the Naval War of 1812.* Garden City, N.Y.: Doubleday & Co., 1956.

Garitee, Jerome R. *The Republic's Private Navy: The American Privateering Business as Practiced in Baltimore during the War of 1812.* Middletown, Conn.: Wesleyan University Press, 1977.

Garraty, John A., and Mark C. Carnes, eds. *American National Biography.* 24 vols. New York: Oxford University Press, 1999.

Gosse, Philip. *The History of Piracy.* 1932. Reprint. New York: Burt Franklin, 1968.

Hagan, Kenneth J. *This People's Navy: The Making of American Sea Power.* New York: Free Press, 1991.

Harper, Lawrence A. *The English Navigation Laws: A Seventeenth Century Experiment in Social Engineering.* New York: Columbia University Press, 1939.

Hearn, Chester G. *Gray Raiders of the Sea: How Eight Confederate Warships Destroyed the Union's High Seas Commerce.* Camden, Maine: International Marine Publishing Co., 1992.

Henderson, Archibald. *The Campus of the First State University.* Chapel Hill: University of North Carolina Press, 1949.

———. *Washington's Southern Tour, 1791.* Boston: Houghton Mifflin Co., 1923.

Hickey, Donald R. *The War of 1812: A Forgotten Conflict.* Urbana: University of Illinois Press, 1989.

Hill, Jim Dan. *Sea Dogs of the Sixties.* 1935. Reprint. New York: A. S. Barnes & Co., 1961.

Hinds, John W. *Invasion and Conquest of North Carolina: Anatomy of a Gunboat War.* Shippensburg, Pa.: Burd Street Press, 1998.

Hoehling, A. A. *Damn the Torpedoes!: Naval Incidents of the Civil War.* Winston-Salem: John F. Blair, 1989.

Holdcamper, Forrest R., comp. *List of American-Flag Merchant Vessels that Received Certificates of Enrollment or Registry at the Port of New York, 1789–1867.* 2 vols. Washington: National Archives, 1968.

Howarth, Stephen. *To Shining Sea: A History of the United States Navy, 1775–1991.* New York: Random House, 1991.

Hughson, Shirley Carter. *The Carolina Pirates and Colonial Commerce, 1640–1740*. Baltimore: Johns Hopkins University Press, 1894.

Johnson, Allen, and Dumas Malone, eds. *Dictionary of American Biography*. 20 vols. New York: Charles Scribner's Sons, 1936.

Johnson, Captain Charles. *A General History of the Robberies & Murders of the Most Notorious Pirates*. 1724. Reprint, with introduction by David Cordingly. New York: Lyons Press, 1998.

———. [Daniel Defoe]. *A General History of the Pyrates*. Edited by Manuel Schonhorn. 1972. Reprint. Mineola, N.Y.: Dover Publications, 1999.

Johnson, William. "Biographical Sketch of Capt. Johnston Blakel[e]y, Late of the U.S. Sloop of War, Wasp." *North Carolina University Magazine* 3 (February 1854): 1–16.

Jones, Virgil C. *The Civil War at Sea*. 3 vols. New York: Holt, Rinehart, Winston, 1960.

Kent, David L. *Barbados and America*. Arlington, Va.: n.p., 1980.

Kert, Margaret Faye. *Prize and Prejudice: Privateering and Naval Prize in Atlantic Canada in the War of 1812*. St. John's, Newfoundland: International Economic Association, 1997.

Kitzen, Michael L. S. *Tripoli and the United States at War: A History of American Relations with the Barbary States, 1785–1805*. Jefferson, N.C.: McFarland & Co., 1993.

Lee, Robert E. *Blackbeard the Pirate: A Reappraisal of His Life and Times*. Winston-Salem: John F. Blair, 1974.

Leland, John G. *Stede Bonnet: 'Gentleman Pirate' of the Carolina Coast*. Charleston: Charleston Reproductions, 1972.

Littleton, Tucker R. "North Carolina's First Steamboat." *The State* 45 (November 1977): 8–10.

Luraghi, Raimondo. *The History of the Confederate Navy*. Translated by Paolo E. Coletta. Annapolis: Naval Institute Press, 1996.

McCrady, Edward. *The History of South Carolina Under the Proprietary Government, 1670–1719*. New York: Macmillan, 1897.

Macintyre, Donald. *The Privateers*. London: Paul Elek, 1975.

Maclay, Edgar Stanton. "The Exploits of Otway Burns, Privateersman and Statesman." *U.S. Naval Institute Proceedings* 42 (May–June 1916): 873–911.

———. *A History of American Privateers*. New York: D. Appleton & Co., 1924.

Mahan, Alfred Thayer. *Sea Power in Its Relation to the War of 1812*. 2 vols. London: Sampson, Low, Marston and Co., 1905.

Mallison, Fred M. *The Civil War on the Outer Banks: A History of the Late Rebellion along the Coast of North Carolina from Carteret to Currituck*. Jefferson, N.C.: McFarland & Co., 1998.

Marvel, William. *Burnside*. Chapel Hill: University of North Carolina Press, 1991.

Merli, Frank J. *Great Britain and the Confederate Navy, 1861–1865*. Bloomington: Indiana University Press, 1970.

Moebs, Thomas Truxtun. *Confederate States Navy Research Guide: Confederate Naval Imprints Described and Annotated, Chronology of Naval Operations and Administration, Marine Corps and Naval Officer Biographies, Description and Service of Vessels, Subject Bibliography*. Williamsburg: Moebs Publishing Co., 1991.

Moore, David. "Blackbeard the Pirate: Historical Background and the Beaufort Inlet Shipwreck." *Tributaries* 7 (October 1997): 31–39.

Morgan, Murray C. *Dixie Raider: The Saga of the C.S.S. Shenandoah*. New York: Dutton, 1948.

Nash, Howard P., Jr. *The Forgotten Wars: The Role of the U.S. Navy in the Quasi-War with France and the Barbary Wars, 1798–1805*. South Brunswick, N.J.: A. S. Barnes & Co., 1968.

Naval History Division. *Civil War Naval Chronology, 1861–1865*. 6 vols. Washington: Government Printing Office, 1971.

Newsome, Alfred R. "A Miscellany from the Thomas Henderson Letter Book, 1810–1811." *North Carolina Historical Review* 6 (October 1929): 398–410.

———. "Udney Maria Blakeley." *North Carolina Historical Review* 4 (April 1927): 158–71.

Nicholson, Lee H. "*Snap Dragon*: An American Privateer." *Nautical Research Journal* 27 (December 1981): 206.

"The Opposing Forces in the Operations at New Orleans, La." In *Battles and Leaders of the Civil War*, edited by Robert V. Johnson and Clarence C. Buel, 2:73–75. 4 vols. 1887. Reprint. New York: Thomas Yoseloff, 1956.

"Otway Burns and the Snap Dragon." *North Carolina University Magazine* 4 (November 1855): 407–13; (December 1855): 461–67; 5 (April 1856): 126–31; (June 1856): 205–8.

Owsley, Frank L., Jr. *The C.S.S. Florida: Her Building and Operations*. 1965. New edition. Tuscaloosa: University of Alabama Press, 1987.

Paschal, Herbert R., Jr. *A History of Colonial Bath*. Raleigh: Edwards and Broughton, 1955.

Patton, James W. "Glimpses of North Carolina in the Writings of Northern and Foreign Travelers, 1783–1860." *North Carolina Historical Review* 45 (July 1968): 298–324.

Paul, Charles L. "Colonial Beaufort." *North Carolina Historical Review* 42 (April 1965): 139–52.

Paullin, Charles O. *Commodore John Rodgers: Captain, Commodore, and Senior Officer of the American Navy, 1773–1838*. 1909. Reprint. Annapolis: Naval Institute Press, 1967.

Perkins, Bradford. *Prologue to War: England and the United States, 1805–1812*. Berkeley and Los Angeles: University of California Press, 1963.

Perry, James M. "The U.S. Sloop of War *Wasp*." *U.S. Naval Institute Proceedings* 87 (February 1961): 84–93.

Petrie, Donald A. *The Prize Game: Lawful Looting on the High Seas in the Days of Fighting Sail*. Annapolis: Naval Institute Press, 1999.

Porter, David Dixon. *The Naval History of the Civil War*. New York: Sherman Publishing Co., 1886.

Powell, William S., ed. *Dictionary of North Carolina Biography*. 6 vols. Chapel Hill: University of North Carolina Press, 1979–96.

Pratt, Fletcher. *Preble's Boys: Commodore Preble and the Birth of American Sea Power*. New York: William Sloane Associates, 1950.

Rankin, Hugh F. *The Golden Age of Piracy*. Williamsburg: Colonial Williamsburg, 1969.

Rediker, Marcus. *Between the Devil and the Deep Blue Sea: Merchant Seamen, Pirates, and the Anglo-American Maritime World, 1700–1750*. Cambridge: Cambridge University Press, 1987.

——. " 'Under the Banner of King Death': The Social World of the Anglo-American Pirates, 1716–1726." *William and Mary Quarterly*, 3rd ser., 38 (April 1981): 203–27.

Reed, Rowena. *Combined Operations in the Civil War*. 1958. Reprint. Lincoln: University of Nebraska Press, 1993.

Reilly, John C., Jr. *The Iron Guns of Willard Park*. Washington: Naval Historical Center, 1991.

Roberts, William P. "James Dunwoody Bulloch and the Confederate Navy." *North Carolina Historical Review* 24 (July 1947): 315–66.

Robinson, William M., Jr. *The Confederate Privateers*. 1928. Reprint. Columbia: University of South Carolina Press, 1990.

Roosevelt, Theodore. *The Naval War of 1812, or the History of the United States Navy during the Last War with Great Britain to Which is Appended an Account of the Battle of New Orleans*. 1882. Reprint. Annapolis: Naval Institute Press, 1987.

Sauers, Richard A. *"A Succession of Honorable Victories": The Burnside Expedition in North Carolina*. Dayton, Ohio: Morningside House, 1996.

Scharf, J. Thomas. *History of the Confederate States Navy from Its Organization to the Surrender of Its Last Vessel*. New York: Rogers and Isherwood, 1887.

Sherman, Richard P. *Robert Johnson: Proprietary and Royal Governor of South Carolina*. Columbia: University of South Carolina Press, 1966.

Shingleton, Royce. "The Atlanta: A Civil War Blockade Runner," *Atlanta Historical Bulletin* 20 (Fall 1976): 11–16.

——. *High Seas Confederate: The Life and Times of John Newland Maffitt*. Columbia: University of South Carolina Press, 1994.

——. *John Taylor Wood: Sea Ghost of the Confederacy*. Athens: University of Georgia Press, 1979.

Shomette, Donald G. *Pirates in the Chesapeake: Being a True History of Pirates, Picaroons, and Raiders of the Chesapeake Bay, 1610–1807*. Centreville, Md.: Tidewater Press, 1985.

Silverstone, Paul H. *Warships of the Civil War Navies*. Annapolis: Naval Institute Press, 1989.

Simpson, Bland. *Into the Sound Country: A Carolinian's Coastal Plain*. Chapel Hill: University of North Carolina Press, 1997.

Snider, William D. *Light on the Hill: A History of the University of North Carolina*. Chapel Hill: University of North Carolina Press, 1996.

Spencer, Warren F. *The Confederate Navy in Europe*. Tuscaloosa: University of Alabama Press, 1983.

Stick, David. *Graveyard of the Atlantic.* Chapel Hill: University of North
Carolina Press, 1952.

——. *The Outer Banks of North Carolina, 1584–1958.* Chapel Hill: University
of North Carolina Press, 1958.

Still, William N., Jr. *The Confederate Navy: The Ships, Men and Organization,
1861–65.* Annapolis: Naval Institute Press, 1997.

——. *Iron Afloat: The Story of the Confederate Armorclads.* 1971. Reprint.
Columbia: University of South Carolina Press, 1985.

——. "Shipbuilding and Boatbuilders in Swansborough, 1800–1950."
Tributaries 5 (October 1995): 7–13.

Symonds, Craig L. *Confederate Admiral: The Life and Wars of Franklin
Buchanan.* Annapolis: Naval Institute Press, 1999.

Thurston, Arthur. *Tallahassee Skipper: The Biography of John Taylor Wood.*
Yarmouth, N.S.: Lescarbot Press, 1981.

Trotter, William R. *Ironclads and Columbiads: The Civil War in North
Carolina.* Volume 3, *The Coast.* Greensboro: Signal Research, 1989.

Tucker, Glenn. *Dawn Like Thunder: the Barbary Wars and the Birth of the U.S.
Navy.* Indianapolis: Bobbs-Merrill, 1963.

Tyler, Leon G., ed. "William Howard the Pirate." *Tyler's Quarterly Historical
and Genealogical Magazine* 7 (July 1919): 36–39.

Watson, Alan D. *A History of New Bern and Craven County.* New Bern: Tryon
Palace Commission, 1987.

——. *Wilmington: Port of North Carolina.* Columbia: University of South
Carolina Press, 1992.

Wheeler, John Hill. *Reminiscences and Memoirs of North Carolina and Eminent
North Carolinians.* 1884. Reprint. Baltimore: Genealogical Publishing Co.,
1966.

Whipple, A. B. C. *To the Shores of Tripoli: The Birth of the U.S. Navy and
Marines.* New York: William Morrow & Co., 1991.

Wideman, John C. *Naval Warfare: Courage and Combat on the Water.* New
York: Metro Books, 1997.

Wise, Stephen R. *Lifeline of the Confederacy: Blockade Running during the
Civil War.* Columbia: University of South Carolina Press, 1988.

Index

Barron, Samuel (1804), 106, 107

Barron, Samuel (1861), 175; in North Carolina, 20, 126–27; in Paris, 210, 211, 212, 218

Bashaw, 107

Bath, N.C., 39, 42, 44, 47, 60

Beaufort, N.C., 4, 25, 26, 121, 132; pirates in, 39, 60–61; Burns in, 75, 90; *Snap Dragon* in, 80, 81, 82, 84, 86, 87, 88; description of, 122; Cooke in, 122, 123. *See also* Maritime Museum, North Carolina

Beaufort, CSS, 19, 125, 128, 129, 181, 182

Beaufort Inlet (N.C.), xii, 19, 148; excavation of shipwreck at, 25–29, 50; artifacts from shipwreck at, 27–28. See also *Queen Anne's Revenge*

Bell, William, 42

Benjamin, Judah P., 183, 196, 206

Bering Sea, 221, 222

Bermuda, 21, 41, 163–64, 167, 210

Bequia (Grenadines), 35

Blackbeard, 8, 24, 25, 33, 56, 57, 59, 71, 121; image of, xi, 29, 30, 32, 49–50; early years of, 29–30; names of, 30; description of, 30–31; wives of, 30, 41; as privateer, 32; commands *Revenge* (first), 33–34; commands *Queen Anne's Revenge*, 35; deposes Bonnet, 36, 59; blockades Charleston, 37–38; at Beaufort, 38–39, 60; commands *Revenge* (second), 39, 41; at Bath, 39–41; at Ocracoke, 42–43; in battle at Ocracoke, 44–47; death of, 46; relationship to governor, 49; song about, 52

Black Warrior, CSS, 128, 129, 130

Blakeley, Jane Anne Hoope, 109, 116–17

Blakeley, Johnston, 15, 24; youth of, 97–99; family connections of, 97–99, 101; at university, 99–101; appointed midshipman, 102; on *President*, 104; on *John Adams*, 105, 107; commissioned lieutenant,

106; on *Congress*, 106; on *Constitution*, 106; commands *Enterprise*, 107–9; at New Orleans, 108; marriage of, 109–10; commands *Wasp*, 109–14; in English Channel, 110–14; defeats *Reindeer*, 111; success of, 111–12; at L'Orient, 111–13; defeats *Avon*, 113–14; lost at sea, 114–15; significance of, 114–15; promoted to captain, 115; recognition of, 115, 117; ballad about, 116; widow and child of, 116–17

Blakeley, Udney Maria, 116–17

Blockade, Union, 18, 19, 20, 126, 194

Blockade running, 21–22, 154–55, 165, 167, 191, 210. *See also* Charleston, S.C.; Wilmington, N.C.

Bogue Banks (N.C.), 39, 90, 121

Bombshell, CSS, 138, 139, 140

Bombshell, USS, 136

Bonnet, Allamby, 55

Bonnet, Edward, 55

Bonnet, Mary, 55

Bonnet, Mary Allamby, 55

Bonnet, Stede, 8, 24, 30; in Nassau, 33, 56; deposed as captain, 36, 59; life in Barbados, 52–53; family connections of, 54–55; off Virginia capes, 56, 61; off Carolinas, 56; wounded, 56; description of, 57; in Delaware Bay, 57, 61–63; off Spanish Main, 59; at Beaufort, 60; as Captain Edwards, 61; as Captain Thomas, 61; at Cape Fear, 63–67; in battle at Cape Fear, 65–67; as prisoner in Charleston, 67, 70; trial of, 69–70; execution of, 71–72

Bonnet, Stede, Jr., 55

Bonnet's Creek (N.C.), 63

Boston, Mass., 37, 50, 116, 117, 145, 163

Brand, Ellis, 43, 44, 47–48

Brandywine, USS, 173

Brant Island Shoal Lightboat, 92

Breckinridge, John C., 177, 196, 197

Bretton, Baron Joseph von, 117
Brooke, John M., 132, 179, 200
Brown, James, 84, 85
Buccaneer: origin of term, 6
Buchanan, Franklin, 158, 159, 173;
    commands CSS *Virginia*, 180, 181,
    182, 183
Buchanan, James, 176, 177
Bulloch, James D., 23, 155–56, 165,
    209, 210; acquires CSS *Shenan-
    doah*, 200, 211, 212, 223, 224
Burns, Jane Hall, 90
Burns, Jane Smith, 92
Burns, Joanna Grant, 75, 90
Burns, Otway, 15, 121; commemora-
    tion of, 73; death of, 74, 92; signifi-
    cance of, 74–75, 90, 92–93; youth
    of, 75; marriages of, 75–76, 90, 92;
    on *Snap Dragon*, 76; in New Bern,
    76–77; first cruise of, 77–82; in Vir-
    gin Islands, 78–79; on Spanish
    Main, 79–82; commands *Snap
    Dragon*, 84; off Newfoundland,
    84–86; second cruise of, 84–87;
    success of, 86–87; off South Amer-
    ica, 87–88; third cruise of, 87–88;
    in Beaufort, 90; postwar businesses
    of, 90; in legislature, 90–91; bank-
    ruptcy of, 92; in Portsmouth, 92
Burns, Owen, 76, 90
Burnside, Ambrose E., 127; expedi-
    tion commanded by (1862), 20–21,
    127–30
Butler, Benjamin F., 126, 207

Caleb Cushing, 163
Camm, Robert A., 128–29
Camouflage, naval: Confederate use
    of, 22, 159, 165
Campeche, Bay of (Mexico), 33
Cape Charles (Va.), 33, 56
Cape Fear (N.C.), 5, 19, 56, 69, 70,
    167
Cape Fear River (N.C.), 90, 98, 135,
    192, 194; Bonnet on, 56, 63, 64;
    battle on, 65–67

Cape Hatteras (N.C.), 27, 128, 153
Cape Henry (Va.), 61
Cape Lookout (N.C.), 5, 84, 88
Cape of Good Hope, 216
Cárdenas, Cuba, 157, 197
Carrieville, 149
Cartagena, Colombia, 81, 83
Carter, Robert R., 200, 211
Cecile, 154–55
Charleston, S.C., 177, 188, 209; priva-
    teering in, 19; Blackbeard at, 37–
    38, 60; Bonnet in, 56, 67, 69,
    71–72; pirates in, 63, 64, 65, 70–71;
    pirate trials in, 67–70; Blakeley in,
    97, 107–8; Maffitt in, 148–49, 152;
    blockade running in, 155, 167, 210
Charlotte, N.C., 195, 196
Charter Oak, 215
Chesapeake Bay (Va.), 56, 128, 162,
    226; naval raids on, 71–72, 185,
    186–87
Chickamauga, CSS, 194, 199
City of San Francisco, 225
Clarence, CSS, 162
Clarke, Jonathan, 63–64, 69
Clubfoot and Harlow Creek Canal
    (N.C.), 90
Coakley, Benjamin D., 85
Coast Survey, U.S., 148–50
Concorde, 34–35, 57, 233–34 (n. 16).
    See also *Queen Anne's Revenge*
Congress, C.S., 18, 137–38
Congress, U.S., 92, 102, 115, 116–17,
    177
Congress, USS (1799), 106, 110
Congress, USS (1839), 131, 181, 182,
    183
Constitution, USS, 96, 103, 122, 123;
    in Barbary Wars, 106, 107; in
    Greece, 143–44, 145
Cooke, James W., 21, 120, 145, 148,
    166, 169, 191; family connections
    of, 121–23; appointed midship-
    man, 122; commands *Relief*, 123;
    commissioned lieutenant, 123;
    described, 123; marriage of, 123;

resigns from U.S. Navy, 124–25; commissioned lieutenant, C.S. Navy, 125; commands *Edwards*, 125–27; commands *Ellis*, 127–30; in battle at Roanoke Island, 128; in battle at Elizabeth City, 129–30; wounded, 130; commands *Beaufort*, 131; promoted commander, 131; commands *Albemarle*, 133–36; in battle at Plymouth, 137; congressional citation of, 137; in battle on Albemarle Sound, 138–40; commands inland waters of North Carolina, 141; promoted captain, 141; death of, 142

Cooke, Lechmere Rittenhouse, 123

Cooke, Mary Elizabeth Ann Watts, 123

Coosawhatchie, S.C., 154

Corbett, Peter, 200, 211, 213

Cotton Plant, 138

Croatan Sound (N.C.), 127, 128

Crusader, USS, 151–52

Cuban junta (N.Y.), 169

Cumberland, USS, 20, 131, 174, 181, 182

Curlew, CSS, 127, 128

Cushing, William B., 141

Dale, Richard, 103–4

Dalton, John, 63, 64

Davis, Jefferson, 120, 220; on privateering, 18; and Maffitt, 152, 159; and Wood, 172, 176, 179, 183, 185, 191, 195, 196

Davis, Varina H., 195, 196

Decatur, USS, 123

Declaration of Paris, 16

Delaware Bay, 33, 34, 57, 68

Delphine, 218

Dismal Swamp Canal, 129, 166

Dolphin, USS, 150

Doughty, William, 109

Drewry's Bluff (Va.), battle of, 184–85, 208–9

Dudley, Thomas H., 156, 200, 213

Eden, Charles, 39, 40, 41, 42, 44, 48, 49, 60

Edmondston, Catherine D., 123, 134, 136, 142, 162–63

Edwards, Captain. *See* Bonnet, Stede

Edwards, CSS, 19, 125, 126, 127. See also *Forrest*, CSS

Edwards Ferry, N.C.: construction of *Albemarle* at, 133–34, 135, 141, 142

Elizabeth City, N.C., 21, 129, 132

Ellerslie, 145, 149, 151, 152

Elliott, Gilbert, 133, 134, 135, 137, 141

Elliott, Jesse D., 143, 144, 145

Ellis, John W., 18, 19, 125

Ellis, CSS, 19, 125, 127, 128–29, 130

Enterprise, USS, 104, 105, 110; commanded by Blakeley, 107–9

Ericsson, USS, 163

Fairfax County, Va., 123

Fanny, CSS, 127, 128, 129

Farragut, David, 159, 207, 208

Fawn, HMS, 80

Fayetteville, N.C., 144–45, 149

Fernando de Noronha (Brazil), 162

Florida, CSS, 23, 199, 209, 214; commanded by Maffitt, 156; description of, 156; in Nassau, 156–57; commissioned, 157; in Cuba, 157; runs Mobile blockade, 158; in Mobile, 158–59; commerce raiding of, 159–65; in Barbados, 160–61; off Brazil, 162; in Bermuda, 163–64; at Brest, France, 164–65; captured, 245 (n. 56). See also *Oreto*

Florie, 165

Flusser, Charles W., 137

Fly, 109

Forrest, CSS, 127, 128, 130. See also *Edwards*, CSS

Fort Branch, N.C., 135, 142

Fort Caswell, N.C., 167, 192

Fort Clark, N.C., 19, 126

Fort Fisher, N.C., 22, 26, 165, 167, 192, 194, 195

Fort Hampton, N.C., 87, 122